US politics today

MANCHESTER
1824

Manchester University Press

Politics Today

Series editor: Bill Jones

US politics
today

Third edition

Edward Ashbee

Manchester University Press
Manchester and New York

distributed exclusively in the USA by Palgrave

The right of Edward Ashbee to be identified as the author of this work has been asserted by him in accordance with the Copyright, Designs and Patents Act 1988.

Published by Manchester University Press
Oxford Road, Manchester M13 9NR, UK
and Room 400, 175 Fifth Avenue, New York, NY 10010, USA
www.manchesteruniversitypress.co.uk

Distributed in the United States exclusively by
Palgrave Macmillan, 175 Fifth Avenue, New York,
NY 10010, USA

Distributed in Canada exclusively by
UBC Press, University of British Columbia, 2029 West Mall,
Vancouver, BC, Canada V6T 1Z2

British Library Cataloguing-in-Publication Data
A catalogue record for this book is available from the British Library

Library of Congress Cataloging-in-Publication Data applied for

ISBN 978 0 7190 82191 paperback

First published 2012

Typeset in Photina
by Servis Filmsetting Ltd, Stockport, Cheshire
Printed in Great Britain
by Bell & Bain Ltd, Glasgow

Contents

List of tables

Preface

The first edition of *US Politics Today* was published in 1999, well before the fiercely fought presidential contest of 2000. Inevitably, much of the material and many of the events and sources upon which the book drew had happened, or been published, during the 1980s and early 1990s. The second edition of the book was published in 2004 and took account of the events and developments that followed in the wake of the attacks 11 of September 2001.

Self-evidently, much has happened during those years. In 1999, the Governor of Texas was contemplating a presidential run although the economic boom led almost all political commentators to predict a safe victory for Vice-President Al Gore. Barack Obama was a member of the Illinois state senate and about to lose a primary race to secure the Democrats' nomination for a seat in the US House of Representatives. There was a mildly isolationist mood as many Republicans and some Democrats feared the dangers of embroilment in the former Yugoslavia and other trouble-spots. There was uncertainty among policymakers about the purposes to which the federal government budget surplus should be put.

At the same time, the study of politics has moved on. As Chapter 8 notes, there is a divide between the study of US politics in Europe and study in the US itself. In the US (and in many sub-fields within European political science), there is an emphasis on testable hypotheses and quantitative, data-based methodologies. The traditional focus on the nation-state as a primary unit of analysis is being displaced by comparative transnational approaches. Instead, in Europe, there is a close association between the study of US politics and contemporary history as well as the broader multidisciplinary field of American Studies.

Over the coming years, the study of US politics in Europe will undergo a fundamental change in character. Research assessment mechanisms and structural shifts in the provision of higher education both in the United Kingdom and in other countries will lead to a quasi-Darwinian process of natural selection. At this point, the eventual outcome is uncertain.

The character of the subject has changed in another way. Since 1999, the publishing market has changed beyond recognition. Students who start out on a US politics course can now pick and choose from a plethora of textbooks, study guides, and periodicals such as *Politics Review*. The third edition of *US Politics Today* is not seeking to make the process of choice more difficult. It does indeed address many of the 'basics' that are to be found at A-level or on undergraduate US government and politics courses. However, the book has another purpose. Alongside the coverage of core topics and themes it seeks to introduce its readers to a broad range of authors, issues, and questions. Some of these are linked to theories and methodologies. Others involve alternative perspectives on the core topics that are not always considered on courses. I hope that the book's readers will be able to use these features to take study of the subject beyond the strict requirements of a course specification.

The process of change has not only extended to the subject, the framework within which it is understood, and the character of the educational publishing market. For my part, I moved some years ago from rural Staffordshire to Copenhagen. I remain immensely grateful to Copenhagen Business School and Denmark for taking me in. I also want to extend my thanks and appreciation to all those who have in all sorts of different ways helped me develop the ideas and approaches that underscore this book and some of my other publications. They include Stephen Amberg, Niels Bjerre-Poulsen, Ray Haberski, Eva Heitmann, Colleen Harris, Bill Jones, Lars Bo Kaspersen, Eric Magee, Kevin McGovern, Carl Pedersen, Grahame Thompson, Alex Waddan, and Andrew Wroe. I am particularly grateful to John Banks, who copy-edited the manuscript. It goes without saying that the responsibility for errors and omissions is mine alone.

Edward Ashbee
Department of Business and Politics
Copenhagen Business School

1

Elections and campaigns

There are countless elections in the United States. They include contests to choose those who serve at federal, state, and local level (such as school or library boards). Positions that in other nations would be assigned through an appointments process, such as judgeships, are contested and voted upon. Furthermore, party candidates are chosen by the voters themselves in primaries, not by party leadership bodies or committed activists alone. Indeed, any citizen can run for office, as neither previous party membership nor a record of political activity is required. During 2011, it appeared for example that Donald Trump, the wealthy property developer and entertainment tycoon, might seek the Republican Party's presidential nomination. For a period, Herman Cain, former head of a pizza company, was a credible candidate. Furthermore, in some states, issues may be decided directly by the voters themselves through referendums.

Despite the frequency and extent of electoral contests, the US electoral system has, however, been subject to sustained criticism. Money and the media, it is said, play too much of a role in federal elections. The length, complexity, and demands of the presidential electoral system dissuade qualified candidates and contribute to low levels of turnout.[1] This chapter considers and assesses these questions.

Electing the president

The president is elected every four years. Since the Twenty-second Amendment was adopted in 1951, no president can be elected to serve more than two full terms. Candidates for the office face a two-stage system structured around the race to secure their party's nomination and the general election contest.

Candidates

Article II of the US Constitution establishes three basic requirements for those who serve as president. An individual must be at least 35 years old, born in the

US (the 'Birther' movement contended that Barack Obama had been born in Kenya and therefore challenged his legitimacy as presidency on this basis), and a resident for 14 years or more. In practice, however, a further 'qualification' is required. Despite frequent talk of a minor party breakthrough (see below), a winning candidate must be a major party nominee. Since March 1853, presidents have been drawn from either the Democratic or the Republican Party. In 2007–8, eight credible Democrats sought their party's nomination in the presidential race. Six were, or had been, members of the US Senate. Another was a state governor (although he had also served at federal level in the Clinton administration) while one sat in the House of Representatives. There were also eight contesting the Republican presidential nomination (a further four withdrew in 2007 before the formal selection process began). One was a senator and another was a former senator. Two were former state governors. Two served in the US House of Representatives. One had served as mayor of New York City while another (who was, in reality, a fringe candidate) had served as a US ambassador to the United Nations. In the contest for the 2012 Republican nomination, there were (by December 2011) seven credible candidates including Texas governor Rick Perry, the former Massachusetts governor Mitt Romney, and Newt Gingrich, who served as Speaker in the House of Representatives between 1995 and 1999.

In recent years, there may have been a shift. Those who have served in the Senate appear to have secured an advantage. Until 2009, four of the past five presidents had served as governors before being elected to the White House. Yet, in 2004, the incumbent president (George W. Bush) was challenged by a serving senator (John Kerry). Then, in 2008, both the Democratic and the Republican parties chose serving senators as their candidates (Barack Obama and John McCain respectively). Arguably, the shift took place because, in the wake of the 11 September 2001 attacks on New York City and the Pentagon, defence policy and 'homeland security' acquired much more importance. Members of Congress, particularly those in the Senate, have some experience of foreign policy deliberations and are thereby more credible candidates. State governors will customarily have a record of involvement only in domestic policymaking. Although 2012 appeared to buck the trend in so far as only one senator was in the race for the Republican nomination, the party's supporters were by the end of 2011 edging towards candidates who had substantial political experience and away from the more radical outsiders.

A president who is seeking re-election may well be unopposed within his own party. Incumbents hold important advantages in terms of status, authority, and funding. In July 2011, well ahead of the 2012 presidential election, it was reported that President Obama had, in addition to his many small donors, recruited about 150 'bundlers' who had each raised half a million dollars for his re-election campaign (Confessore, 2011: 8). At the end of their first terms, Ronald Reagan, Bill Clinton, and George W. Bush faced no serious or credible challengers at the primary stage. However, this is not assured. In 1968,

Eugene McCarthy and Bobby Kennedy ran against President Lyndon Johnson, before he withdrew, in the race to become the Democratic Party's nominee. In 1976, Ronald Reagan almost took the Republican nomination from President Gerald Ford. In 1980, President Jimmy Carter faced a sustained challenge from Senator Edward Kennedy.

The 'invisible primary'

The one- or two-year period preceding a presidential election year has been dubbed the 'invisible primary'. Although it does not have a formal or well-defined status, it is the informal race to secure campaign funds, build a campaign team, attract press coverage, and establish a lead in the public opinion polls. It can be thought of as a process of 'jostling' and has often played a critical role in determining who will eventually secure the party's nomination. As William Mayer, who coined the term, observes: 'In seven of the 10 cases . . . the nominee-to-be had opened up a sizable lead over every other eventual candidate by, at the latest, one month after the preceding midterm election – more than a year, in other words, before the start of the actual delegate selection activities' (quoted in Schneider, 2002) In other words, although the formal selection procedure begins only in January or February of election year, the identity of the parties' most likely presidential nominees is often becoming evident over twelve months before this. (In the 2012 Republican race, however, the 'invisible primary' seemed inconclusive. While those in the party elites and about a quarter of the Republican electorate appeared to back Mitt Romney, many believed that he was not a consistent conservative and had 'flip-flopped' on core issues too frequently.)

How can candidates build up the 'sizable lead' in the polls to which Mayer refers? Observers stress the initial winning of name recognition, the creation of an exploratory committee, the process of attracting campaign teams and strategists (sometimes dubbed the 'talent primary'), participation in candidate debates, courting the different groupings and organisations that are allied with the party, the gaining of endorsements from well-known supporters, and inclusion in lists of credible presidential hopefuls considered by newspaper 'op-ed' columnists and television commentators. The 'straw polls' organised by some of the state parties and organisations such as the Conservative Political Action Conference, have acquired growing importance. The straw poll held in Ames, Iowa, has a particular place in the race for the Republican presidential nomination. This is partly because the Iowa caucuses play a pivotal role at the beginning of election year. Although the result has no formal status it gives 'bragging rights', can boost (or deflate) a campaign and determine a candidate's fundraising prospects. Its structure and character are however reminiscent of premodern electoral systems. Tickets, allowing participation, cost $30 in the 2011 poll. For the most part, this was paid by one of the campaigns, nearly all of which brought in supporters by bus with the promise of food and entertainment. 16,892 votes were cast. The results were victories for Congresswoman Michele Bachmann, a social conservative closely associated with the radical Tea Party movement and Congressman Ron Paul, a veteran libertarian, who came second. Both were 'outsider' candidates who defied the odds and the Republican Party leadership. The outcome was, however, a major setback for Tim Pawlenty, the former governor of Minnesota, who had been seen at an earlier stage as a very strong contender. On the day after the Ames straw poll, Pawlenty announced his withdrawal from the race. Some candidates, including those regarded as frontrunners for the 2012 Republican nomination (most notably the former Massachusetts governor, Mitt Romney), decided not to compete in the poll (although he was listed on the ballot).

During 2007, the year preceding the 2008 presidential election, Democrat presidential hopefuls devoted much of their time to attending forums and debates organised by interest groups, such as the National Association for the Advancement of Colored People (NAACP), NARAL Pro-Choice America, and the Human Rights Campaign (a gay and lesbian organisation), that are closely aligned with the party. The *Washington Post* reported on a forum for the Democrats' presidential candidates organised by the NAACP in July 2007:

> Presidential hopeful Barack Obama drew the loudest cheers of the eight Democratic candidates at a civil rights forum Thursday as he assailed the Bush administration's record on race relations . . . Black voters are a core party constituency. Candidates are in a fierce struggle to capture their support and are refusing to cede it to Obama. Hillary Rodham Clinton, the front-runner, enjoys strong support in the black community and is married to former President Clinton, who was wildly popular among black voters. John Edwards has won praise from black leaders for his commitment to fighting poverty. (Runk, 2007)

However, as Mayer emphasises, a candidate's financial resources are as important as the process of political positioning. A campaign cannot be sustained nor can a candidate secure credibility without a financial 'war chest'. Indeed, its importance is such that some commentators refer to the 'invisible primary' as the 'money primary'. Primary candidates can, if they can demonstrate that they have a credible number of supporters and are ready to be bound by overall expenditure limits, obtain matching funds from the Federal Election Commission (FEC). These funds, which provide dollar-for-dollar assistance, are taken from those taxpayers who have agreed, on their annual income tax returns, that a proportion of the tax that they have paid may be used for this purpose. To qualify for matching funds, and deter marginal candidates, a candidate must raise a total of at least $100,000 in twenty or more states (*Congressional Quarterly*, 1997: 46). In recent years, however, growing numbers of candidates have decided not to seek matching federal funds. In the 2008 Democratic primaries, Barack Obama and Hillary Clinton relied instead on their own fundraising abilities. Amongst the Republicans, John McCain,

Rudy Giuliani, Mitt Romney, and Ron Paul made the same decision. This not only allowed them to spend without limit but was also a demonstration of political and organisational strength. Indeed, the acceptance of federal funding in the primaries increasingly seems to mark a candidate out as being perceived as 'second tier'.

How important is the 'invisible primary'? Much has been made of it by commentators over the past twenty years. However, the 2008 presidential election suggests that its importance may be overstated. Efforts to establish models or 'laws' often founder on the unpredictability and uncertainty of the US electoral process. At the end of 2007, opinion polls conducted amongst likely Democratic primary voters gave Senator Hillary Clinton a clear lead. Barack Obama was a distant second. Among Republicans, the frontrunner was the former Arkansas governor Mike Huckabee. He was followed by the former New York mayor Rudy Giuliani. The former Massachusetts governor Mitt Romney was in third place. So far as fundraising was concerned, Federal Election Commission returns for the period up until the end of 2007 show that Hillary Clinton had a narrow lead amongst the Democratic contenders while Rudy Giuliani and Mitt Romney held the lead in the Republican race. It is worth noting that Senator John McCain, who went on to win the Republican Party's presidential nomination, was far behind in terms of both the opinion polls and fundraising.

Primaries (January–June)

The presidential candidate is formally chosen by majority vote amongst delegates at each party's national convention. Candidates therefore seek to maximise the number of their supporters among the state delegations. Traditionally, convention delegates were chosen by party 'bosses' (who held sway in cities such as Chicago) and factions at a state party convention. However, although there are significant procedural differences between states (and caucuses as well as county and state party conventions can continue to play a role), the primary election has become the norm. The primary allows members of the public, who are registered supporters of a particular party, to participate in the nomination process. By picking a particular candidate to be the party's presidential nominee, primary votes in effect mandate or bind the state party delegates to back that candidate when the national nominating convention is held. The primary 'season' is therefore a race by those seeking the nomination to win national convention delegates.

The proportion of convention delegates chosen on the basis of the primary results in their states grew during the course of the twentieth century. By 1996, 65.3 per cent of Democratic national convention delegates and 84.6 per cent of Republican national convention delegates were selected in primaries (*Congressional Quarterly*, 1997: 141). Of these, some were closed primaries that restricted voting to those who had registered earlier in the year as Democrats or

Republicans. Others were open primaries that do not require pre-registration. In some states, voters are allowed to register as a party voter on the day that the primary is held. In others, they are offered a choice of ballots.

The growth of the direct primary is closely associated with the progressive movement at the beginning of the twentieth century. It sought to modernise the political process by breaking the power of the party 'bosses'. Some states still, however, use caucuses and state party conventions. Caucuses are small-scale meetings. In Iowa, for example, although there are differences between the Democratic and the Republican procedures, meetings (or 'gatherings of neighbours') are held in each of the state's 1784 precincts. They allow discussion of the different candidates' strengths and weaknesses. Participation inevitably tends to be limited to the more committed party activists. On the basis of deliberations in the caucuses, delegates are sent to county conventions, which, in turn, elect delegates to congressional district and state conventions which are held at later dates. These choose the national convention delegates.

In the Democratic Party, the national convention delegates are elected on a proportional basis. Candidates receiving a minimum of 15 per cent of the vote obtain a share of national convention delegates in that congressional district that is proportional to the vote they received (Polsby and Wildavsky, 1996: 120). Among the Republicans, some states adopt proportionality (and in 2012 many of the states holding early primaries had to use a proportional system), while others employ a 'winner takes all' system whereby the candidates with the most votes win all the delegates from that state. The electoral system that is used can have consequence for the character of the primary race. The long and bruising battle between Barack Obama and Hillary Clinton for the Democrats' presidential nomination in 2008 was in part a consequence of proportionality. Each primary victory provided only a relatively small lead in terms of convention delegates. In contrast, Senator John McCain won the Republican presidential nomination by the beginning of March because primary victories in winner-take-all states quickly gave him large numbers of convention delegates.

The overall size of a state party's delegation depends upon factors such as the state's population, its past support for that party's candidates in federal elections, and the number of elected officials belonging to the party. The Democratic convention is significantly larger in terms of delegate numbers.

Although preceded by the Iowa caucuses from 1972 onwards, the first state to hold a primary is, by tradition, New Hampshire. In the past, it was described as pivotal. By winning New Hampshire, it was said, candidates could gain a sense of momentum that would enable them to win in the later primaries. However, the state has rarely chosen the eventual winner. The 1992 Democratic primary was won by the late Paul Tsongas. It was Bill Clinton who secured the presidential nomination. In 1996, the maverick conservative commentator Patrick J. Buchanan won in the New Hampshire Republican primary, but was decisively beaten in the race for the nomination by the former Senate Majority Leader, Bob Dole. In 2000, the New Hampshire Republican primary was won by the Arizona Senator John McCain. Later primaries, however, gave victory to George W. Bush. However, although perhaps not pivotal, New Hampshire should not be dismissed. In 2008, victory in the 'Granite State' allowed Hillary Clinton to continue her campaign after a disappointing third place finish in Iowa. Had she lost New Hampshire her bid to win the nomination would almost certainly have finished there and then. Amongst the Republicans, John McCain's win in New Hampshire established him as the frontrunner.

The primary 'season' traditionally lasts between the beginning of election year and June. There are often tensions about the timetable as states jostle for particular primary dates and party officials seek an early and conclusive victory so that the party can concentrate its efforts on winning the White House. The initial primaries are almost always critical. Although the 2008 Democratic race was an exception, the states that still hold their primaries on a later date may well be consigned to the political sidelines as the losing candidates generally withdraw at an early date. The Iowa caucuses and the New Hampshire primary are the initial tests. However, within the Republican Party at least, the South Carolina primary has become increasingly pivotal. In 2000, George W. Bush's defeat of John McCain (53–42 per cent) established that he would be the overall victor. Where significant numbers of states hold primaries or caucuses on the same day, the results acquire particular significance. In 2008 'Super Tuesday (or 'Super Duper Tuesday' as it was dubbed in some reports) was held on 5 February. Twenty-four states and the American territory of Samoa participated in this.

At this point, there is a snowballing effect. Campaign funds and offers of backing flow towards the frontrunner, who will almost certainly secure the nomination and may win the presidency. For their part, candidates who perform poorly in these early primaries will probably decide to withdraw. Indeed, they may be compelled to, because they may have lost much of their backing from donors. Furthermore, taxpayer funding, administered through the FEC, is restricted to those who gain at least 10 per cent of the vote in at least one of the two final primaries that they contest. This also encourages candidates who perform poorly to withdraw at an early stage. They fear that if they stay in the race they will lose their eligibility for matching funds (*Congressional Quarterly*, 1997: 46). By the end of January 2008, even before Super Tuesday, only Hillary Clinton and Barack Obama remained in the Democratic race. The development of primaries opened up the nomination process, shifted power from party leaders to the ordinary voter, increased participation, and tested the stamina of potential candidates. In a study of the 1992 primaries, Pippa Norris concluded: 'if it ain't broke, don't fix it' (Norris, 1992). However, the primary system has been subject to severe criticism.

First, the primary election 'season' is said to be too long. The length of the campaign imposes unnecessary 'wear and tear' upon candidates (King, 1981: 317).

Second, voting in the states that hold caucuses rather than primaries is open (rather than secret) and those who participate may be unduly swayed by 'groupthink' or subject to peer pressure.

Third, as noted above, 'first tier' primary candidates now turn down the matching (dollar-for-dollar) funds offered by the Federal Election Commission so that they can spend without limit. The pressure to spend is increased by the competitiveness of particular contests and the extent to which a candidate must campaign simultaneously in a number of states. All of this requires high levels of spending. In 2008, Senator Hillary Clinton spent $215,825,248 and lost (Federal Election Commission, 2009).

Fourth, turnout is often low and those who vote in the caucuses and primaries, particularly the caucuses, are socially and politically unrepresentative. Although in the 2008 elections turnout reached 53.6 per cent in New Hampshire, it was just 5.9 per cent In the North Dakota caucuses (United States Elections Project, 2008). A study of those who participated in the 2004 Democratic caucuses in Iowa suggested that turnout was skewed towards those with a college degree who describe themselves as 'liberal'. Arguably, the increasing use of the internet as a mobilising tool (leading to talk of the 'netroots') during the primary season has increased the weight of these groupings still further and tilted the process towards males. This having been said, it would be a mistake to overgeneralise about the character of the primary electorate. There are significant differences between states. In some, for example, independents or those who declare no allegiances can vote. In others, the electorate is restricted to those who have pre-registered as party supporters.

Fifth, the early caucuses and primaries matter most. Traditionally, Iowa and New Hampshire hold the first caucuses and primary respectively. Candidates must, at the least, gain a respectable showing in the state if they are to be considered credible contenders. Critics of the process contend, however, that although Iowa and New Hampshire are accorded a significant role in deciding the fate of presidential hopefuls, they are unrepresentative of the nation in so far as they are largely rural, white, and Protestant. A 2008 poll of Iowa Republican voters suggested that 60 per cent were 'born again' (or evangelical) Christians and 45 per cent regarded themselves as 'very conservative'. Sixty-nine per cent lived in rural neighbourhoods. Thirty-six per cent of New Hampshire Republicans had an annual income of $100,000 or more (Silver, 2011).

Sixth, in the early caucuses and primaries a candidate is judged largely on his or her electoral performance in relation to the expectations that have been set. In February 1992, Bill Clinton gained only 26 per cent of the vote in the New Hampshire primary. He was 9 per cent behind the victor, Paul Tsongas. However, Clinton could call his result a victory, dub himself the 'comeback kid', and go on to win the later primaries because his vote exceeded expectations. However, such expectations are largely set by media forecasts. Net-based sources, the newspapers, radio stations, and television channels thereby gain undue influence.

Seventh, the primary system eliminates peer review from the nomination process. Presidential candidates are generally state governors or serve in Congress. They should, it is said, be judged as candidates by their colleagues rather than by members of the public who will inevitably have little detailed knowledge about their record or suitability. Writing before reforms that extended the franchise in party leadership elections were introduced, Anthony King described the strengths of peer review in Britain:

> The candidates were assessed and voted upon exclusively by their fellow politicians . . . Most of them were on first-name terms with the people they were voting for; they were in an excellent position to know their strengths and weaknesses. More than that, they had a powerful incentive to arrive at the right decision since they personally would have to live with the consequences. They would have to work with the new leader; if they made the wrong decision, they would suffer electorally and possibly also in career terms. (King, 1981: 310)

Eighth, the system of primary elections has, some argue, weakened the American political parties.[2] First, they have removed the parties' ability to nominate their own candidates, thereby causing candidates to become 'public property'. Second, the primaries have encouraged the creation of personal campaign organisations built around the candidates rather than the party (see Chapter 3). Third, the primaries may lead to disunity. The tensions engendered by the Democratic contest between Jimmy Carter and Edward Kennedy in 1980 contributed to the party's defeat later in the year. As Martin Wattenberg notes, even if a popular candidate eventually wins the party nomination, this can be 'insufficient to heal the wounds of the primary season' (1991: 59).

National party conventions (July–August)

Presidential candidates are formally chosen by the Democratic and Republican parties at their national nominating conventions. These are held during the summer months after the primaries and caucuses have concluded.

Historically, the delegates themselves chose the nominee from a number of candidates. This would follow a succession of ballots, compromises and deals in 'smoke-filled rooms.' In recent years, however, the candidate is invariably known months before the convention even begins because most of the convention delegates are pledged to back the candidate who won their state primary or was chosen in the caucuses. Furthermore, in most cases, the losing candidates will have decided to withdraw. Conventions therefore crown an already anointed candidate. In that sense, they are a formality. Since the Second World War, and thus in the period before the primary system became institutionalised, only two nominees, Thomas Dewey (Republican) in 1948 and Adlai Stevenson (Democrat) in 1952, failed to secure a majority of delegate votes on the first ballot. Having said this, there were uncertainties in the 1976 Republican race (when President Gerald Ford narrowly secured the nomination) and in the 1984 Democratic contest when Walter Mondale had to depend upon the votes of the party's 'superdelegates'. There were some forecasts in 2008 that the primary battle between Barack Obama and Hillary Clinton would be resolved only at the convention. However, Obama secured the allegiance of a majority before then.

The convention also considers and agrees upon the party's platform. Nonetheless, its role is limited because, in an era of candidate-centred politics in which a nominee depends upon his or her own organisation rather than the party apparatus, the nominee will not feel bound by it. In a celebrated remark, Senator Bob Dole, the Republicans' 1996 presidential candidate, said that he had not read his party's platform. Furthermore, in contrast with Britain's parliamentary system, a presidential candidate is far from assured, if elected to the presidency, that campaign proposals can be enacted as law. Legislation is invariably a compromise between the White House, the House of Representatives, and the Senate. Nonetheless, although a party's platform should not be seen as a 'manifesto', to which parliamentary candidates are held to account, the words and phrases that are adopted may still be a battleground between different party factions. Platform statements on abortion have proved particularly divisive in the Republican Party.

In the past, the nominee announced his choice of vice-presidential candidate or 'running mate' at the convention. The vice-presidential pick would then be confirmed by ballot. However, the announcement is nowadays made once the overall result of the primaries has become evident. Conventional wisdom suggests that the ticket should be 'balanced'. In other words, the running mate should be drawn from a different part of the country or a different wing of the party. In 1960, John F. Kennedy, a relatively young Catholic from Massachusetts, selected Lyndon Johnson, who was older, a Protestant, and from Texas. In 1988, the Democratic candidate, Governor Michael Dukakis, picked Senator Lloyd Bentsen as his vice-presidential candidate. Dukakis was from Massachusetts and a relatively liberal figure. In contrast, Bentsen was much more conservative and a Texan. At the least, the running mate is selected so as to compensate for a perceived weakness in the personality or politics of the presidential nominee. In 2000, George W. Bush selected Dick Cheney. Bush, who was serving as governor of Texas, had despite his family background relatively little experience of politics in Washington DC or foreign policy. He was widely regarded as weak and perhaps even unqualified in dealing with these matters. Cheney, however, was a consummate Washington 'insider', having formerly served as White House Chief of Staff and Secretary of Defense. For his part, Bill Clinton picked Al Gore in 1992. At first sight, it was an unbalanced ticket. Gore was from Tennessee (which adjoined Clinton's home state of Arkansas), and he shared Clinton's moderate politics. However, he compensated for Clinton's failure to develop ties with organised labour and the environmentalist groupings within the Party, which were cautious towards, or perhaps even suspicious of, Clinton. Senator John McCain, who was 72 by the time of the November 2008 presidential election and, although respected, was distrusted by many Christian conservatives and hardliners, electrified the campaign by picking the Alaska governor, Sarah Palin as his running mate. Palin had committed support among those Republicans whom McCain had failed to energise, particularly those concerned about issues such as abortion. Nonetheless, although the Republican ticket initially gained a 'bounce' in the opinion polls following Palin's selection, questions about her experience and a faltering performance in some television interviews seemed to damage the campaign. Although polling data have suggested that vice-presidential candidates neither win nor lose significant numbers of votes, there is some evidence that Governor Palin's presence on the ticket may have lost the Republicans some support amongst independents. It may have further galvanised the Democratic vote.

The convention has further functions. It is the only opportunity for party activists to meet as a national party, and is therefore a party-building exercise. Party activists are generally organised around local and state elections. At the convention, they can consider the party as a national institution and focus on electing the candidate to the only nationwide office in the US. The convention is, perhaps more importantly, a media event.[3] This was conveyed in a portrait of the 1988 Republican National Convention: 'With a color-coordinated stage; a band playing upbeat, patriotic music; speakers carefully timed, rehearsed, and designed to heighten the campaign themes; balloons set to fall like rain on the nominees and the delegates dressed in all types of garb, the result was pure theater' (Wayne, 1992: 161). Although its scope and scale has been progressively reduced, the convention is a major opportunity to attract free national media coverage and win the attention of voters. Candidates almost always gain a post-convention 'bounce' in the public opinion polls. Bill Clinton secured a sixteen-point increase after the 1992 Democratic Convention. The median increase between 1964 and 2004 was five percentage points (Jones, 2008). Indeed, during this period, only three presidential candidates, George McGovern, John Kerry, and Barack Obama (the Democratic candidates in 1972, 2004, and 2008 respectively), failed to register an increase in support among registered voters increase after their parties' conventions.

The overall size of the 'bounce' depends in part upon the party's stage management abilities. However, other factors are also involved. Stuart Rothenberg argues that it rests upon the public's familiarity with a candidate. The size of Clinton's 1992 'bounce', he asserts, may be attributable to the fact that he had, until then, been a relatively unknown figure. Both Clinton and the Republican challenger, Bob Dole, attracted only small-scale 'bounces' in 1996 because, Rothenberg argues, they were by then familiar to the public (CNN.com, 2000). At the same time, a divided convention can impede the party's prospects. The

1968 Democratic convention was bitterly divided over the choice of nominee, and there were protests against the Vietnam War. The televised scenes did much to ensure that the Republican contender, Richard Nixon, won the November election.

Nonetheless, having said this, the 'bounce' should be placed in its proper context. Although strategists emphasise its importance, it is not pivotal. In 2008, as noted above, Barack Obama failed to secure a 'bounce' while Senator John McCain jumped into a polling lead. It only, however, lasted for about a fortnight.

Post-nomination (September–November)

From 1845 onwards, presidential elections have been held on the first Tuesday after the first Monday in November. In the past, the nominees began their campaigns after the Labor Day holiday in early September. The beginning of the campaigning process has, however, been beginning earlier in the year. Bill Clinton started a nationwide bus tour immediately after the national convention in 1992, thereby giving his campaign a significant boost.

The candidates, who will have been joined in the contest by independents and minor party nominees, are now more likely to frame their appeal in terms of the broader interests of the nation.[4] Although there are exceptions, they will almost certainly have to adopt different themes to those that won them the party nomination, if only because the potential electorate is much larger in size and heterogeneous in character. Television opportunities are pivotal and the campaigns are driven by the need to attract coverage. Increasingly, although candidate-centred, much of the campaigning is undertaken by interest groups and allied organisations (see Chapter 3).

The televised presidential debates, which are usually held in October, have come to occupy an important place in the campaign calendar. They were first introduced in 1960 (although none took place again until 1976), and have become institutionalised and now include one debate between the vice-presidential candidates. Indeed, they sometimes appear to have played a decisive role. John F. Kennedy's victory in the 1960 presidential election is widely attributed to the perception by television viewers of the debate that his Republican opponent, Richard Nixon, looked evasive. However, although the 1960 debate acquired a legendary status, the claim that the debates play a determining role should be qualified. First, although even small shifts can dramatically change electoral outcomes, only relatively small numbers appear to be directly influenced by the debates. In 1996, 92 per cent of those asked in a CBS News poll said that the first debate between Bill Clinton and Bob Dole had done nothing to alter their opinion of the candidates (Bennett, 1997: 24). Second, the debates are often outweighed by other political considerations. In 1988, there was a vigorous exchange in the vice-presidential debate between Lloyd Bentsen and Dan Quayle, Democratic and Republican candidates respectively. However, although Bentsen memorably ridiculed his opponent, the Bush–Quayle ticket won the November election. Third, in so far as the debates do play a role, the data suggest that the important factor is not the debate itself but instead the popular expectations of the candidates' performances. In the 2000 presidential election, there were widely shared expectations that the televised debates would offer an opportunity for Al Gore to display his knowledge and experience. There were also predictions that George W. Bush would stumble when confronted by challenging issues, particularly those associated with foreign policy issues. However, Gore failed to match these high expectations. In contrast, Bush exceeded the low level of expectations that had been set for him. As October progressed, Bush established and consolidated his lead. In 2008, there were predictions that the Republicans' vice-presidential nominee, Governor Sarah Palin, would stumble because of what was widely seen as her lack of political experience and seeming impetuosity. However, she was judged to have avoided serious errors or mishaps and strengthened her position, at least in the eyes of Republican supporters.

The Electoral College

The result of the vote is, almost always, known on the day of the election.[5] Indeed, the television networks announce a victor in, or 'call', states well before voting finishes in many of the other states or the counting of votes has been completed in the state that is being 'called'. In the 2000 election, competition between the television networks led them to 'call' states prematurely. Florida, on which the entire presidential election came to depend, was initially 'called' for Gore. It was later called for Bush. It was finally thrown into an undecided category.

However, despite the televised drama of election night, the formal election takes place, under the terms of the Constitution, only at a later stage, through the Electoral College. Each state is allocated a specified number of Electors or Electoral College Votes (ECV) based on its total Congressional representation. Washington DC has a further three Electors. In all there are 538 ECV. To compensate for shifts in population, the process of reapportionment that is undertaken every ten years, following the census, leads to changes in state representation in the House of Representatives and therefore the Electoral College. Following the 2010 Census, California had, as the most populous state, 55 Electors. Other states with large populations were also well represented. Both New York and Florida had 29 ECV (a loss and a gain of two Electoral Votes respectively). The least populous states (Alaska, Vermont, and Wyoming) each had three Electors.

In every state, except Maine (since 1972) and Nebraska (since 1996), the candidate who wins the most votes (a 'plurality') in that state is allocated all of its ECV. There is a 'winner-takes-all' system. A few weeks after the November contest, the Electors, who are generally officials and loyalists from the party that has won the presidential vote, meet in their state capitals and the District of Columbia formally to elect the president. These gatherings are, almost invariably, a formality. The Electors simply confirm the judgement of the voters in their state. The formal results are dispatched from the state capitals once their Electors have cast their Votes to the vice-president in his role as president of the US Senate. In a joint session of Congress, the tellers read the Electoral Votes from each state. Although little importance is usually attached to the process, there were challenges to the validity of some ECV in 1969, 2001, and 2005.

To win the presidency, a candidate must obtain at least 270 ECV, an absolute majority among the College's 538 Electors. If there is not such a majority, the Constitution specifies that the election is to be conducted by the House of Representatives, although, under the terms of Article II, each state delegation is assigned only one vote.

The Electoral College was established by the Founding Fathers for three principal reasons. First, it offered a degree of reassurance to the states, a number of which saw a danger of centralisation in the US Constitution, that they could play an entrenched and institutionalised part in the selection of a president. Second, an indirect system allowed the states to maintain their own laws governing the extent of the franchise. Indeed, South Carolina did not choose its Electors by popular vote until after the Civil War. Third, although voting rights were severely restricted in the eighteenth century, and were generally conditional upon property ownership, the Constitution's authors feared that the electorate might make an inappropriate choice, and sought safeguards against 'popular passion'. The Electoral College was envisaged as a deliberative institution that could, if necessary, disregard such 'passion' and choose the candidate considered most qualified. The College has however been subject to sustained criticism in modern times by those who see it as an undemocratic relic of an earlier age.

First, the mathematics of the Electoral College can allow a candidate with a smaller share of the popular vote than an opponent to win more ECV. This was vividly illustrated in the 2000 presidential election. The result led to bitter criticism of the Electoral College and challenges to the legitimacy of the Bush administration. The phrase 'Hail to the Thief' was heard. The novelist Gore Vidal talked of the 'Bush–Cheney junta'. Michael Moore, the radical television observer and author of *Stupid White Men . . . and Other Sorry Excuses for the State of the Nation*, said of the College: 'This is a democracy. One person, one vote. We should have done away with this antique long before now' (Moore, 2000). There have, furthermore, been other presidential elections when the winner in terms of the popular vote lost in the Electoral College. In 1876, the Democratic candidate, Samuel J. Tilden, gained 51 per cent of the popular vote, but Rutherford B. Hayes, the Republican, had a one vote majority in the Electoral College and thereby gained the presidency. Twelve years later, in 1888, Grover Cleveland (Democrat) won over ninety thousand more votes than Benjamin Harrison (Republican). However, Harrison won in the Electoral College by 233 ECV to 168.

Second, even when the Electoral College delivers the 'right' result in terms of the overall victor, it distorts the popular vote. This is because the winner in almost every state is allocated all that state's ECV regardless of his or her margin of victory. In 2008, Barack Obama secured 52.92 per cent of the popular vote (thereby becoming the first Democratic presidential nominee to win over half the vote since Jimmy Carter's victory in 1976). However, the Obama–Biden ticket won 365 ECV. The McCain–Palin ticket was just 7 per cent behind (45.66 per cent) but secured only 173 ECV.

Third, the Electoral College assures states of at least three ECV. This, in terms of population, is over-representation for some. Some critics assert that this is, like the system of election to the US Senate that assigns two senators to each state regardless of population size, an undemocratic denial of the popular will.

Fourth, although many states have laws prohibiting it, the system allows the occasional 'faithless Elector' to vote for a candidate who did not win the popular vote in a particular state. In all, there have been 14 instances of this. In 1972, a Nixon delegate from Virginia voted for John Hospers, the Libertarian Party candidate. In 1988, a West Virginia Elector cast her vote for Senator Lloyd Bentsen, the running mate, rather than Michael Dukakis, the Democratic presidential candidate who had won the popular vote in the state. In 2000, one Elector from the District of Columbia abstained in protest against the District's lack of representation in Congress. In 2004, one 'faithless Elector' in Minnesota (perhaps mistakenly) cast an electoral vote for the Democrats' vice-presidential nominee, John Edwards. Although no 'faithless Elector' has changed the outcome of an election, the potential for this in a close race remains.

Fifth, independent and third-party candidates often fare badly in the Electoral College. In 1992, Ross Perot gained 19 per cent of the popular vote but, because his support was dispersed across the country, received no ECV at all. However, having said this, there are exceptions. The popular vote for some minor party candidates has been regionally concentrated. In 1968, George Wallace, who had served as Governor of Alabama and had come to symbolise southern white resistance to desegregation, won in five states, giving him 46 ECV. In 1948, both Henry Wallace, a left-leaning progressive, and Strom Thurmond, the segregationist governor of South Carolina, gained about 2.4 per cent of the national vote. However, because his votes were regionally concentrated, Thurmond won 39 ECV. For his part, Henry Wallace, whose votes were dispersed, gained none.

Sixth, under the terms of the Constitution, the House of Representatives decides upon the presidency and the Senate the vice-presidency if there is no absolute majority in the College. Each state delegation in the House is assigned one vote. Although this happened only in 1800 and 1824 (while the Senate decided upon the vice-presidency in 1836), a shift of only thirty thousand popular votes would have thrown both the 1860 and 1960 elections to the

House (*Congressional Quarterly*, 1997: 128). Such procedures can, however, be seen as a breach of the separation of powers between the legislative and executive branches of government. There is, furthermore, a theoretical possibility that the president and vice-president could be drawn from opposing parties.

Seventh, the College distorts the character of the election campaign. The campaigns concentrate their resources on 'swing' states such as Ohio and Florida. States (including California and Texas) where the result is a foregone conclusion are as a consequence less than full participants in the electoral process.

The reform of the Electoral College has, periodically, been the subject of debate. Many would like to address the problem of the 'faithless Elector' by extending the laws that compel Electors to cast their vote for the winner of the popular vote in their state. There are, however, also calls for more fundamental forms of change. Some, particularly on the left, hope to see the direct election of the president. This, they argue, would ensure a democratic outcome. However, the role of the states and their Electors is entrenched in the Constitution, and this type of reform would require an amendment. It would almost certainly be impossible to secure the required three-quarters majority among the states, because the less populated states gain in terms of their relative number of ECV. If the election was based on the popular vote alone, campaigns would be concentrated in the metropolitan regions, and the more rural areas would be neglected. Furthermore, those who talk of 'states' rights' also fear that such a step would further denude the states of their semi-sovereign role and correspondingly add to the powers of national government. There is also a danger that, if the winner simply required a plurality of the votes, a president could be elected with a relatively small proportion of the votes. The presence of third-party candidates increases the likelihood of this. For this reason, proposals for a direct vote are often tied to an insistence that there should be a threshold. The League of Women Voters, for example, backs a 40 per cent threshold. If no candidate gains this, there would be a second, run-off election. Run-off elections are already used for Congressional elections in Louisiana as well as for local and statewide races in states such as Texas, Arkansas, and Alabama. These, however, draw out and lengthen the electoral process.

Arthur Schlesinger Jr put forward another proposal. He argued for the retention of the Electoral College, but suggested that the winner of the popular vote should be awarded bonus ECV. This would almost certainly guarantee that whoever gained a majority of the popular vote would also win in the College. It would, for example, have ensured that Al Gore gained the presidency in 2000.

Others call for the proportional allocation of Electoral Votes. In place of the winner-takes-all system, a candidate who wins a particular proportion of the popular vote would be assigned that proportion of the ECV. Although thresholds would have to be introduced to prevent the president being elected on a minority vote, this would lead to a fairer, less distorted result, and encourage candidates to campaign across the country. However, in the absence of a Constitutional amendment, it would probably have to be introduced on a state-by-state basis. But the partial adoption of this proposal could give one party an unfair advantage, and, furthermore, it would not address the over-representation of the less populous states.

A more modest proposal would extend the system used in Maine and Nebraska. At present, each state is awarded two Electoral Votes for the state as a whole together with one Electoral Vote for each of its Congressional districts. The Maine and Nebraska system would give only the two statewide votes to the winner in the state as a whole, and would divide the other votes by giving one to the plurality winner in each Congressional district (Center for Voting and Democracy, 2003).

Nonetheless, although the 2002 Help America Vote Act provided some funding for the modernisation of voting technology, far-reaching reform is unlikely. There are two reasons for this. First, there is no consensus on the different alternatives. Second, many types of reform require a Constitutional amendment requiring the backing of two-thirds of Congress and three-quarters of the states. Third, both parties are ambivalent about reform. In recent years, support for both the Democrats and Republicans has been finely balanced. Indeed, some commentators have talked of a '50-50 nation'. Both can rationally hope for victory within the Electoral College.

Inauguration

Although the inconclusive result of the 2010 general election led to a five-day delay as the coalition government took shape, an incoming prime minister in Britain customarily takes office the morning after a general election is held. In the US, a new president is sworn in, traditionally by the Chief Justice, at an inaugural ceremony on 20 January. The two-month transition period allows the president-elect to prepare his administration and appoint its most senior members. The Inaugural Address, delivered once the oath of office has been administered, offers signs of the style and direction that will be adopted by the new administration. In 1933, Franklin D. Roosevelt asserted, in a call for government action against economic depression, that 'the only thing we have to fear is fear itself' (Maidment and Dawson, 1994: 185). In January 1961, John F. Kennedy spelt out the US's commitment to resisting the expansion of communism: 'Let every nation know, whether it wishes us well or ill, that we shall pay any price, bear any burden, meet any hardship, support any friend, oppose any foe to assure the survival and success of liberty' (quoted in Maidment and Dawson, 1994: 190). At his inauguration in 2009, Barack Obama told a crowd estimated to have been over a million: 'The state of our economy calls for action: bold and swift. And we will act not only to create new jobs but to lay a new foundation for growth. We will build the roads and bridges, the electric grids and digital lines that feed our commerce and bind us together.' Obama included an implicit criticism of his predecessor in the White House: 'we will restore science to its rightful place and wield technology's wonders to raise health care's quality' (*The New York Times*, 2009).

Electing Congress

Whereas senators serve six-year terms, members of the House of Representatives are elected every two years. Elections are held using the plurality or first-past-the-post system. With some exceptions because all states must have at least one member of the House, Congressional districts are roughly equal in population (with about 700,000 adults in each) and are subject to a redrawing process every ten years on the basis of shifts in population.[6] The process, known as *redistricting*, is carried out in a majority of states by their legislatures. It often favours incumbents but can at times be bitterly partisan. This has been particularly evident in Texas. In the 2002 elections, the Democrats won a majority of Texas's seats in the House of Representatives (17 seats to the Republicans' 15). Two years later in 2004, following a controversial and bitterly fought redistricting battle, the Republicans won 21 seats to the Democrats' 11. Senators, who represent the entire state, are spared the traumas of redistricting.

Like the race for the presidency, Congressional elections have a two-stage character and rest on the use of either closed or open primaries. In the past, a few states, such as Washington, have held 'blanket primaries'. These allow voters of all persuasions to vote to select the nominees for any of the parties. In 1996, following the passage of Proposition 198, California also adopted the blanket primary. However, it was prohibited by the US Supreme Court in *California Democratic Party* et al. *v. Jones* et al. (June 2000). Despite reform efforts, Louisiana continues to use a second-ballot system. The top two candidates face a run-off contest.

Two further characteristics of Congressional elections should be noted. First, the threat of a primary challenge, and the competition for money and workers with campaigns for other elective offices, mean that Congress members retain their own personal campaign organisation. They are not dependent upon their party apparatus. Second, incumbents enjoy a decisive advantage. Once elected, members of Congress are almost certain to be re-elected (see p. 41). Relatively few elections, unless they are held in 'open seats' in which there is no incumbent, have a genuinely competitive character. This, some suggest, contributes to relatively low levels of overall turnout.

Financing campaigns

US elections inevitably require large-scale financial resources. Although 'independent' organisations increasingly contribute to electoral mobilisation efforts (see below), the candidates' campaigns have to fund television advertisements and other forms of media activity, staff salaries, and travel costs.

Although commentators usually focus on presidential elections, Congressional (and some state) elections also impose heavy financial demands. Senate (and some gubernatorial) elections in the more populous states involve an electorate of many millions. In the 2010 race for the governorship of California, Meg Whitman, the former eBay chief and Republican candidate, spent $178.5 million, $144 million of which was taken from her own funds.[7] For their part, presidential candidates must reach the primary electorate in the first half of the year and the wider voting public in the key 'swing' states in the run-up to the November contest.

There have been sustained efforts over more than a century to regulate the raising of funds and election spending. Indeed, President Theodore Roosevelt expressed concerns about uncontrolled election spending as early as 1905. The political process would, it was argued, be corrupted if candidates could be 'bought' by wealthy anonymous donors. Election victories, it was increasingly argued, should not depend upon a candidate's ability to out-spend opponents.

By the early 1970s, such fears had become acute. Congress responded by passing the Federal Election Campaign Act (FECA) of 1971 which was then amended in 1974 in the aftermath of the Watergate scandal. As the scandal had unfolded, it had become clear that President Nixon's re-election campaign had in part been funded by anonymous donations that had then been used to fund illegal activities. As a consequence of the Act's passage, taxpayer funds administered through the Federal Election Commission (FEC) have been offered to candidates in every presidential election from 1976 onwards. In the primaries, candidates are, subject to stringent conditions, eligible for matching FEC funding (see p. 4). To qualify, candidates must raise their own funds and agree to respect overall spending limits in each of the states so as to ensure a broadly level playing-field. The candidates must also allow a full audit of their campaigns. The spending limit is increased every four years so as to keep pace with inflation. In 2008, primary candidates were limited to an overall expenditure limit of $42.05 million. This was divided between the states on the basis of their voting-age population. The figure for California was $18,279,300 (Federal Election Commission, 2008). In the post-nomination, or general election, phase, the Federal Election Campaign Act envisaged that the candidates nominated by the major parties would receive almost all their funding from the FEC. They were not to spend above and beyond this. In 2004, for example, the Bush and the Kerry campaigns were each assigned $74.6 million (Cantor, 2005: 6). Candidates from the minor parties are given some funding, based on a sliding scale, if they attract over 5 per cent of the vote. In 2000, Patrick Buchanan, who was nominated by the Reform Party, was given $12.6 million because the Party's 1996 candidate, Ross Perot, had won 8 per cent of the vote. The principal parties also receive funding for their national conventions. In 2004, both parties received $14,924,000.

The law also imposes constraints on the individual, political action commit-tees (PACs), and the parties as well as the campaigns. In 2011–12, individuals were legally restricted to contributions of $2500 for each election, making a total of $5000 for a primary and general election together (Federal Election Commission, 2011a). Some PACs could contribute $2500 while others could give $5000. Donations and spending conforming to the limits set under the law are known as 'hard money'.

Nonetheless, the process of regulating electoral finance and limiting spend-ing to 'hard money' totals inevitably faces severe difficulty. Efforts to regulate may be judged to run counter to rights assured in the US Constitution. More importantly, as Justices Sandra Day O'Connor and John Paul Stevens wrote in the case of *McConnell v. Federal Election Commission* (2003), 'money, like water, will always find an outlet'. And, despite regulation, more and more money is required. The size of the voting-age population has grown and is growing. Competition between candidates is often intense because of both growing partisanship and polarisation and, at the primary stage, the extent of differences within the parties. Campaigns 'sell' their candidate at every opportunity and therefore seek to maximise their spending. Negative advertis-ing can lead to a vicious circle whereby candidates seek to defend themselves against the charges that have been made and then themselves make counter-attacks. New production techniques and technology offer further campaign advertising opportunities. Campaigns have been extended in length and are now more professionalised. They will engage in 'micro-targeting' relatively narrow demographic niches and are dependent upon the services of polling organisations. These test public opinion through both conventional sampling techniques and the use of focus groups. These latter are representative gather-ings of potential voters who inform pollsters about their responses and feelings towards the candidate, the opponent, and different campaign strategies.

At the same time, partisan attachments and ideological zeal for particular candidates encourage giving by individuals, a process facilitated by online mechanisms. For many organised interests donations are regarded as essen-tial. They seem to offer access if a candidate is victorious. There is, furthermore, always a residual fear that competing interests will gain a foothold if they contribute more.

Against this background, there are repeated efforts to undermine and cir-cumvent the different forms of legal regulation. Put another way, the institu-tional architecture governing electoral finance is always subject to a process of erosion.

First, following the 1976 US Supreme Court ruling *Buckley v. Valeo*, those who do not seek matching funds are not bound by the limits imposed under FECA. It is now accepted that 'top-tier' candidates in both the Republican and Democratic presidential primaries do not take matching funds and their spending is thereby unlimited (see above). However, the 2008 election estab-lished a first. A major party nominee – Barack Obama – declined FEC funding during the general election campaign. If the primaries and the general election are taken together, he spent $729,288,031 much of which was raised from individuals through Web-based appeals. His Republican opponent, Senator John McCain, who accepted FEC funding in both the primaries and the general election campaign, was limited to a spending total of $202,082,251 in the primaries and to just $84.1 million in the general election although his campaign was boosted by the Republican National Committee (Federal Election Commission, 2009).[8] In September 2008, the Obama campaign outspent McCain in advertising by a ratio of about 4 to 1.

Second, *Buckley v. Valeo* also established that 'independent' campaigns by individuals or political action committees (which before 2010 offered the only vehicle through which an interest group, union, or corporation could engage in electioneering) either in support of or in opposition to a particular candidate could not be restricted. Such restrictions would, the Court ruled, breach the First Amendment's guarantee of free speech. Thus, providing there is no formal connection with a candidate's organisation, campaign advertisements may expressly state opinions about candidates.

Third, increasingly, the major parties also collected and spent 'soft money' (as funds that evaded the 'hard money' limits set by the FEC came to be called). Although it could not be used to back candidates directly, it was directed towards issue-advertising, voter registration efforts, and get out the vote campaigns. Commentators agree that, in practice, there has always been a very thin line between 'issue-ads' and forms of advertising that directly urged a vote for or against a particular candidate.

Fourth, '527s' (campaigning organisations named after Section 527 of the tax code which gives them task exempt status) have also been formed by those seeking to influence election outcomes. There are no legal limits on spending or fundraising (although donations must be disclosed). 527s cannot co-ordinate their efforts with candidates' campaigns and may not call for a vote for or against a particular candidate. However, some have increasingly crossed this particular line. Following the 2004 presidential election, the Federal Election Commission fined a number of organisations including the Swift Boat Veterans for Truth (which had sought, with effect, to undermine Senator John Kerry's Vietnam war record) and MoveOn.org which backed the Democrats.

There have been efforts by lawmakers to rebuild the regulatory frameworks of earlier years. In 2002, Congress passed a significant amendment to FECA known as the Bipartisan Campaign Reform Act (BCRA) or, after the names of its principal Senate sponsors, the McCain–Feingold Act.[9] BCRA sought to restrict the parties' use of 'soft money'. National party committees were prohibited from raising or spending funds other than 'hard money' in elections at all levels and barred from producing 'issue-ads'. At the same time, the Act took aim at issue-ads. It banned advertisements that named a particular candidate in presidential or Congressional elections within 30 days of a primary or 60 days of a general election. It also prohibited corporations (including 'non-profits') from spending their funds on issue-ads.

Despite BCRA, the process of erosion continued. Indeed, the Act was subject to different forms of circumvention and legal challenge. Although barred from raising 'soft money', national party committees could make 'co-ordinated' expenditure with candidates' campaigns as well as 'independent' expenditure. The Republican National Committee spent large 'co-ordinated' sums in the 2008 election (Dwyre and Kolodny, 2003: 92).

Although the US Supreme Court upheld much of BCRA in *McConnell v. Federal Election Commission* (2003), later rulings struck down core provisions. In *Federal Election Commission v. Wisconsin Right to Life* (2007), and perhaps reflecting the appointing of John Roberts and Samuel Alito, the Supreme Court struck down the Act's ban on issue-ads during the run-up to elections. As Roberts and Alito recorded in their opinion, 'the First Amendment requires us to err on the side of protecting political speech rather than suppressing it' (FindLaw, 2007). A 2010 US Supreme Court ruling (*Citizens United v. Federal Election Commission*), broadened the reach of the First Amendment and weakened BCRA still further. It established that companies, unions, and advocacy groups could issue independent 'electioneering communications' without limit (although they still cannot make direct contributions to candidates). While its supporters saw the ruling as a victory for freedom of speech, its opponents (including President Obama) argued that it would permit 'special interests' to exercise disproportionate influence in the electoral process.

However, despite the importance of money in the US political process, some qualifications should be made. First, while the sums are large, they should be seen alongside other forms of expenditure. As Stanley C. Brubaker observes, total spending in the 1996 elections was less than half the spending by Americans on cologne and perfume during the same period (1998: 38). Second, although the critics claim that money can 'buy' elections, Congressional votes, and presidential decisions, there is little hard evidence to support this. As Congressional election results show, the outcome depends on factors other than finance and the television advertising that can thereby be purchased. Third, the marginal gains from television advertising may be limited. In other words, it may be of only limited additional political value to show an advertisement twenty rather than ten times. In the 2010 Senate elections, Linda McMahon (the Republican candidate) spent $49.9 million in the Connecticut race but was still defeated. In Nevada, Sharron Angle, the Republican nominee, spent $27.5 million in her unsuccessful bid to defeat Harry Reid, the Senate majority leader (*Left and Right News*, 2010). The part played by election finance is limited in other ways. Much money is given to candidates who are already in a strong electoral position or have already adopted a favourable policy position from the perspective of the donor, rather than to those who might change their vote. Many PACs give money to competing candidates in the expectation that they will be given a chance to put forward their case before the Congress member takes a position, whoever wins. While incumbents are most successful at raising money, there is little evidence that this increases their likelihood of re-election. However, this having been said, financial resources may matter more for challengers. A well-funded campaign may allow them to compensate for all the advantages held by incumbents.

The role of the media

The character of the political communication process (and thereby that of election campaigns) is changing dramatically. The process in the US and other advanced industrial economies is now structured around digital technologies (Norris, 2011: 353). New technology has transformed the opportunity cost ratios associated with media production thereby allowing a proliferation of twenty-four-hour cable news networks, talk radio channels, websites, social networking, and smartphone applications. All of these are interactive in ways that could not have been visualised just a few years ago.

Nonetheless, as in other countries, there is differential access to media outlets and resources. Although a 2010 report to Congress indicated that 65 per cent of people had broadband access, the figure was (as Table 1.1 shows) significantly lower amongst some groupings.

Attitudes towards the media, particularly television broadcasting, differ. Within western countries, there are those who take a libertarian approach (and therefore resist all forms of government media regulation) and those who argue the case for a 'socially responsible' media system. They look towards the 'public service' broadcasting traditions of the BBC and its system of funding through a licence fee (Norris, 2011: 355). From this perspective, television and perhaps radio broadcasting should educate and inform through, for example, balanced coverage of political debates.

Although there are some limited forms of 'public broadcasting' in the US (through National Public Radio) and the Federal Communications Commission (FCC) has a regulatory role, much more is left to the free market in the US. Television networks are for the most part funded by commercials or

Table 1.1 *Broadband adoption rates by demographic groupings (%)*

National average	65
Rural Americans	50
Low income (under $20,000/year)	40
Older Americans (65+)	35
Less educated (no high school degree)	24

Source: adapted from US General Accounting Office (2010), *Report to Congressional Requesters – Telecommunications: National Broadband Plan Reflects the Experiences of Leading Countries, but Implementation Will Be Challenging,* US General Accounting Office, 18, http://democrats. energycommerce.house.gov/Press_111/20101012/GAO.Report.Broadband.2010.pdf.

subscription. There is open competition. The calls of those who hope for 'social responsibility' have been engulfed by commercial pressures and rapid techno-logical change which, as noted above, has facilitated the growth of countless terrestrial, cable, satellite and online outlets. Some seek a broad target audi-ence while others are 'micro-targeted' at particular demographic or geograph-ical tranches. Furthermore, in 1987, the Reagan administration abolished the 'fairness doctrine' which (as in the UK and other European countries) had required television and radio broadcasters to offer balanced coverage of politi-cal issues.[10] This opened the way for talk radio stations offering an unrestricted political and partisan message and in October 1996 the launching of the Fox News Channel. Although Fox News describes its own television coverage as 'fair and balanced', and insists that commentaries and news coverage are separated out, much of its reporting is closely aligned with conservative issue positions. Although not always uncritical Republican partisans, the chan-nel's most well-known and influential anchors (such as Sean Hannity, Bill O'Reilly, and formerly Glenn Beck) adopt a resolutely conservative approach to both economic and cultural issues. Their coverage of elections, critics charge, has been unremittingly tilted towards the Republicans. Furthermore, the network's news agenda, it is said, largely restricts itself to issues that the conservative movement seeks to advance. There was for example extensive coverage of claims that President Obama was not born in the US and not there-fore constitutionally entitled to serve as president. Before leaving the channel, Glenn Beck highlighted what he regarded as the radical political backgrounds of White House staff members. The issues that the network promotes are, it is claimed, co-ordinated with other groupings and interests within conserva-tive and Republican circles. Furthermore, critical commentators argue, by promoting such a hardline conservative message, Fox News has contributed to the degradation and impoverishment of political discourse (reducing it to a form of 'shouting') and reinforced partisan tensions. Republican legislators, it is charged, dare not seek political compromise because this would lead to criticism by Fox News and other outlets thereby jeopardising their re-election prospects.

Nonetheless, despite all these claims, a 2011 national survey by Public Policy Polling found that 42 per cent trusted Fox News's coverage, a figure margin-ally higher than that for other more mainstream news channels such as CNN and NBC although lower than that for PBS (the Public Broadcasting Service, a non-profitmaking channel) (Public Policy Polling, 2011).[11] Certainly, Fox News's viewing figures are way ahead of the channel's competitors. Table 1.2 shows the viewing statistics in early August 2011. It should be noted that Fox News is even further ahead of its rivals if its individual prime-time evening shows such as *The O'Reilly Factor* are considered.

Fox News's message is bolstered by many of the talk radio hosts, amongst whom conservatives are disproportionately represented. Rush Limbaugh, another hardline conservative, generally commands the largest audience

Table 1.2 *Viewing figures for the leading cable news channels, August 2011 (thousands)*

	Viewers aged 25–54	*Viewers aged 35–64*
Fox News Channel	336	638
CNN	148	196
MSNBC	126	220

Source: adapted from R. Seidman (2011), 'Cable News Ratings for Wednesday, August 10, 2011', *TV by the Numbers*, http://tvbythenumbers.zap2it.com/2011/08/11/cable-news-ratings-for-wednesday-august-10-2011/100248/.

share, drawing more than 15 million listeners a week. He was followed in 2010 by Fox News's anchors who also have radio shows, Sean Hannity and Glenn Beck (*Atlanta Journal-Constitution*, 2011).

MSNBC has increasingly sought to challenge Fox News's hegemony by offering a left-leaning counterpart (although Fox News often claims that CNN is also slanted towards the left). Anchors such as Rachel Maddow and (before he and the network parted company) Keith Olberman have adopted a similar format and style to that pioneered by Fox News. The network has had some successes. In the run-up to the 2008 presidential election, it beat CNN (as it usually does amongst those aged between 25 and 54) and occasionally came ahead of Fox News (Carter, 2008). However, its viewing figures, as noted above, generally lag far behind those for Fox News.

Having said this, those who lean leftwards, are in the younger age cohorts, or have only a limited interest in the political process may not have embraced MSNBC but have proved to be a large and faithful audience for *The Daily Show with Jon Stewart* and *The Colbert Report*. These fuse politics and entertainment in a way that commands a significant market share. Viewing figures for *The Daily Show* averaged 2.3 million in 2011, far ahead of the cable news channels. When Barack Obama made a guest appearance on *The Daily Show* just ahead of the 2008 presidential election, the number of viewers hit 3.6 million (Carter, 2008). Furthermore, although much is made of the influence that *Fox News* and to a lesser extent other news outlets enjoy, relatively few would argue that even the most partisan and ideologically transparent media forms (or paid advertising by candidates and allied organizations) significantly shift opinion. Viewers and listeners are not passive recipients but are instead pro-actively selective. They choose what they watch or hear and will interpret the information or opinions that are broadcast in different ways. For the most part, they select outlets conveying views with which they agree. A *New York Times* / CBS News poll conducted in September 2010 suggested that 78 per cent of viewers (who were at the same time likely voters in the 2010 mid-term elections) were Republican supporters. They were disproportionately male, upper- or upper-middle class, conservative and drawn from the older age group (Thee-Brenan, 2010).

Nonetheless, this does not mean that media influence should be dismissed or disregarded. Although media networks do not pull the political loyalties of their audiences across the political spectrum, scholarly studies suggest that they do play a role in *agenda-setting, framing,* and *amplification* processes. Agenda-setting theories suggest that that the media play a significant role in shaping the political issue that are subject to debate and controversy. Some would, for example, argue that Fox News gave undue weight in its coverage to particular individuals who had associations with Barack Obama in earlier years and the 'Birther' controversy (see p. 2). The network thereby shifted the political agenda towards these issues. 'Framing' refers to the framework within which events, developments, and processes are understood. The conservative media may have contributed to the ways in which the economic crisis was increasingly perceived as a problem of 'big government' (which it was said suppressed economic enterprise) rather than a consequence of unrestrained market forces. This allowed the Tea Party movement (which campaigned for minimal taxes and limited government) to grow and paved the way for Republican victories in the 2010 mid-term elections. 'Amplification' suggests that particular sentiments are intensified and strengthened by partisan or overtly ideological media coverage. Again, it has been said that Fox News built upon widespread hostility to President Obama amongst those of the right and, through the character of its coverage, increased the intensity of these feelings.

Assessing the electoral system

The character of the primaries and the role of money have already been considered. However, other features of the electoral system have also been subject to criticism.

First, although the 2012 election campaign was slow to start, the electoral cycle is generally said to be too long. Campaigning for the House of Representatives is a constant process. The institutionalisation of the 'invisible primary' has extended the presidential contest well into the pre-election year. The primary and caucus season extends over five months.

Second, campaigns are governed by negative 'attack-ads'. Particular advertisements are said to have swung elections. In 2004, as has been noted, Senator John Kerry, the Democratic contender, was undermined by The Swift Boat Veterans for Truth which mounted a series of television advertisements asserting that Kerry had, during the Vietnam war, betrayed the other soldiers with whom he was serving. In 1988, advertisements placed by Republican supporters suggested that the Democratic candidate, the Massachusetts Governor Michael Dukakis, was weak towards criminality. They highlighted the case of Willie Horton, who had attacked a woman while released on weekend leave from a Massachusetts prison. In a brutal phrase employed by the Republican Party Chairman, Horton became Dukakis's 'running mate'.

Third, although turnout levels may sometimes be boosted by the campaigns that have been organised by voluntary and advocacy groups, the US has one of lowest voting turnouts of all western democracies. In 1988, barely half the voting-age population (50.1 per cent) cast a vote. The turnout improved slightly in 1992 to 55.1 per cent, but declined again in 1996 to 49.1 per cent. It then rose to 51.3 per cent in 2000, 55.3 per cent in 2004 and 57.5 per cent in 2008. There is a striking contrast between the US and many other nations. In the 1997 UK general election, the turnout was 71.5 per cent although it was 65.1 per cent in 2010.

Nonetheless, the form of measurement that is customarily used (whereby turnout is measured as a proportion of the voting-age population) paints an unduly pessimistic picture. The figure includes all adults resident in the US whereas only US citizens are eligible to vote. Furthermore, some individuals are barred from voting. Many states have laws limiting the voting rights of those convicted of a felony. These apply not only to prison inmates but also to those on parole or probation. In some states, the right to vote is permanently forfeited. This has a significant impact on African-American voting patterns in particular. An estimated 15 per cent of black males have either temporarily or permanently lost the right to vote (Flanigan and Zingale, 1998: 31).

Eligibility to vote depends also upon registration. Although overall voting rates are low, and while there are significant differences across the racial and ethnic groupings, the proportion of those registered who then vote is relatively high. What are the reasons for this? Some say that the registration process is difficult. However, the 1993 National Voter Registration Act (the 'motor-voter law') simplified procedures by allowing citizens to register when applying for a driving licence or other forms of documentation from government agencies. Nonetheless registration requirements still differ markedly between states. Whereas some states allow voters to register on the day of the election, others require pre-registration.

However, registration barriers provide only a partial explanation of US turnout levels. Estimates suggest that, if they were to be lowered, this would increase overall turnout by about 8 per cent (Flanigan and Zingale, 1998: 45). Other factors should also be considered. There is a high level of geographical mobility in the US, particularly among the young. Inevitably, if people settle in a different state, they will know less about the process of registration and local candidates and races. Some observers, most notably Robert Putnam, point to a decline in the US civic culture. Individuals are more isolated and detached from the social fabric than in the past (Putnam, 2000). Changes in the character of party organisation may also have played a part. In the past, neighbourhood party organisers encouraged turnout. However, urban redevelopment swept away the cohesive and relative homogeneous neighbourhoods in the inner-city areas and there are far fewer party activists at precinct and county level. Others argue that the very large number of elections discourages turnout. Voters, they say, become bored and confused. Although the evidence is unclear, there are suggestions that many contests can be considered 'low-stimulus elections'. This may be because the outcome is regarded as a foregone conclusion. The low level of turnout in the 1996 presidential contest between Bill Clinton, then the incumbent president, and Bob Dole might be explained by its lack of competitiveness. Clinton was widely expected, as he did, to win re-election.

Conclusion

There is a striking contrast between US federal elections.[12] Whereas Congressional contests are governed by predictability in so far as incumbents are almost certain to be re-elected (see p. 41), there is often a significant degree of unpredictability in the presidential election process. Although there have been contests where the eventual outcome has been evident long before, the result of the elections in 1980, 1992, 2000, or even 2004 could not have been foretold with confidence. And very few would have forecast a year ahead of the November 2008 election that it would have been a contest between Barack Obama and John McCain. At that stage many were talking of a fight between Senator Hillary Clinton and the former New York City mayor, Rudy Giuliani. For some, all this is the essence of democracy. For others (see Chapter 8) such uncertainty adds to the relative weakness and disorder of the American state.

Notes

1 The number of elections also adds to the 'porousness' of the US state apparatus and, perhaps, 'ungovernability' (see p. 144).
2 Although it is often discussed, references to the 'weakening' of the US political parties should however be treated with caution. See pp. 49–54.
3 The national convention also provides an early opportunity for figures who may be considering a presidential run four years later to introduce themselves to a wider party audience. Barack Obama, who had not at that point won his US Senate election, addressed the 2004 Democratic National Convention. His speech, which referred to 'the audacity of hope', established him as a national figure.
4 In 2008, minor party candidates included Bob Barr, a former Republican Congressman who stood as the Libertarian Party nominee, and Ralph Nader who had previously stood in 1996, 2000, and 2004. See Chapter 3.
5 Although regulations and procedures differ between states, postal and online voting increasingly takes place well before election day. Estimates suggest that about 39.7 million or 30 per cent were cast early, an increase from about 20 per cent four years previously (United States Election Project, 2010).
6 A US Supreme Court ruling in *League of United American Citizens v. Perry* in 2006 established that there is no barrier to further redistricting during a decade.

7   Despite this level of spending, Whitman was defeated.

8   'Coordinated party expenditures are not considered contributions and do not count against a publicly funded campaign's candidate expenditure limit' (Federal Election Commission, 2011b).

9   It was however the House of Representatives' version of the bill that passed into law.

10 The 'fairness doctrine' did not in practice restrict the broadcasting of vigorous Cold War anti-communist messages and evangelical Christian programming.

11 The figure is however heavily skewed towards conservatives, whites, and the older age cohorts. Only 22 per cent of Democrats and 6 per cent of liberals expressed trust in the channel (Public Policy Polling, 2011).

12 This chapter has not considered state and local elections.

References and further reading

All Other Persons (2008), *Post Election Analysis: Outside the South, Obama Gets Almost Half of the White Vote*, 11 November, http://allotherpersons.wordpress. com/2008/11/11/post-election-analysis-outside-the-south-obama-gets-almost-half-of-the-white-vote/.

Atlanta Journal-Constitution (2011), 'Rush Limbaugh tops talk radio rankings for fifth year in a row', *Atlanta Journal-Constitution*, 9 February, http://blogs.ajc.com/ radio-tv-talk/2011/02/09/rush-limbaugh-tops-talk-radio-rankings-for-fifth-year-in-a-row/.

Bennett, A. J. (1997), *American Government and Politics 1997*, Godalming, the author.

Brubaker, S. C. (1998), 'The limits of campaign spending limits', *The Public Interest*, 133, Fall, 33–54.

Cantor, J. E. (2005), *The Presidential Election Campaign Fund and Tax Checkoff: Background and Current Issues*, Congressional Research Service, http://fpc.state.gov/documents/ organization/105185.pdf.

Carter, B. (2008), 'Election's over, so what's next for the cable news channels?', *The New York Times*, 15 November, www.nytimes.com/2008/11/15/arts/ television/15netw.html.

Center for Voting and Democracy (2003), *Reform Options for the Electoral College*, www. fairvote.org/e_college/reform.htm#50Runoff.

CNN.com (2000), *Stuart Rothenberg: Understanding the Convention 'Bounce' Not Always Simple*, 3 August, edition.cnn.com/ALLPOLITICS/analysis/rothenberg/2000/ 08/03/.

Cogent Politics (2011), 'A brief look at campaign contributions', *Cogent Politics*, 23 February, http://cogentpolitics.blogspot.com/2011/02/brief-look-at-campaign-contibutions.html.

Confessore, N. (2011), 'Obama has early lead over Republicans in fund-raising', *International Herald Tribune*, 18 July.

Congressional Quarterly (1997), *Selecting the President: From 1789 to 1996*, Washington DC, CQ Press.

Dwyre, D. and R. Kolodny (2003), 'National political parties after BCRA', in Michael J. Malbin (ed.), *Life After Reform: When the Bipartisan Campaign Reform Act Meets Politics*, Lanham: Rowman and Littlefield, pp. 83–99.

Federal Election Commission (2008), *Presidential Spending Limits for 2008*, www.fec. gov/pages/brochures/pubfund_limits_2008.shtml.

Federal Election Commission (2009), *Presidential Pre-Nomination Campaign Disbursements December 31, 2008*, www.fec.gov/press/press2009/20090608Pres /3_2008PresPrimaryCmpgnDis.pdf.

Federal Election Commission (2011a), The FEC and the Federal Campaign Finance Law (updated February 2011), http://www.fec.gov/pages/brochures/fecfeca. shtml#Contribution_Limits.

Federal Election Commission (2011b), *General Election Funding*, www.fec.gov/pages/ brochures/pubfund.shtml#General.

FindLaw (2007), *Federal Election Commission v. Wisconsin Right to Life Inc.*, appeal from the United States District Court for the District of Columbia, http://caselaw. lp.findlaw.com/scripts/getcase.pl?court=US&vol=000&invol=06-969.

Flanigan, W. H. and N. H. Zingale (1998), *Political Behavior of the American Electorate*, Washington DC, CQ Press.

Jones, J. M. (2008), 'Conventions typically result in five-point bounce', 20 August, www.gallup.com/poll/109702/conventions-typically-result-fivepoint-bounce.aspx.

King, A. (1981), 'How not to select presidential candidates: a view from Europe', in A. Ranney (ed.), *The American Elections of 1980*, Washington DC, American Enterprise Institute for Public Policy Research, pp. 303–328.

Left and Right News (2010), 'Top spenders of the 2010 elections', *Left and Right News*, 27 December, http://www.leftandrightnews.com/2010/12/27/ top-spenders-of-the-2010-elections/.

Maidment, R. and M. Dawson (1994), *The United States in the Twentieth Century: Key Documents*, London, Hodder and Stoughton in association with the Open University.

Moore, M. (2000), 'Stop Bush's theft of the people's will', *disinformation*, www.disinfo. com/pages/article/id515/pg1/.

The New York Times (2009), 'Barack Obama's Inaugural Address', *The New York Times*, 20 January, http://www.nytimes.com/2009/01/20/us/politics/20text-obama.html.

Norris, P. (1992), 'The 1992 US primaries: if it ain't broke don't fix it', *Parliamentary Affairs*, 45:3: 428–436.

Norris, P. (2011), 'Political communication', in D. Caramani (ed.), *Comparative Politics*, Oxford, Oxford University Press, pp. 352–370.

Polsby, N. W. and A. Wildavsky (1996), *Presidential Elections: Strategies and Structures in American Politics*, Chatham, Chatham House.

Public Policy Polling (2011), *Press Release – PBS the Most Trusted Name in News*, Public Policy Polling, 19 January, http://www.publicpolicypolling.com/pdf/PPP_Release_ National_0119930.pdf.

Putnam, R. D. (2000), *Bowling Alone: The Collapse and Revival of American Community*, New York, Simon and Schuster.

Runk, D. (2007), 'Obama draws cheers at NAACP Convention', *The Washington Post*, 12 July.

Schneider, W. (2002), 'Let the "invisible primary" begin', *The Atlantic Online*, 24 December, www.theatlantic.com/politics/nj/schneider2002-12-24.htm.

Silver, N. (2011), 'Sizing up Iowa without Huckabee', FiveThirtyEight (Nate Silver's

Political Calculus), *The New York Times*, 16 May, http://fivethirtyeight.blogs. nytimes.com/2011/05/16/sizing-up-iowa-without-huckabee/?hp.

Thee-Brenan, M. (2010), 'From poll, a snapshot of Fox News viewers', 29 September, *New York Times* (Politics – The Caucus), http://thecaucus.blogs.nytimes. com/2010/09/29/from-poll-a-snapshot-of-fox-news-viewers.

United States Elections Project (2008), '2008 presidential nomination contest turnout rates', 8 October, http://elections.gmu.edu/Turnout_2008P.html.

United States Elections Project (2010), *(Nearly) Final 2008 Early Voting Statistics*, http://elections.gmu.edu/Early_Voting_2008_Final.html.

Wattenberg, M. P. (1991), *The Rise of Candidate-Centered Politics*, Cambridge, MA, Harvard University Press.

Wayne, S. J. (1992), *The Road to the White House 1992: The Politics of Presidential Selection*, New York, St Martin's Press.

2

Political parties and voting behaviour

Political parties have been defined as organised groupings 'sharing common policy preferences' that 'seek, or have, political power' (Robertson, 1985: 252). They have traditionally had six principal functions:

- They have a nomination or recruitment function, because they put forward candidates for public office and generally offer the only secure route for individuals seeking political advancement.
- They direct and organise election campaigns on behalf of candidates. These, and other forms of party activity, require substantial funding.
- By providing a conduit between the citizen and the decision-making process, the parties have a communication function. Traditionally, they organised meetings and gatherings allowing the electorate to hear the views of candidates and, in what was a process of dialogue, put forward their own opinion.
- Parties have a mobilisation function. Party activists would traditionally ensure, through canvassing, that voters who back the party turn out on election day. They bring together diverse political views and fuse them so as to construct an agreed platform. The role of parties in uniting divergent interests and structuring compromises has been described as an 'integration' or 'brokerage' function.
- They have a co-ordination function. Without parties, legislatures would be anarchic and unwieldy. Every vote would involve the construction of fresh alliances and voting blocs. Parties offer a degree of leadership and discipline, and they thereby structure and facilitate the passage of legislation. They can also provide ties between public officials in the different branches and tiers of government. This has particular importance in a system such as that in the US which is based upon separated institutions. Despite tensions stemming from accountability to different electorates, the parties traditionally offered a mechanism enabling the White House and members of Congress to work together in co-ordinating the passage of legislation.

- Parties have a policy or issue development function. They are compelled by the process of electoral competition to generate new proposals and policy options within a broad framework set by their core values. As Clinton Rossiter argued, the parties 'are perhaps best fitted of all agencies to convert formless hopes or frustrations into proposals that can be understood, debated, and, if found appealing, approved by the people' (1964: 50).

Parties also offer a basis for political identification and choice. The voter can swiftly recognise the political leanings and allegiances of candidates. This simplifies the electoral process and makes it accessible to those who have only limited political knowledge. As Martin Wattenberg has observed: 'it would probably take an individual approximately the amount of time required for one or two college-level courses a year in order to cast a completely informed vote for all of these offices in all of these elections. Therefore, voters need shortcuts, or cues, such as partisanship to facilitate their decision-making' (1996: 14).

For a long period political parties across both Europe and North America at least broadly shared these defining characteristics. Nonetheless, there were always some significant differences between the European parties and those found in the US. First, the American parties were traditionally broad coalitions drawing upon different regional and sectional interests. In contrast, the European parties emerged, or were formed, on the basis of adherence to particular political principles such as conservatism or socialism or to represent relatively narrow interests such as those of farmers. Second, as a consequence of this, the US parties long encompassed broad and sometimes irreconcilable spans of opinion. For many years, the Democrats included southern white segregationists in their ranks as well as those African-Americans in the northern states who had secured the right to vote. During the 1960s, there were divisions in both parties about civil rights legislation. For many years, votes in Congress and the state legislatures could not be predicted with certainty. As Clinton Rossiter put it, the parties 'are creatures of compromise, coalitions of interest in which principle is muted and often even silenced. They are vast, gaudy, friendly umbrellas under which all Americans, whoever and wherever and however-minded they may be, are invited to stand for the sake of being counted in the next election' (1964: 20). Third, the American parties are not membership-based. In contrast with Europe, where party membership rests upon payment of an annual subscription and adherence to formal enforceable rules, the term 'party member' is applied in the US to all those who register (usually at the time when they register to vote) as party supporters. Fourth, the US parties have traditionally been decentralised. In Rossiter's words, they have been 'loose confederacies' (1964: 21). The national party leaderships have always been relatively weak, and there has instead been an emphasis upon the autonomy of state parties and localism. Fifth, the parties, particularly the Democrats, were for long periods associated with the 'machine politics' of party bosses, such as Mayor Richard Daley of Chicago, who often maintained their position through their ability to offer municipal employment or other material advantages to some within the immigrant communities.

Origins, party systems, and voting behaviour

The American parties had their origins in the small groups and factions created by politicians seeking office at both state and federal level. Those around Thomas Jefferson established the Democratic-Republicans. They put forward a vision of a decentralised nation, and sought support from artisans and farmers. Alexander Hamilton's supporters, known as the Federalists, were backed by commercial interests and argued for stronger forms of national government. These groupings were, however, only partially recognisable as political parties:

> They were neither deeply rooted in the political soil nor all-encompassing in their influence and importance. To be sure, some coordinated efforts were made to select candidates, manage campaigns, attract voters, and bring legislators and other officeholders under the discipline of a party . . . Nevertheless, there was always an intermittent, *ad hoc* quality to all of these efforts and a casual attitude toward the partisan forms. There was little coordination between the national level and the political battles in the states of party warfare. (Silbey 2002: 3)

Mass parties, extending beyond caucuses of elected officials, grew with the broadening out of the right to vote or *franchise*. President Andrew Jackson was elected in 1828 through the efforts of the newly established Democratic Party. Although it drew on the backing of agricultural interests, Jacksonianism also rested on the opportunities that westward expansion offered to the ordinary citizen. At the same time, Jackson's critics came together and coalesced to form the Whigs.

The modern party system, based around Democrats and Republicans, emerged on the eve of the Civil War as slavery came to dominate national political debate. Those who opposed the extension of slavery into the newly created states and territories that westward expansion had opened up formed the Republican Party or GOP (Grand Old Party). The Republican candidate, Abraham Lincoln, was elected to the presidency in 1860. Throughout the century that followed, the white South (which had in the wake of Lincoln's election sought to secede from the nation), as well as the waves of newly arrived immigrants from Europe, remained loyal to the Democratic Party.

Nonetheless, although the US political process has, since the 1850s, been dominated by the Republicans and Democrats, there have been significant shifts in their character and the nature of the relationship between them. There have been different *party systems*.

Many influential scholars have understood this in terms of *realignment* theory. This focuses on the groupings from which the parties, as broad coalitions, draw their support. It also suggests that the history of the parties can be divided between distinct eras. For his part, Walter Dean Burnham talked about 30–36-year periods. Within each of these periods there is a dominant and a subordinate party. In a celebrated metaphor Samuel Lubell talked about one party as the sun and other as the moon. The 'sun party' is electorally predominant and largely sets the political and ideological agenda. Although the 'moon party' will periodically win national contests in 'deviating elections', it is on the terms defined by the 'sun party'. Although realignment theorists concede that there can be a drawn-out process of 'secular realignment' such as the change in the voting patterns among white southerners as they shifted from the Democrats to the Republicans, there is an emphasis on 'critical' elections. Commentators generally point to 1828, 1860, 1896, and 1932 (Mayhew, 2002: 7–12). A critical election marks the dividing line between eras. It will often be preceded by a period of electoral uncertainty: 'The critical realignment is characteristically associated with short-lived but very intense disruptions of traditional patterns of voting behaviour. Majority parties become minorities; politics which was once competitive becomes non-competitive or, alternatively, hitherto one-party areas now become arenas of intense partisan competition; and large blocks of the active electorate – minorities, to be sure, but perhaps involving as much as a fifth to a third of the voters – shift their partisan allegiance' (Walter Dean Burnham, quoted in Davis, 2009: 9).

From 1896, which (like 1828 and 1860 in the ante-bellum period) is regarded as a realigning election, the Republicans were predominant. They were the party of industrial capitalism and Protestantism. Despite the growing numbers of immigrants from southern and eastern Europe, the Republicans occupied the White House for 28 of the years between 1897 and 1933.

The 1932 election (which brought Franklin Roosevelt to the White House) inaugurated a period of Democratic hegemony. Although there were interruptions when the GOP seemed on the edge of a long-run recovery, the Democrats remained predominant for 40 years. Their election victories were constructed around a broad alliance, or *bloc*, of economic, racial, religious, and regional interests that collectively formed the Party's core vote. The 'New Deal coalition' embraced white 'hard hat' industrial workers (many of whom were trade unionists), those employed in the growing public sector, Jews, Roman Catholics, African-Americans, and white southerners who had backed the Party since the Civil War.

The bloc was held together between the 1930s and 1960s by the promise of basic social provision, government economic activism, and a degree of acquiescence towards the white South's efforts to maintain the segregationist order. Like all political coalitions, it was, however, subject to inherent strains. As the civil rights movement asserted itself in the 1950s and 1960s, the Democratic Party had to choose between the political goals of African-Americans and those of the white South. In the 1960 and 1964 elections, the Democrats' presidential campaigns chose the former, and blacks came to constitute the Democrats' most loyal constituency. In the 2000 presidential election, for example, Al Gore won 90 per cent of black votes. In 2008, the figure reached 95 per cent. However, large swathes of white southerners, and those, such as Senator Strom Thurmond of South Carolina, who served as their political representatives, responded to the party's growing identification with the civil rights movement (as well as its increasing identification with liberalism) by defecting to the Republicans. Although the shift to the GOP took an uneven form, and Democratic public officials continued to be elected at the sub-presidential level, the extent and scale of the shift should not be underestimated. In the 1950s, as Marjorie Randon Hershey notes: 'The south was the most dependably Democratic region of the country; to be openly Republican was a form of deviance' (1997: 228). Such was the region's loyalty to the Democrats that it had become known as the 'solid South'. In 1952, for example, 85 per cent of southern whites identified with the Democrats. By 1988, however, the proportion had fallen to 46 per cent (Wayne, 1992: 73). In 2008, Barack Obama secured just 30.2 per cent of the white vote in the southern states (compared with 53 per cent across the nation). In Alabama and Mississippi, it was 10 per cent and 11 per cent respectively (All Other Persons, 2008).

There were other, parallel, trends. Many white industrial workers in the northern states including those in Democratic heartland cities such as Chicago turned away from the Democrats at the same time because of their growing associations with the anti-war movement and cultural liberalism. The Party had become tied to 'amnesty, abortion and acid'. During the same period, white evangelical Christians moved towards the GOP. Supreme Court rulings establishing abortion rights and outlawing school prayer in public schools, and the Democrats' identification with what appeared as an assault against long-established values, led to a weakening of traditional political affiliations. Although the evangelicals had initially, in 1976, supported Jimmy Carter's candidature for the presidency, soon the Republicans were 'seen as more attractive, resisting cultural change and an increasingly intrusive government' (Durham, 1996: 26). Evangelical Christians gave decisive support to Ronald Reagan in 1980 and to subsequent Republican presidential candidates.

Against this background, there was growing talk of a further *realignment*. Commentators claimed that the New Deal party system had come to a close and the Republicans had become dominant or hegemonic. The year 1968, or in some accounts 1980, is depicted as a *critical* or *realigning* election. From then onwards, the US entered an era of Republican dominance. The Senate had a Republican majority from 1981 until 1987, and the GOP won a majority in both houses of Congress from 1994 onwards. Although the Democrats won the White House in 1992 and 1996, Bill Clinton (at least after his first two years in office) seemed to embrace the free market policies associated with 'Reaganomics'.

What explains this? In part, notions of 'critical elections' based upon realignment suggest a cyclical theory of history. There is also an overlap with the theories of Stephen Skowronek considered in Chapter 6 (see p. 147). There also however seem to be other reasons why the 'New Deal era' came to a close and was displaced by an anti-government mood. The economic difficulties of the 1970s seemed to suggest that government was, to paraphrase Ronald Reagan, the problem rather than the solution. Furthermore, the loss of faith in the Democrats might also be attributed to the shift from an industrial to a post-industrial society. The age of large-scale manufacturing industry demanded the forms of 'big government' with which the Democrats are associated. The modern era has however been characterised by the break-up of monopolies and the growth of smaller enterprises. Public opinion has been increasingly marked by a 'new mood of doubt' about the role and purpose of government (Ladd, 1996: 171). This led voters towards the GOP.

Nonetheless, although the closing decades of the twentieth century were dominated by Republican victories and the hegemony of the conservative policy agenda, only some observers have been willing to accept that there has been a Republican realignment. Although some point to GOP successes in, for example, 1972 and 1980 and, if Congressional elections are also considered, 1994, there has been no realigning election that can be compared with 1896 or 1932. Despite George W. Bush's victories, and GOP successes in Congressional elections, talk of a Republican realignment seemed to lack credibility by the beginning of the new century. Had it not been for the mathematics of the Electoral College, Al Gore would have won the White House in 2000. Bush secured only a narrow victory in 2004. Some Commentators speak, with some justice, of a '50–50 America' in which the parties are finely balanced. At times, others went further and began to suggest, following the party's Congressional victories in 2006 and Barack Obama's triumph in 2008, that there had been a Democratic realignment. Amidst the post-election euphoria, Harold Meyerson wrote in *The Washington Post*:

> Even though Obama's victory was nowhere near as numerically lopsided as Franklin Roosevelt's in 1932, his margins among decisive and growing constituencies make clear that this was a genuinely realigning election. (Meyerson, 2008: A19)

Republican gains in the 2010 mid-term elections and President Obama's poll ratings during 2009 and 2010 put a significant question mark against judgements such as this.

In place of a search for a 'dominant' party or a realigning election, it is perhaps more legitimate to see the contemporary US as, in party terms, a 50–50 nation. Although each draws its support from very different coalitions, both parties are relatively finely balanced in electoral terms.. This is not immediately apparent if the figures for partisan identification (the party that individuals say that they back) are considered. As Table 2.1 suggests, the Democrats have had a decisive long-term advantage over the Republicans.

Table 2.1 *Partisan identification, 1952–2008 (%)*

	1952	1960	1970	1980	1990	2000	2002	2004	2008
Democrats	59	53	54	52	52	50	49	50	51
Republicans	36	37	33	33	36	37	43	41	37

Note: independents have been excluded while 'leaners' (who 'lean' towards one party or the other but do not regard themselves as firm identifiers) are included.
Source: adapted from American National Election Studies (2011) *Party Identification 3-Point Scale (revised in 2008) 1952–2008*, www.electionstudies.org/nesguide/toptable/tab2a_2.htm.

Table 2.2 *Ideological self-identification, 1972–2008*

	1972	1980	1990	2000	2002	2004	2008
Extremely liberal / liberal / slightly liberal	18	17	16	20	23	19	22
Moderate / middle of the road	27	20	24	23	22	25	22
Slightly conservative / conservative / extremely conservative	26	28	26	30	35	31	32
Don't know / Haven't thought	28	36	33	27	22	25	25

Source: adapted from American National Election Studies (2011) *Liberal-Conservative Self-Identification 1972–2008*, www.electionstudies.org/nesguide/toptable/tab3_1.htm.

However, if ideological identification is considered instead, the picture is different. Three points emerge. First, the proportion of conservatives always exceeds the proportion of liberals, sometimes by a very large margin. Second, the proportion of conservatives has grown markedly since the beginning of the 1990s. It remained high in 2008 despite the relatively unpopularity of the Republican 'brand'. Furthermore, whereas, if Tables 2.1 and 2.2 are compared, the gap between the proportion of conservatives and the proportion of Republicans is relatively small, there is a large gap between the proportion of liberals and the proportion of Democratic identifiers. Third, large sections of the population either define themselves as 'middle of the road' or alternatively haven't categorised their political beliefs.

Therefore, a significant proportion of the Democratic Party's voters either is not liberal or at the least shrinks away from the liberal label. Democratic candidates, many of whom are liberal on core economic and cultural issues, cannot take their allegiance or votes for granted. At the same time, although the Republicans have much lower partisan identification figures than the Democrats, there are large numbers of ideologically uncommitted who can be, and are, won over in both presidential and Congressional elections.

Although ideological allegiances are important in shaping voting behaviour (78 per cent of conservatives backed John McCain in the 2008 presidential election and 89 per cent of liberals supported Barack Obama), other variables come into play particularly amongst the large numbers who are self-defined moderates or haven't considered ideological preferences (CNN ElectionCenter, 2008). Although there is no precise dividing line, these can be divided between long- and short-term variables.

Voting patterns are, on a long-term basis, related to significant demographic variables, in particular race, ethnicity, income, education, religion, and gender. The impact of these is however mediated by socialisation processes. The family, schools, and peer-groupings provide important 'transmission mechanisms'.

First, there is a close correlation between race and ethnicity and voting behaviour. This was particularly evident in the 2008 presidential election. 95 per cent of African-Americans, 67 per cent of Hispanics, and 62 per cent of Asian-Americans voted for the Obama–Biden ticket. In contrast, the figure was 43 per cent amongst whites (CNN ElectionCenter, 2008). As noted above (p. 36), the number was far below this in some of the southern states. Why is there a racial and ethnic divide? Part of the answer lies in income levels. Minorities are disproportionately represented at the lower end of the income scale. African-Americans have furthermore been the Democrats' most loyal constituency since 1964 when much of the party turned its back on the white segregationists and backed the civil rights movement while the Republican presidential candidate, Senator Barry Goldwater, embraced 'states' rights'. Latinos are less firmly wedded to the Democrats and there have been times when the Republicans seemed to be making electoral inroads. As Texas Governor, George W. Bush had significant Latino backing. However, Republican Party backing for propositions put to the California electorate withdrawing state benefits from illegal immigrants and ending affirmative action programmes created a widely shared feeling that the GOP was hostile to minorities. Even Asian-Americans, whom conservatives had long regarded as the 'model minority', because of their seeming commitment to conservative values and the entrepreneurial ethos, joined the swing to the Democrats. This was partly because immigration has been changing the character of the Asian-American communities. They increasingly included low-income workers from countries such as Laos and Cambodia.

Second, although many accounts speak of the 'American dream' and the extent to which individuals can climb the economic ladder (although studies suggest that mobility is relatively limited) there is a close relationship between income levels and voting behaviour. In 2008, Obama led by 22 percentage points amongst those earning less than $50,000 annually. Among those earning $50,000 or more, Obama and McCain drew level (CNN ElectionCenter, 2008). There is however a twist that becomes evident if educational attainment is brought into the picture alongside income. There is no simple class divide. The Democrats drew disproportionate levels of support from those at the top as well as the bottom of the income and educational scale. More voters earning $200,000 a year or more and holding postgraduate qualifications voted for Obama. In other words, Democratic voting support is bifurcated.

Third, there is a significant gender gap in US politics. This has been evident since the 1980 presidential election. Whereas 56 per cent of women backed Obama in 2008, the figure was just 49 per cent (although still a plurality) among men. The gender gap has been explained in different ways. Some suggest that the Republican Party's associations with 'family values' and 'pro-life' policies have alienated women. Others point to the disproportionate representation of women in low-income occupations. The Democrats' ties with the more protective aspects of government (such as healthcare) may be significant. However, having said this, the focus on women may be misplaced. The gender gap has arisen in large part because men have shifted towards the Republicans. This may be tied to resentment about declining real wages and the destruction of traditionally male occupations. It may also be that the Republicans' identification with 'hawkish' foreign and defence policies has masculine associations. There is a parallel 'marriage gap'. There was a 3 per cent lead for John McCain among the men and women who were married. Unmarried men without children (and to an even greater extent unmarried women without children) backed Obama overwhelmingly. All of this is in part tied to age. The unmarried tend to be younger. However, it may also be that there is a correlation between marriage and parenthood and more conservative values.

Fourth, religion is also of pivotal importance. Although there have been variations in their turnout rates, white 'born again' evangelical Protestants are the Republicans' most faithful constituency. 74 per cent backed the McCain–Palin ticket in 2008. Indeed, Senator McCain may have chosen Governor Palin as his vice-presidential 'running mate' because he hoped her presence on the Republican ticket would energise grassroots evangelicals. However, the 'religion gap' goes beyond the divide between evangelical and 'mainline' faiths. Regular and frequent worshippers of all denominations are more likely to vote Republican. In contrast, in 2008, more than two-thirds of those who never attend church (about 16 per cent of the electorate) voted for the Democrats (CNN ElectionCenter, 2008).

Long-term variables however provide only part of the answer. Significant numbers of voters decide at a relatively late stage. In 2008, for example, 60 per cent said that they had decided on their vote before September. The remainder decided during the final two months of the campaign (CNN ElectionCenter, 2008). Although there is a case for scepticism about some of these poll findings, there is evidence that the number of late deciders with no firm political attachments has grown: 'while class, religion, and geography are still related to party identification and voting behaviour, they are not as strongly related as they were in the past. Voters are less influenced by group cues. They exercise a more independent judgement on election day, a judgement that is less predictable and more subject to be influenced by the campaign itself' (Wayne, 1992: 77). Some portray the electorate as 'consumers' who will 'shop around' for policies that correspond to their interests and switch their vote when they are dissatisfied.

The process is partly retrospective. People make a rational assessment of a party or candidate's record in office. As Morris Fiorina argues, voters keep 'a running tally of retrospective evaluations of party promises and performance' (quoted in Wayne, 1992: 67). However, the electorate looks forward as well as backwards. There are widely shared concerns such as the prospects for the economy and the future of education. Particular issues 'pull' voters towards either the Democratic or the Republican candidates. In 2008, 60 per cent of those who were 'very worried' about economic conditions supported Obama. 96 per cent who strongly approved of the US war in Iraq backed McCain (CNN ElectionCenter, 2008). The end result of all this will however depend upon the importance, or *salience*, of a particular issue. In 2008, the 9 per cent of voters who saw the threat posed by terrorism as the most important issue overwhelmingly supported McCain. About the same proportion saw health-care as the most important issue. Three-quarters of them backed Obama (CNN ElectionCenter, 2008).

However, the assessments that voters make may not always be clinically rational appraisals of the economy, overall performance, or policy commit-ments. The campaign strategy, and the images that candidates construct, also play a role. The Obama campaign, which built upon the personal charisma of the candidate and at the same time exploited all the forms of communication offered by the new social media, generated high levels of enthusiasm. 30 per cent of 2008 voters (some of whom were McCain backers) said that would be 'excited' by an Obama victory (CNN ElectionCenter, 2008).

Voting behaviour in Congressional elections

Congressional elections usually have significantly different dynamics. In par-ticular, mid-term contests attract a significantly lower turnout rate than those held in a presidential election year. The composition of the mid-term electorate tends therefore to be different from that in the elections two years earlier and later.

That having been said, incumbency is crucial. The senator or Congress member who holds the post is almost certain to be re-elected, and will remain in office until she or he chooses to stand down. The importance of incumbency as a determinant of election outcomes is graphically illustrated if the figures are considered in percentage terms. Even in the November 2010 mid-term elections, when the Republicans regained the House of Representatives and made major electoral gains, 85 per cent of incumbent members in the House and 84 per cent of those in the Senate were re-elected. In 2004, the figures reached 98 per cent and 96 per cent respectively (OpenSecrets.org, 2011).

Although the incumbency figures may be misleading, because weak incum-bents can decide not to run If they fear that they will lose the election, incum-bency is still an important feature of the American electoral process, and requires explanation. In many states, legislatures are responsible for redistricting every ten years. The boundaries between Congressional districts may well be drawn so as to offer an advantage to many incumbent members of the House. At the same time, office-holding at both state and federal level provides substantial built-in advantages including access to the mass media, name-recognition, the provision of constituency services, and the ability to attract large-scale campaign contributions. Serving legislators and office-holders can also press for, and play a part in allocating, federal government 'pork'. (This refers to the provision of government funding projects for members' own districts or states.) Self-fulfilling prophecies may also be a relevant variable. Potential opponents and the other party will generally believe that an incumbent is electorally safe, and they will not therefore mount a credible challenge or devote resources to the campaign. The incumbency factor shapes the outcome of all Congressional elections. Very few seats in which there is an incumbent will be competitive. The overall result of the elections and the composition of Congress therefore depend upon the number of 'open seats' in which there is no incumbent.

The second important characteristic of Congressional elections is that, traditionally at least, district and state issues have come to the fore. In the celebrated words of Tip O'Neill, who was Speaker of the House of Representatives between 1977 and 1986, 'all politics is local'. As Marjorie Randon Hershey notes: 'Typically, an incumbent emphasizes a record of service to the district and individual constituents and at the same time criticizes that distant institution called "Congress" whose members inexplicably waste so much public money' (1997: 206).

Nonetheless, despite O'Neill's comment, the 'local' character of Congressional elections should not be exaggerated. National factors also play a role.

First, in presidential election years, there can be a 'coat-tails' effect. A wave of support for a particular presidential ticket can lead increased numbers to vote for Congressional candidates belonging to the same party. This is measured by looking at whether there is a larger swing or a smaller swing to the presidential candidate when compared with the party's Congressional candidates. In 1964, Lyndon Johnson's presidential victory was accompanied by a Congressional swing to the Democrats. The coat-tails effect may however be in decline. Barack Obama ran ahead of the Democrats' House candidates in just 36 House districts across the country. Having said this, as Rhodes Cook argues, a coat-tails effect is not always fully captured by the data. The presidential candidate can have a 'tonal' effect in so far as the presidential candidate establishes a rhetorical and ideological framework for both the presidential and the Congressional campaigns (Cook, 2009).

Second, some observers explain the outcome of the mid-term elections that are held between presidential contests in terms of 'surge and decline': 'There is a surge in support for the President's party and in turnout in the presiden-

tial election, which is then followed by a decline in the mid-term elections
. . . between one fifth and one quarter of those who voted in congressional
elections in a presidential year failed to do so two years later' (Owens, 1995:
3). The November 2010 elections could be seen in this way. The sweeping
Republican victories could be understood as a reaction against President
Obama's victory two years previously. However, there is no set pattern. The
party that had won the White House two years before made gains in both the
1998 and the 2002 mid-term elections. This suggests that, in place of cyclical processes, the results of Congressional elections are determined by other,
perhaps rather more short-term, variables.

Third, national campaigns may also play a role although it may be more
limited than it sometimes appears to commentators. In 1994, the GOP won
majorities in both houses of Congress after House candidates adopted the
Contract with America, which committed them to conservative policy goals,
as a national platform. In 2010, House Republicans led by John Boehner
structured their campaign around The Pledge to America which, they said,
constituted a 'governing agenda'.

The minor parties

Although the Democrats and the Republicans dominate studies of the
American party system, the US is an economically, politically, and cultur-
ally heterogeneous nation, and there has always been, as a consequence, a
plethora of minor or 'third' parties. In a classic study, first published in 1960,
Clinton Rossiter divided such parties into six categories, although some of the
labels that he applied had a distinctly pejorative character (1964: 14). There
were, he asserted, 'one-issue obsessionists', such as the Prohibition Party,
which has long opposed the manufacture, sale and consumption of alcoholic
drink. He also identified 'left-wing splinter parties', such as the Socialist Party,
the Socialist Workers' Party, and the Communist Party of the USA. At the
same time, there are one-state parties. Wisconsin had a Progressive Party in
the 1930s. There was a Farmer–Labor Party in Minnesota during the inter-
war years. However, although the party won both the state governorship
and its seats in the US Senate, it progressively lost support and merged with
the Democrats in 1944.[1] New York still has its own Conservative and Liberal
Parties. Some minor parties, Rossiter notes, are 'the personal following of
the dissident hero'. He cites the Bull Moose movement of 1912, which was
organised around the former president Theodore Roosevelt, as an example
of this. There are also minor parties that have emerged from the dissident
wing of a major party. In 1948, the 'Dixiecrats', who drew their support
from white southerners seeking to maintain the system of racial segregation,
deserted the Democratic Party and put forward South Carolina Governor
Strom Thurmond as their presidential candidate. Similarly, in 1968, the

Alabama Governor George Wallace broke with the Democrats so as to form the American Independent Party. Lastly, there are those that Rossiter describes as 'true minor parties' that, he suggests, have the potential, in certain circumstances, to win major party status. He points to the People's Party (often referred to as the *populists*). In the closing decades of the nineteenth century, they campaigned for currency reform and against the railroad companies and other 'trusts' that had, they asserted, a monopoly hold over a particular market or sector of the economy. The populists won particular backing in the agricultural regions of the West and South that had been ravaged by economic depression during those years. In 1890, the party won control of the Kansas state legislature. However, they were increasingly divided between those who hoped to use the party so as to change the political character of the Democrats and those who sought to maintain the party's independent identity.

Many contemporary third parties can be considered 'true minor parties'. The Libertarian Party (LP) was founded in December 1971. It is committed to 'a world of liberty; a world in which all individuals are sovereign over their own lives, and no one is forced to sacrifice his or her values for the benefit of others' (Libertarian Party, 2010). The LP puts forward a platform based around free market economics, the abolition of welfare provision, and minimal government. However, the Party distances itself from others on the right by calling for the legalisation of all victimless 'crimes', for example drug taking, and an end to restrictions on all forms of consensual sexual activity. Although the Greens may appear to be 'one-issue obsessionists', they have raised a range of issues associated with radicalism and feminism. During the 2000 election, when Ralph Nader stood as their candidate, they campaigned against the large corporations. The Reform Party could also be included within this category, although there is a case for adopting James Q. Wilson's typology and categorising it as an economic protest party (*Congressional Quarterly*, 1997: 117). The party, which emerged in the wake of Ross Perot's 1992 presidential bid, drew upon the discontent that accompanied the recession at the beginning of the 1990s. It called for reforms to the political process, such as the imposition of term limits on federal lawmakers, and the adoption of protectionist policies so as to protect American jobs. However, by the end of the decade, against a background of relative economic prosperity, the party disintegrated.

Minor party candidates attracted only a handful of votes in the 2004 and 2008 presidential elections and, although there were fears that Ralph Nader might again take votes from the Democratic ticket in 2004, they made no measurable impact on the course of the campaign. Indeed, although minor parties have sporadically attracted significant numbers of votes, no minor party has made a sustained electoral breakthrough since the Republican Party established itself in the years before the Civil War. Why have they failed?

First, many of the attempts to build alternatives to the Republicans and Democrats have been made by groupings associated with the political fringes. Their thinking is often removed from the American mainstream. The

Constitution Party (which secured almost two hundred thousand votes in the 2008 presidential election) is committed to cultural and economic uncompromising conservatism. The Libertarian Party (which attracted just over half a million votes in 2008) campaigns for free market economic policies (which alienate many on the left) and personal freedom so far as personal and sexual issues are concerned (which conflicts with the commitment of many on the right to moral traditionalism).

Second, many minor parties have been ridden by factional rivalries and internal tensions. The disintegration of the Reform Party in 2000 is instructive. It was torn between different ideas. These included 'progressive' calls for the 'cleaning up' and modernising of government institutions, conservative fiscal theory, and populist demands for the protection of American economic interests against those of outsiders. A further ingredient was added when, in November 1998, Minnesota elected Jesse Ventura, a Reform Party member, as state governor. To the dismay of the party's more traditionalist supporters, he backed the legal availability of abortion and supported the legalisation of cannabis and same-sex marriage (Sifry 2002: 25). Against this background, the party began to fall apart. Ventura and his faction left the party in the spring of 2000. Supporters of Patrick J. Buchanan, the hard right commentator who had sought the Republican presidential nomination in 1992 and 1996, joined the party and promoted his candidature. They won, but only after a bruising and bloody battle with Perot loyalists. In the wake of all this, Buchanan gained just 448,895 votes in the November presidential contest.

Third, there are particular problems facing leftist parties. In striking contrast with the countries of Europe, where socialist and social-democratic thinking took hold during the closing decades of the nineteenth century, leftist ideas never took root in the US. Although there were anarchist and syndicalist protests, these movements were structurally weak and short-lived. Some attribute the failure of American socialism to repression by government authorities. Others stress the hold of individualistic thinking and the material prosperity of the American working class. In a celebrated phrase, Werner Sombart, a German observer, wrote that America was 'Canaan, the promised land of capitalism' where 'on the reefs of roast beef and apple pie socialistic utopias of every sort are sent to their doom'.

Fourth, there are administrative and legal obstacles. Many states require that candidates gain a certain number of signatures before their names can be placed on the ballot. The principal parties need only submit a limited number. The regulations for third parties are, however, much more demanding, and they require many more names. Although Ralph Nader who, in 2000, was the Green Party nominee had widespread name-recognition, he was unable to secure a place on the ballot in seven states. There are also 'sore loser' laws in some states that prohibit those who were defeated in the primaries entering the general election contest. While obstacles such as these are not always insurmountable, they compel minor parties to devote their energies and financial resources to ballot access. The principal parties can, in contrast, concentrate their efforts on campaigning.

Fifth, Congress members represent single-member districts. Presidential elections are structured by the Electoral College (see Chapter 1). Both employ a simple plurality, or 'first-the-the-post', electoral system, and few people will vote for a small party that they believe has no realistic prospect of success. In the 1992 presidential election, Ross Perot attracted 19 per cent of the popular vote across the US, yet gained no Electoral College Votes.

Sixth, minor parties also face financial challenges. Modern election campaigns are capital-intensive. However, with some significant exceptions, most independents and minor parties have only limited financial resources. As noted in Chapter 1, under the provisions of the Federal Election Campaign Act (FECA), candidates contesting the Republican and Democratic presidential primaries are awarded matching funds by the Federal Election Commission. Furthermore, the Democratic and GOP national conventions each attract a subsidy from the taxpayer. In the November general election campaign, the major party candidates have their costs paid in full if they agree not to spend above and beyond this amount. Minor parties must be on the ballot in at least ten states and have gained at least 5 per cent of the poll in the preceding election if they are to receive taxpayer funding. It is then paid on a sliding-scale basis depending upon the share of the vote that the party secured. If it is a new party, these funds are provided only retrospectively rather than when they are most needed.

Seventh, for many individuals and campaigns, lobbying activity offers a more effective avenue of influence than the formation of a party. Those seeking reform and change may therefore be dissuaded from establishing a party. As Chapter 4 argues, the US political system offers countless access points that enable organised interests to reach decision-makers at both a federal and a state level

Eighth, although some commentators, pointing to the growing number of people defining themselves as 'independents', suggest that there has been a process of *dealignment* and argue that this offers a basis for the birth and development of minor parties, significant numbers are still identifiers with the principal parties. In other words, despite strains, loyalties to the Republicans and Democrats remain entrenched.

Ninth, the growing use of primaries in the mid-twentieth century changed the character of the major parties and made them much more porous. Political entrepreneurs from a broad range of political backgrounds have the opportunity to campaign for support within the Republicans and Democrats and there is therefore less of a likelihood that they will establish alternative party organisations. A strategy of 'burrowing from within' faces many difficulties but is likely to prove more successful. David Duke, a former Ku Klux Klan leader, initially attempted to break into politics as the presidential candidate of the Populist Party. He abandoned the Party and contested the 1988 Democratic primaries. In 1989, after success in the primary, he became a Republican nominee for the Louisiana state legislature, to which he was elected. In 1992, he entered the Republican Party presidential primaries, winning 11 and 9 per cent of the poll in Mississippi and Louisiana respectively.

Tenth, the character of the principal parties has denied opportunities to the construction of minor parties. In Europe, the principal parties were structured around ideological differences and social class. In contrast, the principal US parties had at least traditionally much more of a 'catch-all' character. For many years, they drew together strikingly different groups and interests. They have therefore had an integrative character and absorbed new social movements that might have otherwise established separate parties, in a way that was precluded in Europe. As Clinton Rossiter has noted: 'One of the most persistent qualities of the American two-party system is the way in which one of the major parties moves almost instinctively to absorb (and thus be somewhat reshaped by) the most challenging third party of the time' (Rossiter, 1964: 15). Although it was sometimes suggested that the Tea Party movement, which emerged in 2009 and campaigned for lower tax rates and limited government, might lay the basis for a new party, it was always a constituency within the Republican Party's orbit.

Eleventh, most states do not permit electoral fusion. Electoral fusion allows the minor parties to nominate the candidate of another (usually a major) party. This enables the voters to show their support for the minor party but at the same time back a candidate with a credible chance of winning. The few states allowing electoral fusion include New York, Connecticut, and Delaware.

Twelfth, although many of the minor parties often claim that there has been a process of ideological convergence between the major parties and stress the similarities between successive administrations, many of the American public do see differences. Indeed, in 1995, John H. Aldrich concluded, 'this perception of party differences has grown, especially over the past decade, to truly significant levels' (Aldrich, 1995: 174). This gives the two major parties a legitimacy that they would otherwise lack.

Thirteenth, significant minor party votes are often a function of generalised voter discontent with those in authority. At other times, when there is greater quiescence, there is little to sustain their protests against 'establishment' politicians. Ross Perot's 1992 vote reflected disillusionment with Washington DC and anger at the recession. However, the issues that fuelled the anger of the early 1990s lost much of their former salience as the decade progressed.

Nonetheless, although these barriers limit the ability of minor parties to gain votes, they should not be disregarded. In the 1992 presidential election, Ross Perot, a Texan billionaire, won almost one in five of the votes. It was the most successful performance for a third-party candidate since Theodore Roosevelt, the former president, gained 27.4 per cent of the vote in the election of 1912. Perot's showing led to the formation of the Reform Party. Perot stood again, as the Party's 1996 presidential candidate, but won only 8.5 per cent of the vote.

The importance of minor parties also rests upon their ability to remould and restructure the political agenda. For example, many of the ideas around which Ross Perot campaigned were later adopted, albeit in a different form, by major party candidates. These included the need for a balanced federal government budget, the importance of imposing term limits on lawmakers, the elimination of government waste, and the reform of campaign finance.

Having said that, the role of minor parties can extend beyond agenda-setting. As John B. Anderson, a former Congressman who received six million votes when he stood as an independent in the presidential election of 1980, argues, minor parties also ensure that the Republicans and Democrats do not lose touch with the American electorate: 'New parties offer voters better choices and bring important perspectives to political debate. They provide a check on any drift of major parties away from substantial numbers of people' (Anderson, 2001).

Furthermore, the 2000 election illustrated that the role of minor parties can in certain circumstances be decisive. As embittered Democratic Party activists observed in the aftermath of the 2000 election, Ralph Nader probably contributed to Al Gore's defeat. Although Gore won a narrow majority of the votes across the country, the outcome of the entire election came to depend upon the casting of Florida's 25 Electoral College Votes (ECV). In the end, after recounts and a challenge heard by the US Supreme Court, George W. Bush was finally deemed to have won in Florida by a margin of 537 votes. On this basis, he was assigned all the state's ECV and gained the presidency. For his part, Ralph Nader attracted 97,488 votes in Florida. Although the claim has been challenged, analysts have asserted that many of these ballots would have been cast, in the absence of Nader, for Al Gore. Although Nader stood in both the 2004 and 2008 presidential elections, provoking some anxiety and resentment among Democratic activists, his vote was minimal and did not affect the overall result.

In 2000, the Nader campaign also put the Democrats under pressure during the run-up to election day. Gore was compelled to yield campaign resources, in terms of both staffing and finance, into states where Nader appeared to be garnering support, such as Wisconsin, Minnesota, and Iowa. Furthermore, as commentators such as Andrew Sullivan have noted, the Nader campaign shifted the political agenda. Gore was compelled to tack leftwards. His campaign speeches assumed a populist tone as he criticised powerful companies, such as those in the pharmaceuticals industry, for exploitative practices. This rhetoric, Sullivan has suggested, alienated moderate voters and propelled them towards the Republican camp.

Some observers have spoken of minor party votes as the harbingers of electoral realignment. The successes, it is said, presage a fundamental shift in the balance of power between the parties (Mayhew, 2002: 77–78). The electoral statistics do not, however, provide much to sustain such a view. Their role is more modest. Richard Hofstadter, a celebrated historian, offers a more fitting epitaph. Minor parties, he once claimed, were destined 'to sting like a bee and die' (National Commission on Federal Election Reform, 2001). In other words, while they make a significant impact, it is invariably short-lived.

The 'party decline' thesis

Some decades ago, many commentators spoke of 'party decline'. The thesis was spelt out in David Broder's 1971 book, *The Party's Over. It* suggested that, if the trends then evident continued, the principal parties would no longer perform many of the functions outlined at the beginning of this chapter. The thesis has been succinctly summarised:

> the two parties are in full retreat in all the areas that they have traditionally dominated. No matter whether it is selecting candidates, fundraising, running campaigns, mobilising voters, or co-ordinating government, the argument is that the parties have become less and less relevant. In short, the parties are no longer doing the things which parties are even minimally expected to do. (Bailey, 1990: 12)

These points should be considered in more detail. The rise of primaries and caucuses, which enabled ordinary voters to select the parties' candidates, began as an attempt to dislodge the party 'bosses' and 'machine' politicians who had offered rewards, principally municipal employment, to those who backed them. However, as a long-term consequence, the nomination function was progressively transferred from the parties to the broader public.

The first primary was held in Wisconsin in 1905. By 1912, 32.9 per cent of the delegates attending the Democrats' national convention, which formally chooses the Party's presidential candidate, had been selected in primaries. By 1976, the proportion of delegates selected in the Democratic primaries had risen to 72.6 per cent, although old-style political leaders were able to influence or even dictate the primary results in some states until the 1960s (Hays Lowenstein, 1992: 67). Many of the delegates will have been 'pledged' or mandated to vote for the candidate who won in their state's primary.

The role of the primary was entrenched by the McGovern–Fraser reforms. These were drawn up by the Commission on Party Structure and Delegate Selection that was established by the Democrats in the wake of the 1968 presidential election. In 1968, the Democratic nominee had been former the Vice-President Hubert Humphrey, a late entrant into the race, who, although backed by party leaders, had not stood in the primaries. It was a 'top-down' selection process, and there were allegations from supporters of Senator Eugene McCarthy, a more radical candidate who had contested the primaries on a platform opposing America's military intervention in Vietnam, that the system by which national convention delegates were selected had been rigged to deny them proper representation.

The Commission's report and the basis for the reforms, *Mandate for Change*, was published in 1970. It led to amendments to state law, and thereby compelled both the parties to make rule changes. Caucuses, the meetings that are held by some state parties to decide on candidate selection, were made more open. In the Democratic Party, the proportionality rules, which ensured that the delegation's voting at the national convention reflected the votes cast in the primary, were introduced. The Commission also stipulated that delegations should become more socially representative by including women, minorities, and young people 'in reasonable relationship to their presence in the population of the state'. The reforms, which were put into effect at the 1972 national convention, placed strict limits on the influence of party organisers and made primaries pivotal in delegate selection. A mere 1.1 per cent of the delegates were chosen by the state party committees (*Congressional Quarterly*, 1997: 28).

The institutionalisation of the nominating primary in the selection of candidates has had consequences for the political character of the parties. As noted in Chapter 1, it has lessened the party's hold over its elected officials. They have led to candidate-centred forms of politics, because those who are electorally victorious owe their success to the campaign organisations that they established during the primaries rather than to the party apparatus. In 1972, for example, President Nixon's successful bid to win a second presidential term was organised around the Committee for the Re-election of the President (CREEP). In 2008, the Obama campaign was directed from Chicago, not from the Democratic National Committee's headquarters in Washington DC, by his personal appointees, most notably David Plouffe and David Axelrod.

The parties were also said to have lost their role as fundraisers. Presidential candidates became eligible for taxpayer funding under the provisions of the amended Federal Election Campaign Act (FECA) of 1974. Although Congressional candidates are not eligible for financial assistance from the Federal Election Commission, the parties contribute only a small proportion of their overall campaign funding. Instead, they built their campaigns around contributions from individual donors, their own resources, and money given by political action committees. In the 2009–10 election cycle nearly $4 billion was spent by candidates. Of this, about $1.5 billion was donated by 797,579 individual donors who gave amounts exceeding $200 (which have to be registered). The remaining $2.5 billion was given by individuals who donated less than $200, corporations, political action committees, and the candidates themselves (many of whom had substantial financial resources) (*Cogent Politics*, 2011).

Traditionally, the parties would hold meetings and organise processions in support of their candidates, particularly in the close-knit urban neighbourhoods. However, urban redevelopment, television, and modern technology (including the internet and new forms of social networking) appear to have weakened the parties' communication function. Although the focus of attention in 2008 was on social networking, the use of television entered a new phase. The Obama campaign's financial resources allowed it to show a 30-minute 'infomercial' on almost all the major networks.

The rise of the modern media and the changing character of the American city have had consequences. Whereas party meetings were at least to some extent a two-way process, Television and radio are a one-way medium. Furthermore, some observers argue, a candidate's prospects have come to depend upon the way in which he or she is represented by the media, particularly television. The construction of image has become pivotal. As Anthony King recorded in the aftermath of the 1980 contest: 'the great majority had never been in the physical presence of any of the candidates . . . Instead they were forced to form their own impressions from what they could read in the printed media or see on television . . . the performances that mattered were not in high office but on the small screen' (King 1981: 316).

Furthermore, much of the part that the parties traditionally played a large part in 'getting out the vote' on election day has been taken over by advocacy organisations and interest groups. Many are broadly associated with and have coalesced around one or other of the major parties. They concentrate their attention on campaigning activities intended to back the party and maximise turnout levels among those sections of the population most likely to support their aims and objectives. In the 2008 election, the Human Rights Campaign, the largest of the gay and lesbian organisations, launched a $7 million election mobilisation campaign. The National Organization for Women (NOW) called voters across the country and its political action committee made specific candidate endorsements. Both organisations are closely aligned with the Democrats. Their efforts may contribute towards election victories at federal and state level but also give the organisations leverage if the candidates they back win the contests.

The parties have also increasingly abandoned the process of policy development. This is the exploration, researching and popularising of new policy ideas. It is undertaken by interest groups, advocacy organisations, and, to a greater extent, 'think tanks'. Conservative 'think tanks' such as the American Enterprise Institute (AEI), the libertarian Cato Institute, and the Heritage Foundation have, for example, been influential in Republican Party circles. Heritage was founded in February 1973 amidst concerns that the Republican Party was being pulled towards the pragmatism of centre-ground politics. The Foundation publishes briefing documents, research papers, and conferences, and supports a website that acts as a clearing-house for a broad range of conservative organisations and campaigns.

There are liberal counterweights to the conservative foundations. The Economic Policy Institute was founded in 1986 and has ties to the trades unions. It 'seeks to broaden the public debate about strategies to achieve a prosperous and fair economy'. The Progressive Policy Institute is closely associated with the Democratic Leadership Council and more moderate Democrats, The Center for American Progress is particularly significant. Its president, John Podesta, a former White House Chief of Staff, headed the Obama transition team In 2008–9 and many members of the Center's staff went on to serve in the Obama administration.

Alongside these trends and developments, some commentators have made much of the differences within both of the parties. There has been, they suggest, a process of splintering and fragmentation. There are at least three distinct factions in the Republican Party.

First, the Christian right was brought into the political arena by developments during the 1970s such as the secularisation of education, successive Supreme Court rulings (particularly *Roe v. Wade*, which established abortion as a constitutional right), and the emergence of the 'gay lobby'. Against this background, evangelical Christians sought the adoption of policies structured around moral traditionalism and family values. In particular, they hoped to outlaw abortion and counter efforts to represent homosexuality and heterosexuality as moral equivalents. Christian conservatives were particularly well represented within the Bush administration. Extended federal funding was, for example, provided for 'abstinence-only' sex education programmes which focus on the maintenance of virginity before marriage rather than providing instruction in the use of contraception. Many of the Bush White House's judicial appointments, particularly the elevation of John Roberts and Samuel Alito to the US Supreme Court bench, were enthusiastically welcomed.

Second, economic conservatives stress the importance of low taxation and minimal government. They call for a return to the principles that, they assert, underpinned the US Constitution and fear the expansion of government that took place, to some extent during the Bush years, and then at an accelerated pace during Obama's period of office. Their ranks include organisations such as the Club for Growth and Americans for Tax Reform. The Tea Party movement, which emerged and grew rapidly during 2009 and 2010, is rooted in economic conservatism. Whereas some economic conservatives share the moral traditionalism of the Christian right, others, such as Grover Norquist of Americans for Tax Reform, fear that social issues may prove divisive.

Third, although recognised as a current within US conservatism since the 1960s, 'neoconservatives' (sometimes called 'national security conservatives') emerged more forcefully during the latter half of the 1990s. Their thinking initially took shape around the Project for the New American Century and the *Weekly Standard*. Although there were few in its ranks, their emergence reflected a shift in mood among some on the right. They called for an assertion of American leadership across the globe based upon 'benevolent hegemony'. Such hegemony would not be based upon business needs, a narrow understanding of the national interest, or the amoral calculus of *realpolitik*. Instead, it was to be informed by moral considerations and the 'export' of American values. After the 11 September 2001 attacks, however, the Project gained greater currency. It increasingly seemed that American national security could be maintained only if the wider world shared the values upon which the US was built, most notably democracy, liberty, and the free market. 'Neoconservative' voices, including that of Paul Wolfowitz at the Department of Defense, seemed to contribute to the US's decision to invade Iraq in 2003. Although the dashing of expectations that there would be a rapid and relatively straightforward transition to western democracy in Iraq led many neoconservatives to retreat ideologically, some retained their commitment to an assertive foreign policy and, for example, backed US efforts to bring about change in Libya during 2011.

Although the dividing lines are sometimes rather more blurred, there are also tensions and cleavages among Democrats. Both the 'Blue Dogs' and the Democratic Leadership Council (DLC) are on the right of the party. The Blue Dogs are, broadly at least, based among the party's few remaining backers in the southern states. They are conservative on economic (particularly fiscal) issues and many lean towards moral traditionalism. Their ranks include committed supporters of gun rights and those who are fearful of free trade. Arguably, the Blue Dogs are a dying breed. Although they had 53 members in the House of Representatives before the 2010 mid-term elections, this number fell to 23 afterwards. This was in part because many Blue Dogs were standing in southern districts that had, on a long-term basis, been becoming steadily more Republican.

The DLC includes some bigger names. Both Bill Clinton and Al Gore were associated with the Council. Formed in the aftermath of the Democratic defeat in the 1984 presidential election, the DLC was formed as an attempt to 'modernise' the party. It talked, in a phrase that was to be adopted by some European social democrats, of a 'third way'. In this spirit, the DLC's *New Democrat Credo* draw on themes associated with both liberalism and conservatism: 'We believe that economic growth generated in the private sector is the prerequisite for opportunity . . . We believe that government programs should be grounded in the values most Americans share: work, family, personal responsibility, individual liberty, faith, tolerance, and inclusion' (New Democrats Online, 2001). Although, the DLC asserts, there should be some pro-active government intervention, it should be confined to certain specific sectors of the economy such as education or innovation. The DLC tends to be rather less associated with moral traditionalism than many Blue Dogs. It also has a greater commitment to the lowering of trade barriers. The New Democrats of the DLC have also lost ground. They took a blow when Senator Hillary Clinton's presidential bid was defeated. They have, furthermore, been challenged by others within the party's ranks. According to Jeff Faux of the Economic Policy Institute: 'Their program cannot hold together. It is a tired mixture of conservative intention watered down with liberal tinkering in the hope that it will fill in the crack in the center' (1995: 173).

In contrast to the DLC, Democratic Party traditionalists see much more of a role for government, particularly in the provision of healthcare and education. They believe that the country has been damaged by growing inequality and slowing rates of social mobility. They are committed to policies that conservative critics have derided as 'tax and spend' and seek to maintain the loose association between the Party and trade (or 'labor') unionism.

There is a third strand in the Democrats' thinking, although it often overlaps and interweaves with other strands of thought within the Party. For some, 'identity politics' are pivotal, and they emphasise the importance of addressing the social and economic disadvantages faced by women and minority groupings. This leads to backing for policy proposals that include abortion rights, affirmative action, and measures to encourage minority entrepreneurship.

'Obamaism' has sought to navigate between some of these differences. It was constructed around an implied rejection of the policies and political style of the Clinton administration although this may in part have been dictated by Obama's rivalry with Senator Hillary Clinton in the 2008 Democratic primaries.[2] In place of 'Clintonism', there were oft-repeated calls for change and claims that partisan divisions could be transcended. In his Inaugural Address, delivered on 20 January 2009, Obama reiterated some traditional Democratic Party goals but sought to distance himself from 'big government': 'The question we ask today is not whether our government is too big or too small, but whether it works, whether it helps families find jobs at a decent wage, care they can afford, a retirement that is dignified' (*The New York Times*, 2009). In so far as 'Obamaism' offered a distinctive philosophy it was sometimes tied to the politics of 'nudge'. Sometimes described as libertarian paternalism, *Nudge* (a book written by Richard Thaler and Cass Sunstein) sought to suggest that government could work most effectively by 'nudging' individuals and groups towards particular outcomes rather than by imposing legal requirements to pursue a certain course.[3]

The contemporary parties

While the 'party decline' thesis was, at least for a period, widely accepted, it is now difficult to sustain.

First, there is little evidence of long-term partisan dealignment within the US electorate. According to the American National Election Studies (ANES), 32 per cent regard themselves as 'strong partisans'. In other words, they identify 'strongly' with either the Democrats or the Republicans. As Table 2.3 suggests, the figure has been broadly constant since the 1980s (American National Election Studies, 2011). There has been a long-term shift among weaker identifiers but this has been confined to the voting blocs associated with the Democrats. As has been noted above, the party disproportionately lost support among white southerners, men, and blue-collar workers from the late 1960s onwards. There was a reaction against desegregation and the

Table 2.3 *Strength of partisanship, 1960–2008 (%)*

	1960	1970	1980	1990	2000	2002	2004	2008
Independent	12	14	15	12	13	9	10	11
Leaning independent	13	18	22	24	28	28	29	29
Weak partisan	39	39	37	34	27	33	28	28
Strong partisan	36	29	26	30	31	31	33	32

Source: adapted from American National Election Studies (2011) *Strength of Partisanship 1952–2008*, http://www.electionstudies.org/nesguide/toptable/tab2a_3.htm.

Democrats' growing associations with 'big government' and cultural liberalism. The picture is, however, very different for the GOP. Indeed, Republican partisanship (taking strong and weak identifiers together) was at the same level (28 per cent) in 2004 as it had been in 1952 (American National Election Studies, 2011).

Having said this, there has, as a corollary to the long-term decline in identification with the Democratic Party, been an increase in the proportion of the electorate defining itself as 'independent'. Their ranks include independents who lean towards the Republicans, independents who lean towards the Democrats, and those who might be dubbed 'independent independents'. The proportion of 'independent independents' reached 16 per cent in 1976 and 1976 but then fell back. Between 1998 and 2008 it fluctuated between 13 per cent and 7 per cent (American National Election Studies, 2011). If independents are considered more broadly (so as to include those who call themselves independent but lean towards one of the major parties) the evidence for 'dealignment' becomes thinner still. Although they define themselves as 'independent' their voting record suggests otherwise. As Bruce E. Keith *et al.* noted in 1992:

> They display an impressive tendency to vote for the candidate of the party they feel closer to; indeed, in presidential elections *they are generally more loyal to their party than weak partisans*. In seven of the ten presidential elections since 1952, Independent Democrats gave a higher proportion of their vote to the Democratic presidential candidate than did Weak Democrats . . . On average, since 1952, 89 percent of Independent Republicans have voted for the Republican presidential candidate, compared to 87 percent of Weak Republicans. (Keith, 1992: 65–66)

Second, studies of partisanship met, however to go beyond voting trends. The role of the parties within Congress should also be considered. In the past, some accounts have referred to a process of individualisation within both the House of Representatives and the Senate:

> In our era of debilitated political parties, Washington is run by 536 individual political entrepreneurs – one president, 100 senators and 435 members of the

House – each of whom got here essentially on his own. Each chooses the office he seeks, raises his own money, hires his own pollster and ad-maker and recruits his own volunteers. (Wattenberg, 1991: 165)

However, studies of 'party unity scores' tell a different story. These scores are constructed from roll call votes (those that are formally recorded and are held if requested by at least a fifth of those members who are present) and measure the proportion of such votes in which a majority of voting Democrats oppose a majority of voting Republicans. Although the numbers shown in Table 2.4 are significantly lower than would be found in a whipped parliamentary system such as that in the UK (where disciplinary action can be taken by the party against persistent dissidents and importance inducements are offered to ensure loyalty), they do suggest that there has been a long-term rise in partisan voting.[4] Indeed, as *Congressional Quarterly* recorded, '2009 was the most partisan year ever' (Seabrook, 2010). It is particularly noteworthy that party unity scores in the Senate, traditionally regarded as the more individualistic and less partisan of the two chambers, have often matched those for the House of Representatives.

The growth of party unity is also evident in the decline of organised groupings within the Congressional parties. The 'boll weevils' (southern conservative Democrats) were particularly influential and their backing for policies proposed by the Reagan White House enabled Republican legislation to secure passage. At the same time, there were liberal-leaning Republicans ('gypsy moths') elected in the north-eastern states. These groupings are now more or less extinct and their successors (such as the Blue Dog Democrats) face significant difficulties.

Table 2.4 *Party unity scores, 1960–2009 (%)*

	House Democrats	House Republicans	Senate Democrats	Senate Republicans
1960	75	77	73	74
1970	71	72	71	71
1980	78	79	76	74
1990	86	78	82	77
2000	86	90	90	91
2001	86	94	90	90
2002	90	93	85	88
2003	91	95	90	95
2004	91	93	88	93
2005	91	93	90	90
2006	90	92	89	87
2007	92	85	87	81
2008	92	87	87	83
2009	91	87	91	87

Source: adapted from The Brookings Institution (n.d.) *Party Unity in Congressional Voting*, www.brookings.edu/~/media/Files/Programs/Governance/govwatch/charts/party%20unity.pdf.

Third, another way of considering the role of the contemporary parties is to survey the extent to which members of Congress in a particular party support the president when he belongs to the same party. The year 2009, the first of the Obama presidency, is instructive. It was a period of 'unified government'. Both chambers of Congress and the White House were controlled by the Democrats. Indeed, the Democrats secured 60 seats in the Senate, the figure required to defeat filibusters. In 2009, Obama gained a presidential support score of 96.7 per cent. The previous record was held by Lyndon Johnson who secured 93 per cent in 1965 (Seabrook, 2010).

Fourth, in both parties, the 'establishment' apparatus has made sustained attempts to recapture the nomination process. Within the Democratic Party, there was a steady retreat from the McGovern–Fraser reforms that circumscribed the role of party officials and committees. The Commission on Presidential Nomination and Party Structure chaired by the former Michigan Party Chairman, Morley Winograd, between 1975 and 1980 recommended that party leaders, elected officials, and 'add-ons' should also serve as convention delegates. In contrast with the delegates chosen on the basis of the primary and caucus results, these 'super-delegates' are unpledged and can choose a candidate freely. Furthermore, their political experience reintroduced a degree of peer review into the nomination process. The Winograd proposals were built upon in 1982, when a commission chaired by Governor James B. Hunt of North Carolina recommended a significant increase in their numbers (*Congressional Quarterly*, 1997: 27–31). As a consequence of these changes, 'super-delegates' generally represent about 18 per cent of the total delegate count. In 2008, when it was at one stage thought that the super-delegates could be decisive in choosing between Clinton and Obama, they constituted about a fifth of the total. Within the Republican Party, state governors, members of state legislatures, and other elected officials exercise considerable influence. Their backing was said to be decisive in winning the 2000 presidential nomination for George W. Bush.

Fifth, the parties have also sought to influence the promotion and selection of candidates in Congressional and state-level contests. Although the nomination process for nominees is open to the voting public through primaries and caucuses, Paul S. Herrnson has recorded the activities of party officials: 'They actively recruit some candidates to enter primary contests and just as actively discourage others from doing so . . . Party leaders and staff use polls, the promise of party campaign money and services, and the persuasive talents of party leaders, members of Congress, and even presidents to influence the decisions of potential candidates' (Herrnson, 2002: 63). In particular, the National Republican Senatorial Committee and the National Republican Congressional Committee and their Democratic counterparts (the Democratic Senatorial Campaign Committee (DSCC) and the Democratic Congressional Campaign Committee (DCCC)) have sought to ensure that the candidate most likely to win in the general election is selected as the party's nominee. In the

2006 mid-term elections, the Democrats' efforts were largely directed by the Illinois Representative Rahm Emanuel (who later became President Obama's Chief-of-Staff and then Mayor of Chicago but at that time served as Chairman of the DCCC), and the New York Senator Charles Schumer (Chairman of the DSCC). They targeted particularly winnable districts and states. For example, Jim Webb, a relatively conservative Democrat with a record of military service, was backed in the Virginia primary and then supported heavily in the general election. The state, it was felt, could be won by the Democrats only with a candidate such as Webb. His victory allowed the Democrats to take control of the Senate.

Sixth, a number of US Supreme Court rulings also strengthened the position of parties. Following the 1972 Democratic national convention, the Court ruled in *Cousins v. Wigoda* (1975) that state courts could not interfere with the right of national parties to decide who will be seated at their national conventions. This was confirmed in *Democratic Party of the United States v. LaFollette* (1981) (Plano and Greenberg, 1989: 64). In 1989, in *March Fong Eu v. San Francisco County Democratic Central Committee* (1989), the Court declared that the parties had the right to endorse a particular candidate in the primaries (Hays Lowenstein, 1992: 8).

Seventh, from the late 1970s onwards, there has been extensive party-building activity and infrastructural development. Indeed, there has been a process of professionalisation. As John H. Aldrich has concluded: 'They have become more truly national parties, better financed, more professionalized, and more institutionalized, with greater power to shape the actions of their state and local organizations' (Aldrich, 1995: 260). Having said this, however, a caveat should be entered. Although the parties have become much more professionalised, there are tensions and differences between the different leadership bodies. Within the Republicans, Michael Steele, who served as RNC Chairman between 2009 and 2001, proved controversial. Amongst Democrats, there were bitter battles in the run-up to the 2006 mid-term elections. The DNC Chairman Howard Dean (who had sought the party's presidential nomination in 2004 and then headed the DNC between 2005 and 2009) was committed to a '50-state strategy'. He argued that the Democrats should add to their resources and build up their organisational structures across the entire country. Senior Congressional Democrats, most notably Rahm Emanuel, Chairman of the Democratic Congressional Campaign Committee, argued that the Party should concentrate on those districts where there were close races. Resources would otherwise, he reportedly said, be squandered.[5]

Eight, the national committees, along with the party committees based in Congress such as the National Republican Senatorial Committee, have become major vehicles for fundraising and spending. Although there are limits on the funds the national party committees may accept, party organisations are permitted to make 'coordinated expenditures' (which are organised together with a candidate's campaign team) as well as 'independent expenditures' that will support and assist the party's nominees. As the Federal Election Commission states: 'Coordinated party expenditures are not considered contributions and do not count against a publicly funded campaign's candidate expenditure limit' (Federal Election Commission, 2011). In the 2008 election campaign, the Republican National Committee (RNC) played a pivotal financial role. Although the McCain campaign was limited in its spending (to $84.1 million) because it had accepted FEC funding, the RNC provided 'coordinated' and 'independent' expenditure. The RNC and the state Republican parties also committed large amounts to 'get-out-the-vote' efforts.[6]

Last, it should be noted that the party decline model was structured, if only implicitly, on the premise that there was a past 'golden age' when party structures and identities flourished. The accuracy of this is open to question. A 1956 study of Detroit revealed that fewer than one-fifth of local organisations were operating at their full potential. As a Congressman noted, two years later: 'if we depended on the party organization to get elected, none of us would be here' (quoted in Wattenberg, 1996: 108).

Conclusion

There are therefore dangers in generalising too broadly about political parties. Arguably, those who talked of 'party decline' are guilty of this. Writing in his 1942 textbook, *Politics, Parties, and Pressure Groups*, V. O. Key distinguished between the party in the electorate (the voters), the party in office (elected officials), and the party as organization (Key, 1966). As noted above, those who talk of 'party decline' can cite shifts in the character of parties-as-organisations. In particular, party organisation at local level is weak and at times perhaps non-existent (although the same might also be said about the major parties in many European countries). Arguably, during 2009 and 2010, the Tea Party movement grew rapidly on the edges of the Republican Party because there were few neighbourhood party organisations that could have provided a channel for the antipathy that many on the right felt for the Obama administration. There has been another shift so far as parties-as-organisations are concerned. The relationship between the party and the election campaigns (including the presidential campaigns) is, with the growth of primaries and the move towards candidate-based forms of organisation, more a subject for negotiation and bartering than in the past. Both have substantial political, financial and human resources and there is a process of exchange. However, notwithstanding these shifts, accounts of parties-as-organisations need to incorporate the changes that have taken place at national and state leadership level. As noted above, the parties are much more professionalised than in earlier years. At the same time, despite earlier talk of dealignment, the parties in the electorate are a strong as they were when polling data on this was first collected. There are high levels of partisanship levels. Indeed, during the Clinton and Bush years, there were frequent references to separate 'red' (Republican) and 'blue' (Democratic) nations. Perhaps most significantly of all, the parties in office (particularly at Congressional level) have more distinct and separate identities than, some suggest, at any point since the Civil War.

Notes

1 The Democrats in Minnesota are still known as the Democratic–Farmer–Labor Party.
2 Ironically, significant numbers of former Clinton administration officials, and Hillary Clinton herself, were however appointed to senior positions within the Obama White House.
3 However, despite talk of 'nudging', 'Obamacare' (the health reform enacted in 2010) rested on the individual mandate requiring almost everyone to have a basic level of health insurance coverage.
4 There are always methodological difficulties with statistics such as these. Tables based upon roll-call votes weight all these votes equally. However, some will be of far greater political significance than others.
5 Arguably, Dean's 50-state strategy contributed to the Democrats' victories in the 2006 mid-term elections and helped the Obama–Biden campaign win in traditionally 'red' (or Republican) states in 2008.
6 The parties are however prohibited from accepting 'soft money' contributions (which are not reported to the FEC and are not subject to its limits). This section of the 2002 Bipartisan Campaign Reform Act (often known after the names of its Congressional sponsors as 'McCain–Feingold') was upheld by the US Supreme Court (*McConnell v. F.E.C*, 2003) and reaffirmed in June 2010 when the Court refused to hear an appeal from a lower court (Liptak, 2010).

References and further reading

Aldrich, J. H. (1995), *Why Parties? The Origins and Transformation of Parties in America*, Chicago, The University of Chicago Press.
All Other Persons (2008), *Post Election Analysis: Outside the South, Obama Gets Almost Half of the White Vote*, 11 November, http://allotherpersons.wordpress.com/category/presidential-general-election-2008/.
American National Election Studies (2011), *The ANES Guide to Public Opinion and Electoral Behavior – Party Identification 3-Point Scale (revised in 2008) 1952–2008*, www.electionstudies.org/nesguide/2ndtable/t2a_2_2.htm.
American National Election Studies (2011), *The ANES Guide to Public Opinion and Electoral Behavior – Strength of Partisanship 1952–2008*, www.electionstudies.org/nesguide/toptable/tab2a_3.htm.
Anderson, J. B. (2001), *Testimony of John B. Anderson to the National Commission on Federal Election Reform (Ford–Carter Commission)*, 24 May, http://archive.fairvote.org/administration/cartercommision.htm.

Bailey, C. (1990), 'Political parties', *Contemporary Record*, February, 12–15.

Broder, D. S. (1971), *The Party's Over: The Failure of Politics in America*, New York, Harper and Row.

CNN ElectionCenter (2008), *President – Full Results*, http://edition.cnn.com/ELECTION/ 2008/results/president/.

CogentPolitics(2011),'Abrieflookatcampaigncontributions',*CogentPolitics*,23February, http://cogentpolitics.blogspot.com/2011/02/brief-look-at-campaign-contibutions. html.

Congressional Quarterly (1997), *Powers of the Presidency*, Washington DC, Congressional Quarterly.

Cook, R. (2009), 'Obama and the redefinition of presidential coattails', *Rasmussen Reports*, 17 April, http://www.rasmussenreports.com/public_content/political_ commentary/commentary_by_rhodes_cook/obama_and_the_redefinition_of_ presidential_coattails.

Davis, M. (2009), 'Obama at Manassas', *New Left Review*, March–April, 5–40.

Durham, M. (1996), 'The fall and rise of the Christian right in America', *Politics Review*, 5:4, April, 26–28.

Faux, J. (1995), 'The myth of the new Democrat', in W. D. Burnham (ed.), *The American Prospect Reader in American Politics*, Chatham, Chatham House, pp. 162–173.

Federal Election Commission (2011), *Public Funding of Presidential Elections*, www.fec. gov/pages/brochures/pubfund.shtml.

Hays Lowenstein, D. (1992), 'American political parties', in G. Peele, C. J. Bailey, and B. Cain (eds), *Developments in American Politics*, Basingstoke, Macmillan, pp. 63–85.

Hershey, M. R. (1997), 'The Congressional elections', in G. M. Pomper *et al.*, *The Election of 1996: Reports and Interpretations*, Chatham, Chatham House, 205–239.

Herrnson, P. S. (2002), 'National party organizations at the dawn of the twenty-first century', in L. S. Maisel (ed.), *The Parties Respond: Changes in American Parties and Campaigns*, Boulder, CO, Westview Press, pp. 47–78.

Keith, B. E. (1992), *The Myth of the Independent Voter*, Berkeley, CA, University of California Press.

Key, V. O. (1966) *Politics, Parties and Pressure Groups*, New York: Thomas Y. Crowell Company.

King, A. (1981), 'How not to select presidential candidates: a view from Europe', in A. Ranney (ed.), *The American Elections of 1980*, Washington DC, American Enterprise Institute for Public Policy Research, pp. 303–328.

Ladd, E. C. (1996), 'The 1994 Congressional elections: the postindustrial realignment continues', in B. Stinebrickner (ed.), *American Government 96/97*, Guilford, Dushkin Publishing Group, 167–180.

Libertarian Party (2010), *Libertarian Party 2010 Platform*, http://www.lp.org/platform.

Liptak, A. (2010), 'Supreme Court affirms a ban on soft money', *The New York Times*, 29 June, www.nytimes.com/2010/06/30/us/politics/30donate.html.

Mayhew, D. (2002), *Electoral Realignments: A Critique of an American Genre*, New Haven, Yale University Press.

Meyerson, H. (2008), 'A real realignment', *The Washington Post*, 7 November.

New Democrats Online (2001), *The New Democrat Credo*, www.ndol.org/ndol_ci.cfm?k aid=86&subid=194&contentid=3775.

OpenSecrets.org (2011), *Reelection Rates Over the Years*, www.opensecrets.org/bigpicture/reelect.php.

Owens, J. (1995), 'The 1994 US mid-term elections', *Politics Review*, 4:4, April, 2–6.

New York Times (2009), 'Barack Obama's Inaugural Address', *The New York Times*, 20 January, www.nytimes.com/2009/01/20/us/politics/20text-obama.html?pagewanted=2.

Plano, J. C. and M. Greenberg (1989), *The American Political Dictionary*, Fort Worth, TX, Holt, Rinehart, and Winston.

Robertson, D. (1985), *The Penguin Dictionary of Politics*, Harmondsworth, Penguin.

Rossiter, C. (1964), *Parties and Politics in America*, New York, Signet.

Seabrook, A. (2010), 'CQ: 2009 was the most partisan year ever', National Public Radio, 11 January, http://www.npr.org/templates/story/story.php?storyId=122441095&ps=rs.

Sifry, M. L. (2002), *Spoiling for a Fight: Third-Party Politics in America*, New York, Routledge.

Silbey, J. H. (2002), 'From "essential to the existence of our institutions" to "rapacious enemies of honest and responsible government": The rise and fall of American political parties, 1790–2000', in L. M. Maisel (ed.), *The Parties Respond: Changes in American Parties and Campaigns*, Cambridge, MA, Westview Press, pp. 1–8.

Vicini, J. (2010), 'Supreme Court upholds political party money limits', *Reuters*, 29 June, www.reuters.com/article/2010/06/29/us-usa-court-politics-idUSTRE65S30920100629.

Wattenberg, M. P. (1991), *The Rise of Candidate-Centered Politics*, Cambridge, MA, Harvard University Press.

Wattenberg, M. P. (1996), *The Decline of American Political Parties 1952–1994*, Cambridge, MA, Harvard University Press.

Wayne, S. J. (1992), *The Road to the White House 1992: The Politics of Presidential Selection*, New York, St Martin's Press.

3

Organised interests, lobbying, and advocacy

Organised interests, now sometimes dubbed the 'persuasion industry', have long been a characteristic feature of American politics. Indeed, the right 'to petition the Government for a redress of grievances' is incorporated within the First Amendment. Interests seek to persuade, or 'lobby', decision-makers at federal, state, or local level. In contrast to political parties, they do not seek to win elected office other than in a few exceptional instances as a campaign tactic.[1]

Writing in the 1830s, Alexis de Tocqueville was struck by the plethora of groups and associations: 'In no country in the world', he asserted, 'has the principle of association been more successfully used, or applied to a greater multitude of objects, than in America' (1984: 95). Over the past century, sectoral organisations and advocacy groups have proliferated alongside the religious and civic groupings that Tocqueville described. In 2007, there were an estimated 14,878 lobbyists (sometime dubbed 'hired guns') in Washington DC (OpenSecrets, 2011a).

Some work for specialist lobbying firms while larger companies maintain their own in-house lobbyists. Many of the largest corporations and the peak business associations have become much more assertive and astute in terms of lobbying techniques. Think tanks, many of which are tied to particular ideological perspectives, have secured much more influence. K Street in Washington DC is now synonymous with the lobbying industry There are, furthermore, an estimated 45,000 registered lobbyists active at state level (Repetto, 2006: 2). Why is there so much group activity in the US?

First, the US is a diverse and heterogeneous society. Despite a strong sense of national identity and patriotism, there are significant regional, racial, religious, and sectoral cleavages. Groupings may fear that their interests will be marginalised because of inter-group competition and they therefore seek what is sometimes termed 'a place at the table'.

Second, from the late nineteenth century onwards, as national markets emerged, commerce and industry have increasingly crossed state lines and have therefore been subject to regulatory control by the federal government. Television, radio, and broadband are, for example, regulated by the Federal Communications Commission (FCC). The Federal Energy Regulatory Commission (FERC) has authority over electricity and gas sales as well as hydroelectric provision. Companies and producer groups have, as a consequence, sought to influence those in Congress, the federal bureaucracy, and the courts who shape business activity and set a framework for it.

Third, both the federal government and the state governments provide assistance and entitlements to individuals and those in particular categories. The Small Business Administration offers assistance to promote low-level entrepreneurship. Groups form so as to claim a share. When the incoming Obama administration announced that it was planning a large-scale economic stimulus (ARRA – the American Recovery and Reinvestment Act), to revive the economy, the *Washington Post* reported the extent to which groupings, many of which had ties with the Democratic Party, were seeking advantage. Political processes the newspaper suggested, might well trump economics:

> The potential for massive new spending has touched off a frenzy among interest groups eager to claim their share of the expanding stimulus pie. The profusion of requests from governors, transportation groups, environmental activists and business organizations is spawning fears that the package could be loaded with provisions that satisfy important Democratic constituencies but fail to provide the jolt needed to pull the nation out of a deepening recession. (Montgomery, 2008)

Fourth, although American public culture has always incorporated a distrust of government, there was also for a long period a degree of deference towards those in authority. For example, until the era of Vietnam and Watergate, press coverage of the president was largely respectful, and there was at times a degree of self-censorship. Much that was known at the time about President Kennedy became public knowledge only years after his death. Suspicion of office-holders has fuelled activism and group formation amongst those on both the left and the right. Those on the left fear the disproportionate influence of business interests while conservatives are alarmed by the growth of what they regard as an elite 'political class'.

Fifth, since the mid-twentieth century the US, together with other western nations, has shifted towards 'post-materialism'. In the past, widespread economic insecurity gave rise to materialist values (or what are sometimes called 'survival' or 'scarcity' values) and led to the formation of organisations such as the trades unions that sought higher wages and workplace reform. However, because of economic advances, and despite significant residual poverty, basic, material needs are now assured to a greater extent. This contributed to a fundamental value shift whereby older materialist values were displaced by concerns tied to concepts such as freedom, identity, self-expression, and participation. Against this background, new groups and social movements structured around post-materialist values came to the fore. These included the women's movement, gay organisations, and, for example, environmental campaigns.

Sixth, as Chapter 2 noted, there has been increasingly intense and bitter partisanship in recent decades. There is a significant ideological divide between the major parties. Indeed, some commentators have spoken of 'hyper-partisanship'. Legions of advocacy organisations seeking to counter the claims made by those on the other side of the divide have emerged. Alongside this, large numbers of think tanks have been founded. These are research organisations that publish in-depth reports surveying the rationale behind, and the implications of, particular public policy options. Although many are neutral, a significant proportion is politically aligned. Their tax-exempt status prevents them from lobbying or campaigning directly, but their work often structures the activities of legislators. Indeed, some major bills have been written by think tank staff. The Center for American Progress is broadly liberal in its orientation. The Heritage Foundation and the American Enterprise Institute are conservative.

This chapter considers the work of interest groups. It outlines different types of interest group, assesses the methods that they employ, and asks two questions. To what extent do groups influence decision-makers? Do they play a negative or a positive role in the political process?

Organised interests – a typology

Although the dividing lines are often blurred, interest groups can be classified. Different typologies have been put forward. Some draw a dividing line between *issue* and *protective* groups.

Issue groups, which are sometimes also described as *advocacy* or *cause* groups, are organisations that lobby on behalf of others or campaign for a broad political, social, or cultural cause. For the most part they are structured membership organisations. Many are organised around post-materialist issues and seeking the greater provision of what economists term 'public goods'. Classically defined (although the phrase is sometimes used more loosely), these are forms of provision that nobody can be excluded from using and where one individual's consumption does not reduce that of another. The campaigns that seek a reduction in carbon emissions or seek increased environmental regulation are proto typical examples of issue groups. However, groups organised around particular foreign and defence policy goals and the different 'pro-choice' and 'pro-life' organisations could also be cited. Some issue groups will be social movement organisations. Although they are formally independent and in contrast with movements structured on a membership basis, they are part of a wider social movement. In other words, they are connected through formal and informal networks with other organisations and individuals who collectively share, at least in broad terms, a commitment to a shared ideology and common goals. The National Organization for Women (NOW) is a social movement organisation within the broader feminist movement. The Human Rights Campaign is one of many social movement organisations within the gay and lesbian movement.

Protective groupings (which are sometimes simply termed 'interest groups') defend and promote the declared interests of their membership.[2] They can be divided into a number of categories.

First, there are business groupings, including organisations such as the National Association of Manufacturers and the US Chamber of Commerce. One report puts the Chamber's membership numbers at 300,000 (Hightower, 2010). The Chamber itself claims an 'underlying membership' of more than three million businesses and business associations (National Chamber Litigation Center, n.d.: 1). Although they cautiously backed the passage of the American Recovery and Reinvestment Act at the beginning of 2009, they became increasingly critical of the Obama administration. They feared the additional costs imposed on businesses by health reform and efforts to limit carbon emissions. There were also tensions with the Democrats in Congress. Whereas business organisation hoped for greater trade liberalisation, many Congressional Democrats believed that American jobs would be lost.

Second, there are trades, or labour, unions. As of 2008, 56 and an affiliated membership of 11 million were brought together by the American Federation of Labor–Congress of Industrial Organizations (AFL–CIO), which was formed in 1955. Although the AFL-CIO is, in the language of interest group categorisation, a *peak association*, it has been challenged by the creation of Change to Win in 2005. Change to Win, which claims over 5.5 million affiliated members drawn, in particular, from farm workers, the 'Teamsters' (truck drivers), and service employees (many of whom are minorities and women). Change to Win has organised a series of campaigns aimed at boosting union membership among the low-paid in companies such as Wal-Mart. Although the unions do play a role in American industrial life, they are significantly weaker than in Europe. As of 2010, just 11.9 per cent of workers were union members. In some states, the figure was far lower. In Texas, just 5.4 per cent were unionised. Furthermore, the figure for private sector industry was, at 6.9 per cent, much lower than the national average (Bureau of Labor Statistics, 2011). The unions were badly hit by the recessions in the early 1980s and 1990s, and from late 2007 onwards. They were also affected by the long-term processes of *deindustrialisation* (the decline of the manufacturing sector, where the unions traditionally had a strong hold) and *outsourcing* (whereby production or stages in the production process are transferred overseas where wage levels are lower). Although the service sector has grown in recent decades, it has proved difficult to organise. The public sector has, however, held out against the trend. Indeed, the characteristic union member is now employed by local, state, or the federal government. In 2010, those employed by the national, state, or local governments had a union membership rate of 36.2 per cent. At local government level the figure rose to 42.3 per cent (Bureau of Labor Statistics, 2011).[3]

Third, there are professional associations, such as the American Medical Association (AMA), representing doctors, and the American Bar Association (ABA), which puts forward the interests of lawyers. Together with some other organisations, they exercise a degree of self-government within their occupational sector. For example, the ABA and the AMA provide accreditation to law and medical schools respectively. In contrast, however, with professional organisations in some other countries they cannot regulate admission into or out of the occupation. Indeed, only about a fifth of doctors and medical students belong to the AMA.

Fourth, arguably, sub-governments (state and local governments) and the myriad departments, agencies, and bureaux within the federal government also act as organised interests. Much of this activity is informal. Nonetheless, the individual states are represented through organisations such as the National Governors Association and the National Council of State Legislatures.

Two further points should be noted. First, as well as issue and protective groupings, there are *hybrid* organisations that can be placed somewhere between protective and issue groupings. They act on behalf of their membership, which has its own distinct, sectional interests, but also campaign for others beyond their own ranks. For example, the National Rifle Association (NRA) protects the rights of gun-owners, but also campaigns, more broadly, to uphold the right to 'bear arms'. Second, the role of companies goes beyond the peak organisations (such as the National Association of Manufacturers) noted above. Many of the larger corporations have their own distinct interests and they are engaged in lobbying. Much of this overshadows the activities undertaken by groups. According to a 2010 estimate, there were 11,195 corporate lobbyists in Washington DC. In 2009, corporations spent $2.95 billion on lobbying activities. And, as of April 2010, corporate executives and lobbyists had given a total of $473 million to candidates, party committees, and leadership political action committees (Hightower, 2010).[4]

Influence and access

The degree of influence secured by organised interests and corporate lobbyists depends in large part on three factors. First, the institutional framework (what is sometimes termed the *institutional architecture*) should be considered. Second, influence is also related to the *structure of political opportunity* at a particular point in time. Third, it is dependent upon the *resources* that particular interests have at their command.

Institutional architecture

The institutional character of US government and administration encourages the creation, growth, and efficacy of organised interests. The US government apparatus has a particularly porous character. There are large numbers of openings or 'access points' that enable groups to reach decision-makers. These include the three branches of government in Washington DC, as well as the different tiers of state and local government. Despite the growth in partisanship, the whipping system in both Congress and the state legislatures is weaker than in most European legislatures and this provides openings for organised interests that are seeking to build connections with policymakers. The byzantine structure of the executive branch (based around overlapping and interlocking departments, agencies, and bureaux) creates divided loyalties and uncertainties about jurisdiction. Again, this offers forms of political space to external interests that are denied in those countries governed by more professionalised and hierarchical bureaucracies. Furthermore, both the state and federal courts are open to argument and persuasion by 'outsiders' in a way that is prohibited in many other countries.

However, the character of the institutional architecture gives structural advantages to those interests that have substantial resources (see below). Most of those seeking public office depend during both the primary and the general election campaign upon outside financial contributions and this ensures that the organisations that provide significant funding secure a degree of access to those who are elected.

The system by which those who staff the senior levels within the executive branch are political appointees rather than permanent civil servants adds further to the porousness of the decision-making process. There are legal restrictions including a one-year 'cooling off' period for some 'senior' officials during which time they are prohibited from seeking to influence those still serving in their former departments or agencies (and a two-year period for those who are 'very senior' who are forbidden from lobbying anyone within the executive branch). A day after he came into office, President Obama issued an executive order prohibiting political appointees from lobbying anyone within the executive branch during the lifetime of his administration (Maskell, 2010).

Nonetheless, there is still a 'revolving door'. This metaphor refers to the movement of individuals between the private sector and government service.[5] Members of earlier administrations and Congress have readily found employment as lobbyists in larger firms or the 'umbrella' interest groups that act on their behalf. Furthermore, some of the most senior appointees in the Obama administration have close ties to the financial sector and Wall Street. Commentators suggest that there are therefore close personal affiliations between senior public officials and private sector business. As Open Secrets, a research-based advocacy organisation, records:

Although the influence powerhouses that line Washington's K Street are just a few miles from the U.S. Capitol building, the most direct path between the two doesn't necessarily involve public transportation. Instead, it's through a door – a revolving door that shuffles former federal employees into jobs as lobbyists, consultants and strategists just as the door pulls former hired guns into government careers. While officials in the executive branch, Congress and senior congressional staffers spin in and out of the private and public sectors, so too does privilege, power, access and, of course, money. (OpenSecrets.org, 2011b)

As of July 2011, 86 of the lobbyists employed by the US Chamber of Commerce and 38 employed by the National Association of Manufacturers had a background in government service (OpenSecrets.org, 2011c).[6] Why is the 'revolving door' so controversial? It leads, commentators suggest, to a conflict of interest. Those in government will unduly favour the corporations or organisations that employed them in the past and may well employ them in the future. This lays a basis for networks and connections within government that give a structural advantage to wealthy interests. Nikos Passas from Temple University has put this in graphic terms: '[These officials] take measures that will benefit companies and interests (while in power) and then they take positions with them . . . I call that "deferred bribery"' (Center for Public Integrity, 2003).

The structure of political opportunity

The structure of political opportunity is the political context within which political actors and interests seek to achieve the goals that they set. It is shaped by both events and processes including election outcomes. The opportunity structure offers openings to different interests at different times. It can empower political entrepreneurs who can take advantage of openings but can also constrain them.

The opportunity structure is in part structured around partisan variables. Many organised interests (particularly advocacy organisations) have close associations with one of the two major parties. Indeed, the relationship between interests and parties has become closer in recent decades as the parties have become more polarised (see Chapter 2). The election of George W. Bush in 2000 opened up space for significant numbers of interests tied to Republican constituencies. Organisations associated with the conservative movement gained a hearing at the highest levels. Regular Wednesday meetings convened by the veteran conservative organiser Grover Norquist (the president of Americans for Tax Reform) brought together White House staff, Congressional aides, and representatives from a plethora of conservative organisations. Some (the 'Christian right') emphasised cultural conservatism and the importance of traditional values while others stressed free market economic policies or US national security strategies. Their opinions on court nominations had an influence. Legislative priorities were considered collectively. In response to the calls of the Christian right, funding levels for 'abstinence-only' sex education were significantly increased. In the wake of the 11 September 2001 attacks, neoconservative groupings, which argued for the 'export' of US democratic values and vigorously backed the 2003 invasion of Iraq, came to the fore.

By the same token, the election of Barack Obama in 2008 (and the Democrats' recapture of Congress two years earlier) gave an impetus to the constituencies associated with the Democrats such as the women's movement and minority organisations. Groups that had largely been outsiders during the Republican years secured much more of an insider status.

Resources

Resources take different forms. They can be electoral, financial, economic, informational, attitudinal, or based upon an interest's political and administrative or implementational capacity.

Some organisations have significant electoral resources. In other words, they can influence elections or, perhaps more significantly, they are believed to influence election outcomes. They therefore command respect and a degree of fear. The AARP (the American Association of Retired Persons) has a membership of over 35 million. AARP members are aged 50 or over, a demographic grouping that has disproportionately high turnout levels. Many are well represented in particular districts, giving the Association potential electoral leverage. The size of a particular lobby and its voting potential interact with the level of commitment and participation to be found amongst its supporters. The National Rifle Association (NRA) is one of the most influential interest groups. Indeed, in 2001, *Fortune* magazine published the 'power 25 survey' (based upon the perceptions of Washington 'insiders') and placed the NRA at number one.[7] Although the size of the Association's membership (estimated at three to four million) and its financial resources are important, the commitment of the membership to its goals also plays a role. For many in the NRA's ranks, gun rights are the basis of individual liberty and define their way of life. They will turn out with little notice to lobby a member of Congress or canvass for a candidate. The degree of commitment within the NRA's ranks was powerfully symbolised in May 2000 when the film actor and Association president Charlton Heston aimed remarks at Vice-President Al Gore and other advocates of increased gun control: 'I want to say those fighting words for everyone within the sound of my voice to hear and to heed, and especially for you, *Mr. Gore*: "From my cold, dead hands!"'

Alongside a group's electoral potential, financial resources are self-evidently pivotal. They allow firms, protective organisations, and advocacy groups to make campaign donations (through political action committees [PACs]) and arguably increase the likelihood that they will secure access to elected officials.

Again, however, only some interests (largely corporations and a relatively small number of interest groups) have the substantial financial resources required to make a significant political impact. The number of political action committees (PACs) making donations to candidates increased from 89 in 1974 to 1,622 in 2005. Their spending levels rose from $52 million to $843 million during the period. There was a particularly significant rise in expenditure by corporate PACs, which increased their expenditures from $15 million to $221.6 million (Repetto, 2006: 2).

The US Supreme Court's 2010 ruling *Citizens United v. Federal Election Commission* may well extend corporate intervention into the political process still further. The decision allowed companies (as well as trades unions although their resources are more limited) to spend without limit on political campaigning. *Citizens United* struck down a section of the McCain–Feingold Act that prohibited companies and unions from broadcasting 'electioneering communications' (see p. 21). Writing for the majority, Justice Anthony Kennedy asserted that there was 'no basis for allowing the government to limit corporate independent expenditures . . . The government may regulate corporate speech through disclaimer and disclosure requirements, but it may not suppress that speech altogether' (quoted in *Fox News*, 2010). Those who support the judgement argue that corporate bodies are entitled to the same constitutional protections as individuals and media outlets (who were able to undertake 'independent' campaigning prior to the ruling). Those opposed to *Citizens United* spoke in very different terms. The Wisconsin Senator Russ Feingold, who sponsored the Act with John McCain, feared that large-scale business expenditure would distort and corrupt the electoral process: 'The American people will pay dearly for this decision when, more than ever, their voices are drowned out by corporate spending in our federal elections.' President Obama spoke in similar terms and said the Court had 'given a green light to a new stampede of special interest money in our politics'. It was, he argued, a 'major victory' for Wall Street (*Fox News*, 2010).

Writing in the *Financial Times*, Mark Roe argued that legislators would become more reluctant to enforce regulatory mechanisms that might curb excesses by powerful corporations. He also pointed to the consequences of the Supreme Court decision for the structure of inter-business relationships. Unlimited spending would, he argued, give large and established firms (or sectors) an in-built advantage over firms (or sectors) that were relatively new. The former would in particular provide funding for those decision-makers who would regulate the market so as to create barriers to entry or growth. Whatever their dynamism, new entrants would be squeezed out. All of this will, Roe argues, make the US economy less competitive:

> Consider whether it would have been easy for upstarts with weak funding to emerge to counter-balance, for example, efforts IBM would have been able to make under this new regime to suppress new competitors decades ago? Could Bill

Gates, or Steve Jobs in his garage, really have matched IBM in campaign funding back then? (Roe, 2010)

Financial resources do not only provide a basis for interventions in the electoral process. They also allow firms and groups to use the state and federal courts. Cases can be brought or challenged. This is important because a significant proportion of Supreme Court rulings have direct implications for the business sector. In June 2011, in a ruling that was welcomed by Wal-Mart and other companies, the Supreme Court limited the grounds on which a particular category of individuals could bring a 'class action' case. In *Dukes v. Wal-Mart Stores, Inc*, the Court ruled that women working for Wal-Mart did not constitute a cohesive group and could not therefore bring a case against the company alleging that it was in breach of civil rights legislation by discriminating against women by paying lower wages and giving them lower-level job assignments. At about the same time, the Court struck down a Vermont law that prohibited data companies using and selling information about the medical prescriptions issued by doctors without the patient's consent. The Court ruled that this law violated their First Amendment rights (Hobson, 2010).

In contrast to many European countries where judicial institutions are relatively 'insulated', the US courts are open to a degree of lobbying. Corporate interests and other organisations may submit *amicus curiae* briefs. In the words of the late Chief Justice William Rehnquist, such briefs are issued by 'someone who is not a party to the litigation, but who believes that the court's decision may affect its interest' (Rehnquist 1987: 89). *Amicus* briefs can be put forward at different stages. Some will urge the Court to hear a particular case or, in the language of the Court, grant *certiorari* ('cert'). Some studies suggest that there is a relationship between the number of *amicus* briefs that have been filed and the Court's decision to grant cert. Other briefs urge the Court to rule on a case in a particular way. The organisation will not itself be directly involved in the case (as either appellant or appellee), but at the same time has to show that it has an interest in the outcome.

Amicus briefs, like other submissions to the federal courts, customarily structure their arguments around the Constitution and precedents established by other court rulings. In some cases, however, they call for the overturning of an earlier ruling. When the Supreme Court considered Citizens United, the US Chamber of Commerce submitted an amicus brief. It urged the Court to overturn a 1990 ruling and allow corporations to undertake independent political campaigns.[8] The brief argued that 'the corporate form of a speaker is not a constitutional basis for banning core speech' (National Chamber Litigation Center, n.d.: 4).

Economic resources can be distinguished from financial resources and are tied to the structural position of an interest, organisation, or institution. The term refers to control or leverage over particular economic assets and the ability to take decisions that have significant economic consequences. Corporations make, or have the potential to make, investment decisions such as a planned relocation between states or proposals to transfer production overseas. This gives them substantial political leverage. States will be under pressure to adopt policies that will attract inward investment. They will be deterred from introducing policies that might limit or reduce corporate investment.

Trades unions can undertake industrial action, including a withdrawal of labour. Arguably, however, they are in a weaker position than business interests. Almost half the states have 'right-to-work laws' that prohibit the 'closed shop' whereby union membership is a condition of employment. Many workers are employed on an 'at-will' basis and have little or no job security. There is also, as rational choice scholars argue, a 'free rider' problem. Workers may benefit from the improved wage levels or working conditions secured by a union even if they are not members. There is therefore little incentive to join and pay membership dues.

Some interests, including those that may have very few electoral, financial, or economic resources, have *informational* leverage. In other words, they can secure influence through the knowledge that they hold or their ability to gather and organise information within a relatively short period. Again, the process that led up to the passage of ARRA offers an example. A left-leaning think tank, the Center for American Progress, offered a blueprint for the spending of federal government funds in ways that, it believed, would create jobs within a relatively short period. The depth of the economic crisis, and the sense of urgency that prevailed, compelled policymakers to listen to and adopt the Center's plans. Although there were later changes to accommodate competing interests within Congress and meet the political goals of the White House, the Center played a significant part in shaping the eventual character of the Act. Indeed, it later boasted:

> The Center for American Progress published a report last year setting out 'How to Spend $350 Billion in a First Year of Stimulus and Recovery.' Almost all of our proposals were included in the House plan – and many of these with increased funds to sustain spending for two years. (Ettlinger and Straw, 2009)

Some organised interests have a measure of sympathy or perhaps substantial support amongst sections of public opinion. This provides an organised interest with a degree of legitimacy. The process is not, however, straightforward. Public attitudes are characterised by tensions and ambiguities. There is, in particular, a distinction between the general and the particular. There is widespread hostility towards 'special interests'. But when polling questions are asked about more specific interests, opinion is much more mixed. A Pew Research Center poll conducted at the beginning of 2011 found that, on hearing news of a dispute between businesses and their employees, 43 per cent say that their first reaction is to back the business while 40 per cent say that their first reaction is to support the unions (Pew Research Center for the People and the Press, 2011). When questions were asked by Rasmussen Reports about the AARP in mid-2011, 52 per cent saw the Association in positive terms (either strongly or more weakly) while 34 per cent had an unfavourable view (Rasmussen Reports, 2011). An organised interest's attitudinal resources are largely a function of the way in which that interest and its demands are framed. If, for example, they are seen as 'special' or sectional there is little that can be drawn upon or utilised.

Last, some interests have what might be termed administrative or implementational resources. Some interests (particularly tiers of government but also some voluntary organisations) have the capacity to implement particular government programmes. They secure influence and the ability to shape the character of such programmes because government requires their co-operation and participation. Both welfare provision and the system of reformed healthcare provision passed by Congress in 2010 depend in part on the administrative resources and capacity of the states. Arguably, the Obama administration and the Congressional Democrats were compelled to grant the states extensive leeway, particularly after 2017, in deciding how to develop healthcare within their jurisdictions. Both Vermont and Oregon, which are left-leaning states, have already taken steps to provide more comprehensive health coverage (Vestal, 2011).

Limits and constraints

It would nonetheless be a mistake to present a one-dimensional picture of organised interests. Despite their undoubted influence, some qualifications should be made. There are a number of reasons why the role of interests may, in practice, be more limited than some accounts suggest.

First, although the ties between organised interests and those in Congress or the executive branch lay a basis in Hugh Heclo's phrase for the creation of 'issue networks', they may be trumped by other connections and networks. In a study of organisations representing the farming industry, William P. Browne suggests that Congress members prefer to work with trusted 'confidants' in their home districts or states rather than with Washington-based interest groups. In part, this is because Congress members are increasingly uncertain, given the proliferation of interests, about which has credibility and deserves to be given attention (1995: 281–284).

Second, the parties have gained stronger and more ideological identities and have become more cohesive, (see Chapter 2). As party loyalties and voting discipline have grown within Congress, it becomes more difficult for some interests (particularly those that might in some way be at odds with the party's Congressional leadership) to prise individual members away.

Third, although studies often draw a sharp dividing line between insiders and outsiders and suggest that organised interests with substantial resources (particularly financial resources) are insiders while those that are less well-endowed are inevitably destined to be outsiders, the distinction may in practice vary from issue to issue. Indeed, networks form around particular issues and influence is not necessarily transferred from one issue to another.

Fourth, the evidence suggesting that candidates can be 'bought' with financial contributions is open to argument. There are, firstly, methodological objections. Timothy Groseclose, Jeffrey Milyo, and David Primo argue that: 'The causality can be reversed . . . For example, a member of Congress may represent a district populated by NRA-friendly hunters. The representative may indeed support NRA-backed legislation because he does not wish to alienate voters, not necessarily because the NRA made a contribution' (Groseclose 2001).

Fifth, further legal restrictions have been placed on the lobbying process in recent years. The Honest Leadership and Open Government Act of 2007 was passed after the exposure of the Republican lobbyist Jack Abramoff. Abramoff (who was later imprisoned) had organised networks within which lobbyists gave money, gifts, and holidays to members of Congress and executive branch officials in exchange for political favours. The Act strengthened earlier Congressional rules. As well as restrictions on the 'revolving door' (which were later tightened), severe limits were placed on the giving of presents. The Act also closed off the possibility of another 'K Street project'. This had been organised by Congressman Tom DeLay (who served as house majority leader between 2003 and 2005 and was later convicted of money laundering) and it tied access for lobbyists to the giving of campaign funds and the hiring of the party's personnel. In other words, it was made clear that access to the Republican leadership in Congress depended upon donations to party organisations and candidates and the hiring of Republican staff members. Lobbying firms with ties to the Democrats were frozen out.

Sixth, the principal-agent problem should be considered. Although corporate lobbyists are hired so as to promote the interests of a particular company, lobbying firms have interests of their own. Lobbyists gain when Washington DC is seeking to impose further and more complex forms of regulation. They may make concessions in a deal involving one firm because it will give them an advantage when representing another firm. The company hiring lobbyists does not itself have insider knowledge and therefore cannot 'police' the activities that they are undertaking. Even where a large company has its own lobbying arm it may have interests that are different from those of the more productive sections of the company (Adler, 2011).

Seventh, many interests, particularly advocacy organisations, face an 'equal and opposite reaction'. This reins in their influence. Planned Parenthood and NARAL Pro-Choice America are the most influential 'pro-choice' organisations. They are, however, countered by the Susan B. Anthony List and the National Pro-Life Alliance. Both make contributions to candidates and political action committees.

Eighth, the concept of influence should be carefully considered. A distinction should be drawn between negative influence, through which the proposals put forward by others can be hindered, amended, or halted, and positive influence that enables a group to bring about the forms of change that it seeks. The influence of US pressure groups is almost always negative in character. In 1993–94, interest groups could prevent President Bill Clinton's healthcare plan being adopted. The National Federation of Independent Businesses feared the costs that would be imposed by universal health insurance coverage. Others were concerned that reform might increase the availability of abortion. The Health Insurance Association of America ran a series of television advertisements (based around the fictional characters of 'Harry and Louise') asserting that the Clinton plan would deny people the right to choose their own form of health insurance (Cigler and Loomis, 1995: 401–403). Interest groups did not, however, have the ability to agree upon and ensure the passage of an alternative plan.

Ninth, arguably, many organised interests are weaker than in earlier periods. As Robert Putnam argued in his book *Bowling Alone*, there has been a process of long-term social fragmentation. Whereas the post-Second World War generation was heavily engaged in associations and organisations at neighbourhood level and beyond (such as sports leagues, associations, and the trades unions), there has been a significant decline in social and civic engagement among subsequent generations. Although new organisations have proliferated, and notwithstanding the degree of commitment that underpins some organisations such as the NRA, there has been a loss of social capital (Putnam, 2000).

Criticisms

Few would now echo Alexis de Tocqueville's elegant description of voluntary associations inculcating the habits of self-rule and thereby bolstering democratic government. Instead, as noted above, critics of the US political process emphasise what they regard as the disproportionate leverage of the most wealthy and powerful interests. The process of interest competition is, from this point of view, a profoundly unequal contest. Corporations, it is said, secure access to and influence over legislators and those who staff the executive branch at the most senior levels through the 'revolving door'. There have also been claims, particularly from those on the left, that business organisations have structural advantages over the trades unions and organisations representing disadvantaged groupings.

There are further criticisms. Some point to 'regulatory capture. a term used to describe situations in which a department, agency, or regulatory commission agency is unduly swayed created by commercial or special interests that dominate in the industry or sector for which it is responsible or is charged with regulating. The likelihood of regulatory capture is increased by the 'revolving door' (see p. 68). There have been claims from many on the right that the Department of Education is overly close to the teaching profession. Some accuse the Federal Communications Commission of being too deferential towards the large broadcasting networks. It has, they charge, acquiesced in mergers and created barriers to entry so as to restrict newcomers to the market.

In his book *Government's End*, Jonathan Rauch offers arguments that bear some similarity to the concept of regulatory capture, but he goes further. Rauch points to the way in which the lobbying 'industry' has become a drain on the country's productive capacity. Resources are diverted into a modern form of 'gold digging' by 'Special interests' (and he includes organisations such as the AARP as well as corporations in his strictures) which concentrate on securing subsidies and benefits from government. This also leads to the continuing expansion of government and distorts the structure and character of the government apparatus. Once established because of lobbying by interests, departments and programmes seek to perpetuate their own existence. There is a clientelistic relationship between interests and those who staff the federal government:

> Like the virus that mutates to stay ahead of the latest drugs, programs change, but they do so in ways that preserve their existence and keep their clients happy, rather than in ways that solve any particular social problem with any particular degree of effectiveness. If the business of America is business, the business of government programs and their clients is to *stay* in business. (Rauch, 1999: 18)

Conclusion

Although US politics textbooks and organised interests themselves come together in offering a positive picture of the lobbying process, commentators of all persuasions are critical, sometimes highly critical, of their overall role. Those on the left stress the disproportionate influence of corporate interests and other constituencies that possess substantial resources. The right talk of 'producer capture' and the 'rent-seeking' activities of groupings winning political, legal, or financial advantages for themselves (through, for example, the securing of government subsidies at the expense of others and in a way that distorts efficient market processes).

Notes

1 The dividing line between interests and parties is however rather more blurred in some other countries.

2 The dividing line between issue groups and protective groups is often blurred because protective groups invariably frame their demands and values in terms of broader and more generalised interests. Indeed, they will often claim to be acting on behalf of the nation.

3 The statistics for those who are represented by unions are slightly higher than the figures for membership.

4 Leadership PACs are those established by leading party figures. They will channel funds to particular Congressional candidates. A significant proportion has been formed by those considering a presidential bid. Candidate funding enables such figures to make a national impact and, arguably, create a sense of obligation that may bring later political rewards. In 2009, the former Alaska governor, Sarah Palin, established SarahPAC.

5 Even if there are restrictions on individuals, lobbying is to some extent a family enterprise. Some lobbyists are the children, spouses, or siblings of lawmakers. They can use the contacts that they have acquired because of family associations for private gain.

6 The 'revolving door' extends beyond corporate interests to think tanks, although few can pay the salaries offered by corporations. Thirty-six lobbyists employed by the Center for American Progress, which is tied to influential constituencies within the Democratic Party, have a background in government service (OpenSecrets.org, 2011c).

7 The AARP (the American Association of Retired Persons) was placed second.

8 An 'independent' political campaign is one that is not co-ordinated with a particular candidate for public office.

References and further reading

Adler, J. (2011), 'Policing Beltway lobbyists', *National Review Online*, 2 August, www.nationalreview.com/articles/273355/policing-beltway-lobbyists-jonathan-h-adler.

Browne, W. P. (1995), 'Organized interests, grassroots confidants, and Congress', in A. J. Cigler and B. A. Loomis (eds), *Interest Group Politics*, Washington DC, Congressional Quarterly, pp. 281–297.

Bureau of Labor Statistics (2011), *Economic News Release – Union Membership (Annual)*, www.bls.gov/news.release/union2.t01.htm and http://www.bls.gov/news.release/union2.t05.htm.

Center for Public Integrity (2003), *Hired Guns*, 15 May, www.publicintegrity.org/dtaweb/index.asp?L1=20&L2=10&L3=23&L4=0&L5=0.

Cigler, A. J. and B. A. Loomis (1995), 'Contemporary interest group politics: more than "more of the same"', in A. J. Cigler and B. A. Loomis (eds), *Interest Group Politics*, Washington DC: Congressional Quarterly, pp. 393–406.

Ettlinger, M. and W. Straw (2009), *Recovery Plan Offers Needed Change*, Center for American Progress, 16 January, www.americancongressprogress.org/issues/2009/01/recovery-plan.html.

Fox News (2010), 'Supreme Court removes limits on corporate, labor donations to campaigns', *Fox News*, 21 January, www.foxnews.com/politics/2010/01/21/supreme-court-sides-hillary-movie-filmmakers-campaign-money-dispute#ixzz1RF9ejXEh.

Groseclose, T. (2001), *PAC Contributions: The Mistrust Is Misplaced*, Stanford Graduate School of Business, www.gsb.stanford.edu/research/reports/2001/groseclose.html.

Hightower, J. (2010), 'Hightower: Washington overrun by 11,000 corporate lobbyists and $500 million in Corrupting Donations', *AlterNet*, 29 April, www.alternet.org/story/146643/hightower:_washington_overrun_by_11,000_corporate_lobbyists_and_$500_million_in_corrupting_donations?page=entire.

Hobson, K. (2010), 'Supreme Court: Pharma companies can buy prescription data', *WSJ Blogs*, 23 June, http://blogs.wsj.com/health/2011/06/23/supreme-court-pharma-companies-can-buy-prescription-data/.

Maskell, J. (2010), *Post-Employment, 'Revolving Door' Laws for Federal Personnel*, Congressional Research Service, www.fas.org/sgp/crs/misc/97-875.pdf.

Montgomery, Lori (2008), 'Obama team assembling $850 billion stimulus', *Washington Post*, 19 December.

National Chamber Litigation Center (n.d.), *In the Supreme Court of the United States – Citizens United v. Federal Election Commission, Supplemental Brief of Amicus Curiae Chamber of Commerce of the United States in Support of Appellant*, www.campaignfreedom.org/docLib/20091007_USCoCsupplemental.pdf.

OpenSecrets (2011a), *Lobbying Database*, www.opensecrets.org/lobby/index.php.

OpenSecrets.org (2011b), *Revolving Door*, http://www.opensecrets.org/revolving/index.php.

OpenSecrets.org (2011c), *Revolving Door – Top Organizations*, http://www.opensecrets.org/revolving/top.php?display=D.

Pew Research Center for the People and the Press (2011), *Labor Unions Seen as Good for Workers, Not U.S. Competitiveness*, 17 February, http://people-press.org/2011/02/17/labor-unions-seen-as-good-for-workers-not-u-s-competitiveness/.

Putnam, R. D. (2000), *Bowling Alone: The Collapse and Revival of American Community*, New York: Simon and Schuster.

Rasmussen Reports (2011), *52% Have Favorable Opinion of AARP*, 5 July, www.rasmussenreports.com/index.php/public_content/business/general_business/july_2011/52_have_favorable_opinion_of_aarp.

Rauch, J. (1999), *Government's End: Why Washington Stopped Working*, New York: PublicAffairs.

Rehnquist, W. H. (1987), *The Supreme Court: How It Was, How It Is*, New York, William Monroe and Company.

Repetto, R. (2006), *Best Practice in Internal Oversight of Lobbying Practice*, Yale Center for Environmental Law and Policy, Working Paper No. 200601.

Roe, M. (2010), 'More corporate lobbying is bad business', *Financial Times*, 25 January, www.ft.com/intl/cms/s/0/bd03f92e-09aa-11df-b91f-00144feabdc0.html#axzz1R40hn8tn.

Tocqueville, A. de (1984), *Democracy in America*, New York, Mentor.

Vestal, C. (2011), 'For Oregon and Vermont, health-care waivers a big deal', *The Seattle Times*, 13 March, http://seattletimes.nwsource.com/html/nationworld/2014489486_healthwaivers14.html.

4

The US Constitution

Significant numbers of Americans do not have an accurate knowledge of the US Constitution and its provisions. A 2010 poll of New York voters suggested that only 16 per cent consider themselves to be 'very familiar' with the document. Only two-thirds of those asked knew that the president heads the executive branch, three-fifths were not aware that the legislative branch makes laws, and only 55 per cent understood that the US Supreme Court has the power of judicial review. Nonetheless, at the same time, 76 per cent of respondents believed in the 'central importance' of the US Constitution. Indeed, just 5 per cent disputed its significance (Lane and Barnette, 2011: 7–13). The centrality of the Constitution has political consequences. While the Constitution is often at the centre of political controversy, that debate is generally about the interpretation of the principles upon which it is structured rather than the fundamental value of those principles. Proposals for reform are more often than not put forward as a means by which the spirit of the Constitution can be more fully implemented.

This chapter outlines the principal features of the US Constitution, considers the institutions that were created on the basis of it, and surveys the character of debates about the relevance of the Constitution for contemporary US politics.

Origins of the US Constitution

By the eighteenth century, the original settlements that had been established on the eastern seaboard had evolved into thirteen colonies. As such, although some had begun as corporate or religious ventures, they were British possessions. Nonetheless, despite the appointment of governors by the London authorities, the colonists had a tradition of limited self-government through colonial assemblies. Although the right to participate in civic affairs was, as in Britain, dependent upon property ownership, such ownership was more broadly distributed than in Europe (at least among white men), thereby extending participation to relatively large numbers.

Against this background, and amidst growing talk of 'unalienable rights' and constraints upon the power of government, restrictions on the westward expansion of the colonies, the imposition of taxes, and other limits on trade by the British laid a basis for protests and eventual rebellion. The 1773 Tea Act, which sparked the protests that were dubbed the 'Boston Tea Party', and the 1774 Quebec Act (which extended its boundaries so as to threaten the western expansion of the American colonies) were particularly resented. American leaders responded by establishing the First and Second Continental Congresses, bringing together delegates from the different colonies. The British refused to compromise and demanded that the colonists recognise the authority of Parliament. The Patriots, as supporters of American interests came to be called, began to organise themselves. Attempts by British troops to disarm them and suppress their activities triggered war. In a celebrated speech to the Virginia legislature, which symbolised the shift from protest to rebellion, Patrick Henry said 'Give me liberty, or give me death.'

After eighteen months of fighting, on 4 July 1776, Congress issued the Declaration of Independence. Written principally by Thomas Jefferson, the Declaration on offered a justification for the revolutionary repudiation of British rule:

> We hold these truths to be self-evident, that all men are created equal, that they are endowed by their Creator with certain unalienable rights, that amongst these are life, liberty and the pursuit of happiness. That to secure these rights, governments are instituted amongst men, deriving their just powers from the consent of the governed. That whenever any form of government becomes destructive of these ends, it is the right of the people to alter or abolish it, and to institute a new government. (quoted in Foley, 1991: 31)

The arguments pursued in the Declaration drew upon the notions of liberty, rights, and limited government that defined classical liberalism and drew upon the claims made by figures such as the English philosopher John Locke (1632–1704):

- All people (and not only Americans) have natural rights, most notably 'life, liberty and the pursuit of happiness'. These rights were granted by God and could not be taken away. They were 'unalienable'. The claim that men were created 'equal' is not an egalitarian statement in the modern sense. Instead, it is a repudiation of the divine right of kings and (although Jefferson was himself a slaveholder) an affirmation that men are equally entitled to particular rights.
- The purpose of government and the reason why it is created is to protect these rights. There is a social contract between the people and government in which the people accept a duty to obey the government. In return, those in government have an obligation to protect the people's rights.

- The people have the right to withdraw that consent, and have the right of rebellion if the government fails in its obligation to protect their rights.
- King George III and the British Parliament had, through acts of oppression, broken their side of the social contract. The people had been denied their 'unalienable' rights. The American colonists could therefore justifiably break their side of the contract and deny British authority on American soil.

The Declaration also put forward a list of 27 specific grievances against the British Crown to demonstrate the ways in which the rights of the colonists were being denied. King George III was described in bitter terms: 'He has plundered our seas, ravaged our coasts, burned our towns, and destroyed the lives of our people . . . A prince, whose character is thus marked by every act which may define a tyrant, is unfit to be the ruler of a free people' (quoted in Henretta, Brownlee, Brody, and Ware, 1993: 168).

The Declaration has been portrayed in different ways. For some, it was an assertion of a distinct American nationhood and marked a rupture between America and Europe. Others suggest that the Declaration represented an attempt to reclaim the traditional rights and liberties of the 'freeborn Englishman'. Alongside these claims, there are also less idealistic depictions. The rebels, it is said, were seeking to pursue economic interests that had been placed in jeopardy by the British authorities. Furthermore, the Declaration of Independence spoke in the name of 'men'. Women, blacks, native Americans, and propertyless whites were largely excluded from the political process. The war of independence can justly be described as 'a conservative revolution'.

The British were finally defeated by the Americans, fighting in alliance with the French, in October 1781 at Yorktown in Virginia. The Treaty of Paris, signed in September 1783, recognised American independence.

Articles of Confederation

A year after the writing of the Declaration of Independence, the Second Continental Congress adopted the Articles of Confederation. These laid down a basis for governing the new nation but were not, however, ratified by all 13 of the former colonies, now states, until 1781.

The Articles rested upon a loose and decentralised system and a very weak national government. Each state maintained 'its sovereignty, freedom, and independence', but the Congress, in which each state had one vote, had only limited powers. Important decisions and changes to national law required the backing of nine of the 13 states. There was, furthermore, no separate executive branch. Given this, decision-making was inevitably a slow, cumbersome, and uncertain process.

The powers of the national government were limited for two reasons. First, there was a reaction against the strongly centralised character of British rule.

Second, many of the states jealously guarded their own prerogatives and were unwilling to cede even a limited degree of power. However, although the Articles were eventually ratified, the Confederation faced difficulties from the beginning. These stemmed from the limitations on the powers assigned to the Congress. Congress did not have the authority to raise tax revenue. Furthermore, the states, upon which Congress depended for funds, failed to pay the sums that were required. The state governments also had limited authority. During a period of economic depression, the state of Massachusetts imposed property tax increases so as to pay off debts incurred during the war. When the taxes were not paid, farms and homes were seized. In 1786, many farmers took part in Shays's rebellion as a protest. The rebellion later collapsed; but it appeared to portend growing social discontent. There were at the same time fears that the newly established nation might fragment. At the least, differences and tensions seemed to impede development. The states imposed tariffs and duties against each other so as to protect their own immediate commercial interests. There were incipient tensions between the northern and southern states. In 1783, there was serious discontent and talk of a military coup, the Newburgh conspiracy, within the army. There were, furthermore, fears that foreign powers would seek a foothold for themselves within the new Republic. Britain, France, and Spain all had possessions on the North American continent, and there were concerns that some of the states might be tempted into alliances with these powers that might break up the Confederation.

Philadelphia Convention (1787)

Because of these criticisms, a constitutional convention of delegates from the states was called in 1787 to amend the Articles. Although the delegates who met in Philadelphia were not directly elected by the people, and one state (Rhode Island) was not represented at all, a new constitution emerged from their deliberations. The opening words were imbued with the belief that although the states retained many of their powers and prerogatives, the American nation required a sense of common purpose that had been absent in the Articles:

> We the People of the United States, in Order to form a more perfect Union, establish Justice, insure domestic Tranquility, provide for the common defence, promote the general Welfare, and secure the Blessings of Liberty to ourselves and our Posterity, do ordain and establish this Constitution for the United States of America.

The debate at the convention continued throughout the summer of 1787. The 55 delegates, who became known as the 'Framers' or 'Founding Fathers', considered two alternative models of government.

- The larger states supported James Madison's Virginia Plan. It rested on the 'supremacy of national authority', so that the states would lose much of the autonomy that they had been afforded under the Confederation. The national government would draw its authority from the American people rather than the states. There would be a bicameral legislature that would, in part, be directly elected. The legislature would choose those who would head the executive branch.
- The New Jersey Plan was backed by the smaller states, who were fearful that they would lose their powers. Although it also envisaged a greater degree of political centralisation than under the Confederation, it respected the authority of the states by proposing a unicameral legislature based upon the states, which would be allocated equal representation regardless of size. The states would also be able to remove members of the executive branch.

The different factions at the convention agreed upon 'the Great Compromise'. The larger states favoured a system of government that assigned representation on the basis of population. Therefore, the numbers in the lower chamber, the House of Representatives, were to be based upon a state's population. However, to meet the fears of the smaller states, the Senate was to be based upon equal representation. Each state was to have two Senators, who until the early twentieth century were appointed by the state legislatures rather than elected, regardless of its size or population. The Philadelphia Convention also pursued other forms of political accommodation and reconciliation between competing interests.

First, there were differences at the convention between those who talked in terms of the 'people', although this often referred only to male property-holders, and those who were fearful of unrestrained democracy. It was agreed that some form of democracy was required to act as a check on the abuse of power by the executive, but there were claims that unchecked majority rule might trample on the rights of the individual citizen. In particular, the larger property-owners also feared that their interests might be in jeopardy if the 'mob' had excessive powers. The convention therefore sought to place constraints on the will of the majority. It agreed that only the House of Representatives would be directly elected by the people. The president was to be indirectly elected through an electoral college. Senators would be chosen by the state legislatures. The judiciary would be appointed.

Second, there were tensions between free states and the slave states. There were some anti-slavery sentiments in the northern states, but the five southern states would have refused to join the US if slavery had not been permitted. As a consequence, slavery was not addressed in the Constitution, although there was a provision that, for the purposes of representation, slaves would be counted as three-fifths of citizens. This was at the insistence of the free states, who wanted to limit the political influence of the slave states.

Third, there was also a debate between advocates and opponents of a strong, centralised executive branch of government. Some of the founders, most notably Alexander Hamilton, argued that there had to be 'energy in the executive' so as to unify the nation. They called for a single executive that would have far-reaching powers. Others feared, however, that the placing of so much power in the hands of a single figure would lead to tyranny. They therefore agreed upon a single executive – the president – but restricted the powers of the office. These were concentrated in foreign policymaking, where swift and decisive action might be required. In the domestic sphere, the powers of the executive branch were to be more limited.

Fourth, the Constitution also sought to establish a compromise between those who feared that the states would lose their independence and authority and 'nationalists' who believed that a stronger form of national government was required if the country was to survive. However, the character and extent of the 'states' rights' afforded by the US Constitution have been the subject of subsequent controversy at the time of the Civil War but also thereafter. Some, including President Ronald Reagan, have portrayed the US as a compact between the states. This implies that the states have far-reaching rights that cannot be abrogated. Others argue that the American people as a whole have *sovereignty*. From this perspective, the rights of the states are much more limited and the constraints placed upon the states in the Constitution are of particular importance.

Adopting the Constitution

The Constitution was eventually accepted – or *ratified* – by the states between 1787 and 1790. However, there was a fierce debate between supporters of the new Constitution, known as the Federalists, and opponents, the Anti-federalists.

The Federalists argued that the Constitution offered a basis for a system of government that had strength and cohesion but would not threaten the fundamental rights and liberties of either the states or the American people. They wrote a series of newspaper articles – *The Federalist* – in its defence. The principal authors were James Madison, Alexander Hamilton, and John Jay, who collectively wrote under the pseudonym of 'Publius'.

The Anti-federalists feared that the Constitution would lead to an over-centralisation of power in the hands of the federal government and that this would inevitably threaten the independence of the states and the rights of the citizen. Although the Anti-federalists lost the debate, the concerns that they expressed still resonate in American politics today. So as to secure majorities in some of the states, the Federalists promised to amend the Constitution so that the powers of the federal government would be contained and the rights of the states assured. As a consequence, ten amendments were added in 1791. These amendments, the Bill of Rights, placed constraints upon the powers of the national government. In later years, the US Supreme Court would progressively extend these limits so that the liberties extended to individuals in the Bill of Rights also had to be respected by the state governments as well as the national government.

Principles of the Constitution

The Constitution has five core principles.

First, it offered a form of government based, in part, upon the representation of the people. Indeed, the Constitution rests upon the belief that a government's right to rule – its *legitimacy* – depends upon the consent of the governed. The principle of consent marked out the US from the autocratic regimes that dominated Europe at the time when the US Constitution was written.

Second, nonetheless, the representation of the people takes a constrained form. The Constitution promised a 'republic' that would be responsive but also responsible. The Founders' search for a compromise between democratic participation and constraints that would prevent a majority infringing or denying the rights of individuals led them towards constitutional mechanisms that would allow government to act only when there was a widely shared consensus on a clearly and widely accepted public good. Although President Abraham Lincoln later spoke, in the 1863 Gettysburg Address of 'government of the people, by the people, for the people', the Constitution not only sought to prevent impulsive decision-making but was informed by a *counter-majoritarian* spirit.

Third, the Constitution was structured around a *separation of powers* or, in some accounts, *separated institutions sharing powers*. Political systems involve legislative, executive, and judicial responsibilities. These terms refer to the making, implementation, and interpretation of the law. The Constitution established that these three responsibilities would be exercised by three separate institutions: Congress, the presidency, and the federal courts. Yet although these are often described as the legislative, executive, and judicial branches of government, each of the three branches plays a part in the legislative, executive, and judicial processes. As Richard Neustadt, author of *Presidential Power and the Modern President*, notes, the president is, for example, involved in the making of law. The Constitution allows him to veto bills or to mould the character of legislation by threatening the imposition of a veto: 'The Constitutional Convention of 1787 is supposed to have created a government of "separated powers." It did nothing of the sort. Rather, it created a government of separated institutions sharing powers' (Neustadt, 1991: 29). In 1959, President Dwight Eisenhower reportedly insisted: 'I am part of the legislative process'. He probably had his veto power in mind. It allowed him and other presidents (who head the executive branch) to shape the legislative process. The three branches of government are assigned different powers, methods of election or appointment, and terms of office.

Fourth, the Constitution also rested on *checks and balances*. The Founding Fathers built a degree of conflict between the branches of government into the fabric of the constitution. They sought to ensure that no single branch could become over-powerful or oppressive. The Constitution therefore required that many decisions must have the backing of more than one branch. For example, presidential appointments for the most important positions in the executive branch and to the federal judiciary have to be made with 'the advice and consent' of the Senate.

The Constitution was based, fifthly, on federalism. The powers of government are divided between the national and the individual state governments. Although the character of the relationship is not defined with precision the Constitution emphasised the essential unity of the US in its relationships with other nations. Foreign policy powers were to be the sole prerogative of the federal government. According to Article I of the Constitution, states may not conclude treaties with other countries, impose taxes on imports and exports, or maintain their own troops in times of peace. These stipulations were intended to ensure that the US came together as a single diplomatic, economic, and military entity. Article I also specifies that the US Congress has the authority to pass laws for the 'general welfare of the United States'. It also, in what became known as the 'interstate commerce' clause, permitted Congress to regulate trade and business between the states. The wording of these phrases, and the *expansive* interpretation that the US Supreme Court subsequently put upon them, provided a basis for the growth of the federal government and its role in American society. At the same time, the Constitution offered certain specific assurances to the states. Article II assigned a formal role, through the Electoral College, to the states in the choosing of a president. In Article IV, the states are assured that they will be defended from invasion, that their boundaries will not be changed without their consent, and that they will be given equal representation in the US Senate. Article V specifies that the Constitution can be amended only with the assent of three-quarters of the states. Furthermore, the Tenth Amendment, which formed part of the Bill of Rights, and was added in 1791, was intended to ensure that these states' rights were not subsumed by the national authorities. It states that 'the powers not delegated to the United States by the Constitution, nor prohibited by it to the States, are reserved to the States respectively, or to the people'. In other words, those decision-making powers not specifically assigned to the federal government are the prerogative of the individual states.[1]

Structure and contents

The Constitution consists of one single document of only seven thousand words. It is divided up into sections or *Articles*. These mostly consider the powers, responsibilities, and characters of the three different branches of government.

Article I: Congress

Congress, the national legislature, was to be the principal source of law and policy. *The Federalist* stated that 'in republican government, the legislature necessarily predominates'. Congress is also assigned specific powers. It has the right to declare war and the 'power of the purse'; it decides upon the levying of taxes and the allocation of federal government spending. In a phrase that progressively acquired greater significance as the US became a modern industrial economy stretching from coast to coast, Congress has the power to regulate 'interstate commerce'.

Some observers suggest that the Framers thought in terms of Congressional hegemony. From this perspective, the role of the president was in large part to serve as a check should Congress exceed its bounds. Many of the early presidents (although Thomas Jefferson, Andrew Jackson, and Abraham Lincoln are important and noteworthy exceptions) appear to have seen their role in this way. It was not until the twentieth century that the president came to assume the prominence he has today (see Chapter 7).

Congress was given a *bicameral* structure. It was, in other words, divided into two chambers. The Senate and the House of Representatives were to be elected in different ways and with different but sometimes overlapping powers. The House of Representatives was to be the popular, directly elected chamber. The House's members were and are elected every two years (in single-member constituencies or *districts)* so as to ensure its responsiveness and answerability to the electorate. Every state was guaranteed at least one Representative or 'Congressman' but otherwise representation was based on the population of a particular state. To take account of population shifts, there was to be a process of *reapportionment* and, within each state, *redistricting* every ten years following the census.

The Senate is sometimes described as the upper chamber although they are constitutionally co-equal. It was intended to represent the individual states and have a more thoughtful and deliberative character. Through the six-year terms of office that each senator serves, the chamber would be, according to James Madison, the stable 'anchor' of Congress, thereby acting as a check on the more populist House and, at the same time, offering accumulated experience, or what the historian Garry Wills has termed an 'institutional memory' (Wills, 1999: 74). A rolling system of election was adopted, so that one-third of the Senate is subject to re-election every two years. This was established so as to ensure that the Senate would not surrender to the 'passions and panics of the moment' to which the House would be prone.

Every state, regardless of numerical size, is entitled to two senators, from large states such as California to the least populous states such as South Dakota and Wyoming. Senators were originally elected by the state legislatures but since 1913 have been directly elected by the voters of the state. If a senator resigns from office or dies, a special election is held although in some states, the state governor can select a nominee to serve on a short-term basis.

The governor will almost certainly pick an individual from his or her own party. This can, at times, have significant consequences for the overall balance between the parties in the Senate.

Article II: the president

The president is elected for a four-year term by an electoral college. The college was originally composed of elder statesmen chosen by the different state legislatures. It now plays a nominal role, in so far as all the 'Electors' almost always confirm the choice made by the voters in each state. However, the first-past-the-post electoral system on which the college rests can distort the popular vote and, in exceptional circumstances, can lead to the election of a president who has lost the popular vote. This happened in 2000 (see Chapter 2). From 1951 onwards, the president has been restricted to two elected terms of office.

The founders believed that the executive branch of government should be headed by a single person so as to ensure that the federal government had direction and foreign policy had the necessary degree of purpose and coherence. He has constitutional powers although they are relatively few in number. These included his position as commander-in-chief of the armed forces and his ability to negotiate treaties with other countries. His domestic powers were more limited still. He had a responsibility to ensure that the laws were carried out. He was also given the right to veto bills so as to provide a further check on the impulsive tendencies of the House of Representatives and the passage of populist legislation. A vice-president was also to be elected. He was to take the president's place in the event of death or incapacity but his powers were otherwise ill-defined and unspecified.

Article III: the Supreme Court

In contrast with the preceding Articles, Article III is relatively brief. It simply states that 'the judicial power of the United States shall be vested in one Supreme Court'. It also allowed Congress to establish 'inferior' courts.

At the same time, however, Article III assigned the federal courts a number of specific powers and responsibilities. Their jurisdiction included legal disputes between the national government and other institutions and the resolution of conflicts between state governments. It was only later, through a process of political and judicial evolution, that the Supreme Court established the power of *judicial review* and the power to declare a law or action undertaken by the federal or a state government unconstitutional.

Article IV: federalism

Although it also extended some assurances to them, the principal purpose of Article IV was to encourage closer co-operation between the individual states.

For example, it laid down in the 'full faith and credit clause' that each state should recognise 'the public Acts, Records, and judicial Proceedings of every other State'. The exact meaning of this has long been debated. Some states have, for example, refused to accept inter racial or, more recently, same-sex marriages undertaken in other states. Article IV also allowed for the admission of new states to the USA, and guaranteed that every state should have a republican (or representative) form of government.

Article V: amending the Constitution[2]

The process of changing, or amending, the Constitution was made intentionally difficult. It is dependent upon 'supermajorities'. An amendment must be proposed by either a two-thirds majority in both houses of Congress or by a special constitutional convention that would have to be convened by two-thirds of the state legislatures. Any amendment arising from Congress or the convention has then to be ratified by three-quarters of the states. Congress has generally imposed a seven-year deadline for this, although the period allowed for the ratification of the Equal Rights Amendment (ERA), which would, if it had been rectified, have entrenched legislation prohibiting discrimination on the basis of gender by government agencies, was extended for a further three years.

No constitutional convention has been held since the Framers met in 1787. Nonetheless, over ten thousand amendments to the Constitution have been proposed in Congress. However, of those, only 33 gained the required Congressional supermajority, and a mere 27 have been ratified by the states. The first ten of these, forming the Bill of Rights, were adopted just four years after the Constitution was written. Indeed, they are widely regarded as a part of the original constitution. Other, subsequent amendments extended the right to vote, added to civil rights, increased the power of the federal government, and made limited alterations to the institutions of government:

The amendments forming the Bill of Rights were intended to ensure that there were further restraints on the central government than those provided in the 1787 Constitution. Indeed, the provisions in the Bill of Rights were originally understood to apply to the central government alone. State governments were not bound by them. It was only during the latter half of the nineteenth century that the federal courts drew upon the Fourteenth Amendment and the concept of *substantive due process* so as to rule that the states also had to respect the liberties assured in the Bill of Rights and subsequent amendments. The amendments are based on a negative conception of rights in so far as they restrict government rather than require some form of action or provision from it. (Negative rights have a 'leave me alone' character.)

- The First Amendment is widely known. It protects freedom of speech and religion. The Second Amendment guarantees the right to 'bear arms' and is, to this day, the subject of intense controversy.

- A series of later amendments established that the right to vote could not be denied on grounds of race (Fifteenth), and granted the vote to women (Nineteenth), the citizens of Washington DC (Twenty-third), and those over eighteen (Twenty-sixth). The Twenty-fourth Amendment, which was adopted in 1964, prohibited laws that tied the right to vote in federal elections to the payment of poll taxes. Such taxes had been used in a number of southern states to deny the right to vote to African-Americans.
- Civil rights were extended in the aftermath of the Civil War (1861–65) with the abolition of slavery (Thirteenth), and the assertion that all citizens were entitled to 'the equal protection of the laws' (Fourteenth). However, the protections offered by the 'equal protection' clause were in practice institutionally denied to African-Americans for a century after its passage. The Sixteenth Amendment, adopted in 1913, allowed the federal government to raise an income tax. This added to the powers of the federal government.
- In contrast to other amendments, many of which added to rights, the Eighteenth Amendment was restrictive. It prohibited the manufacture and sale of alcohol across the US, but, after 13 years of Prohibition, it was repealed by the Twenty-first Amendment.
- Other amendments have reformed the institutions of government. The most significant of these, the Seventeenth Amendment, established that all US senators should be directly elected by the people, thereby extending popular participation in the legislative process. The Twenty-second Amendment, which was introduced in the wake of Franklin Roosevelt's years in the White House, restricted the president to two terms of office.

During the 1990s and in the early years of the new century, conservatives put forward and campaigned for a series of proposed constitutional amendments. These included the Flag Desecration Amendment (which sought to protect the US flag from being burnt or otherwise damaged in political protests), the Balanced Budget Amendment, the Human Life Amendment (outlawing abortion), a Term Limits Amendment (which would have restricted the terms of office served by members of Congress), the Federal Marriage Amendment (forbidding same-sex unions), and a School Prayer Amendment. None, however, was successful.

The most recent amendment to be incorporated into the Constitution was ratified in 1992, more than two hundred years after it was originally proposed. The Twenty-seventh Amendment states that Congressional pay increases cannot take effect immediately; instead members of Congress must wait until after the next election so that voters have the opportunity to pass judgement.

Assessing the Constitution

The goal of the founders was to create a system of government that would be effective but limited. It would be efficient in undertaking its responsibilities, but would at the same time respect and protect the rights of both the citizen and the states. Subsequent debates around the Constitution have sought to assess the extent to which these goals have been achieved. Whereas some assert that the federal government has only limited capacity, others claim that it has excessive powers.

Liberals and radicals argue the case for more activist forms of government, although, despite some calls to extend statehood to Washington DC and, in the wake of the 2000 presidential election, for the abolition of the Electoral College, relatively few have put forward Constitutional amendments.

Many on the left assert that the system of government established by the Constitution prevents the successful resolution of the many pressing economic and social problems facing the nation. These include the needs to close the gap between rich and poor, to constrain the activities of the large corporations, and to address climate change. However, it is said, the system of government has developed in such a way that the 'energy in the executive' required by Alexander Hamilton has been lost. Commentators make two principal claims.

First, in practice, checks and balances have created *gridlock*. More often than not, legislation cannot be passed because there is insufficient agreement between the different branches of government. The difficulties that arise from the Constitution itself have been compounded by later developments most notably the adoption of a Senate rule effectively requiring a supermajority for the passage of legislation. In contrast with the countries of western Europe, the US has, many liberals argue, been unable to establish a welfare state because the decision-making process allows some interests, particularly those that are well-financed, to block reforms even if they have majority backing. The governmental system is structured around mechanisms that prevent reform and, although Congress considers a wealth of legislative proposals, they are rarely enacted.

Second, it can also be argued that, through the separation of powers and federalism, the Constitution established a particularly open, or *porous*, political system. There are countless access points (see Chapter 3). Lobbying, particularly by wealthier and more powerful interests, is institutionalised. The assurances in the Bill of Rights have been used to obstruct many of the reforms that might limit the power of money in politics. At the same time, modernisation processes have been hindered. The government apparatus continues to rest upon byzantine structures and still depends upon very large numbers of political appointees who have little specialist knowledge and few professional skills. As a consequence, despite its size, the federal state has only limited capacity and constrained resources. Its inability to address domestic crises was brutally highlighted by the inadequacy of its response to Hurricane Katrina and the flooding in New Orleans in 2005. It simply could not cope. In a celebrated phrase, Stephen Skowronek has described the American state as a 'hapless giant' (Skowronek, 1982: 290). It is, he argues, 'a hapless confusion of institutional purposes, authoritative controls, and governmental boundaries' (Skowronek, 1982: 287). For their part, Desmond King and Lawrence Jacobs refer to: 'the administrative state's generally porous, easily penetrated boundaries; its consistent (though not uniform) lack of independent expertise to independently assess and respond to the behavior of markets and individuals; and multiple and competing lines of authority that stymie even necessary intervention' (King and Jacobs, 2010: 798). In 1987, when the US political parties still appeared weak in contrast with those in Europe, the Committee on the Constitutional System, which sought comprehensive constitutional reform, claimed that:

> The separation of powers, as a principle of constitutional structure, has served us well in preventing tyranny and the abuse of high office, but it has done so by encouraging confrontation, indecision and deadlock, and by diffusing account-ability for the results. Because the separation of powers encourages conflict between the branches and because the parties are weak, the capacity of the federal government to fashion, enact and administer coherent public policy has diminished and the ability of elected officials to avoid accountability for govern-mental failures has grown. (Committee on the Constitutional System, 1987: 3)

Critiques such as this have led to calls for the adoption of the parliamentary model of government. In a parliamentary or prime ministerial system, such as that in the UK, the government is formed by a party leader who can command majority support in the legislature. Unless there is a 'hung Parliament', in which no single party has an overall majority in the legislature (as happened following the 2010 general election), or serious unrest within the governing party, the leader, who becomes prime minister, will have few difficulties when his or her legislative proposals are considered. Indeed, although there will be some amendments, they are more or less certain to become law. In con-trast, the US president faces a separately elected legislature and, even when his own party has a majority, his legislation may be lost or amended beyond recognition.

In contrast, many on the right assert that government, particularly the federal government, has become excessively powerful and intrusive. It is now, they say, much more interventionist than the founders intended. They point to high levels of taxation, the federal government's role in regulating business, and its progressive involvement in state prerogatives such as education and social policy. In simple terms and in contrast to liberals, conservatives assert that the federal government does far too much rather than too little.

Nearly all those on the right not only accept but revere the Constitution. Why, however, has it failed to check the growth of federal government? From a conservative perspective, there are three principal reasons.

First, the US Supreme Court and the lower federal courts have abused their power of judicial review by engaging in judicial activism. They have repeatedly sought to establish further national 'rights' (such as the 'right' to an abortion), facilitated governmental interventionism, and curtailed individual freedom of action. They have colluded in destroying the powers and prerogatives of the states.

Second, the federal government has, through financial incentives and legislation that led to an expansion of its role, gained control and influence over many responsibilities that were the traditional prerogatives of the states. In the 1930s, the New Deal established the executive branch as 'manager of the economy'. The economic prosperity of the states came to depend upon judgements made in the nation's capital. Measures such as the 1935 National Labor Relations Act laid down national standards for both capital and labour. Employment projects, most notably the Tennessee Valley Authority, which brought hydroelectricity to the rural south, cut across state lines. At the same time, the states became increasingly financially dependent upon the federal government. Washington DC had begun giving *grants-in-aid* (or financial transfers) in 1887 so as to assist the states in the development of agricultural research, education, and highway programmes. The number and size of these transfers increased dramatically during the 1930s. In 1925, grants-in-aid amounted to $114 million. By 1937, this had risen to nearly $300 million. Under the 1935 Social Security Act, Washington DC used grants-in-aid to provide the beginnings of a rudimentary welfare state. There was material assistance for some dependent children, the elderly, and the unemployed. V. O. Key has recorded the consequences of these measures: 'The federal government . . . had been a remote authority with a limited range of activity . . . Within a brief time, it became an institution that affected intimately the lives and fortunes of most, if not all, citizens' (quoted in Conlan, 1988: 5). The process of centralisation went further during the Great Society years of the 1960s. President Lyndon Johnson committed the federal government to ending poverty in both the inner-city neighbourhoods and the rural areas. Despite his 1968 election pledges, the growth of 'big government' continued during President Nixon's period of office. In 1970 alone, grants-in-aid to the states rose by 19.3 per cent on the previous year. Some commentators rushed to offer a rationale for the centralising trend. As James Sundquist argued, effective governance required 'close federal supervision and control to assure that national purposes are served' (quoted in Dye 1990: 8). From this perspective, the Tenth Amendment, which circumscribed the powers of the national government and offer assurances to the states, had seemingly been forgotten.

Third, 'special interests' have come to dominate the decision-making process. This has led to dramatic increases in federal government expenditure. Furthermore, some of these interests have been able to secure legislation, such as the minimum wage or other barriers to entry in a particular sector, that excludes newcomers and confers monopoly privileges.

From this perspective, actions, measures, and reforms are required that would place further checks upon the scope and prerogatives of government.

In particular, conservatives would assert that the only appointees who should be placed on the federal court bench should be those who would respect the original intentions of those who wrote it.

Furthermore, and most importantly of all, constitutional amendments are required so as to rein in the excesses of the federal judiciary and circumscribe the powers of government. Many have been proposed in recent years. Liberal activists, who are increasingly the federal courts' most committed backers, suggest that the many efforts to amend the Constitution are undermining the Court's authority and legitimacy. As Kathleen M. Sullivan argued in *The American Prospect*:

> Increasing the frequency of constitutional amendment would undermine the respect and legitimacy the Court now enjoys in this interpretive role. This danger is especially acute in the case of proposed constitutional amendments that would literally overturn Supreme Court decisions, such as amendments that would declare a fetus a person with a right to life, permit punishment of flag burning, or authorize school prayer. Such amendments suggest that if you don't like a Court decision, you mobilize to overturn it. (Sullivan, 1995)

Conclusion

Although the US Constitution is sometimes hailed as a model, there has always been some caution on the part of other countries about a number of its provisions. Indeed, as Robert Dahl has noted, 'among the countries most comparable to the United States . . . and where democratic institutions have long existed without breakdown, not one has adopted our American constitutional system' (quoted in Scialabba, 2002). Few nations, in particular, have adopted constitutions that detach the executive branch from the legislature to such an extent, a 'first-past-the-post' electoral system that almost invariably discriminates against minor parties, and an upper chamber based upon a highly unequal form of representation.

Nonetheless, the US Constitution has survived over two hundred years without being fundamentally altered. It has adjusted to the diversity and complexity of contemporary American society. It is striking that few political actors or commentators believe that the Constitution requires radical change, and even those most critical of the current political system still claim that the essential principles it embodies remain valid. The survival of the Constitution can be attributed to the amendments that have been adopted. The most important of these modernised those sections of the Constitution that were most deeply rooted in late eighteenth-century thought.[3] The Constitution's resilience can also, in part, be tied to the process of judicial review (see Chapter 7). Many of the Constitution's provisions have an 'elastic' character that the US Supreme Court has 'stretched' (or at times 'released') in the light of changing social and economic circumstances. Most importantly of all, the US has since its founding seen off the threats posed by radical disorder, secession, and foreign powers. In most countries (France is a striking example), far-reaching constitutional change and the founding of a new republic have been tied to invasion, occupation, or internal collapse. The US, through its rise as a world *hegemon*, has been spared such a fate.

Notes

1 Because the US has a federal system of government there are significant public policy differences between the states. Levels of healthcare vary considerably. Regulations regarding marriage and divorce differ. The sales tax that is paid on retail goods and services varies between the states. States also have their own income taxes. Driving is subject to a range of laws and regulations. Legal punishments also differ. The majority of states, for example, have the death penalty on their statute books. Twelve, including, for example, Vermont, do not. Some, most notably Texas, carry out executions on a regular basis. In most other states, they are a very rare occurrence. Euthanasia is also a matter for state policymakers. Following a referendum in 1994, Oregon passed the 1997 Death with Dignity Act, allowing doctors to prescribe drugs so that the terminally ill can end their own lives.
2 Article VI considered government debt and established that the Constitution represented 'the supreme law of the land'. Article VII addressed the process by which the Constitution should be ratified.
3 The defeat of the South in the Civil War (1861–65) was followed by the passage of amendments to the Constitution that sought to give a measure of protection to the former slave population. Under the Fourteenth Amendment, every state had to ensure that all those living within its jurisdiction were accorded 'the equal protection of the laws' and that no person could be deprived of 'life, liberty, or property, without due process of law'. The Fifteenth Amendment required that the right of US citizens to vote could not be denied 'on account of race, color, or previous condition of servitude'. However, some qualification is required. Despite these amendments, white rule was re-established in the southern states by the 1880s, and the black population progressively lost the limited rights that it had won in the aftermath of the Civil War. A system of racial segregation, a form of institutionalised racism under which blacks were consigned to separate and inferior public facilities, and the voting 'tests' that kept the right to vote in white hands made a mockery of the Fourteenth and Fifteenth Amendments until the 1960s.

References and further reading

Committee on the Constitutional System (1987), *A Bicentennial Analysis of the American Political Structure*, Washington DC, Committee on the Constitutional System.
Conlan, T. (1988), *New Federalism: Intergovernmental Reform from Nixon to Reagan*, Washington DC, The Brookings Institution.

Dye, T. R. (1990), *American Federalism: Competition Among Governments*, Lexington, MA, Lexington Books.

Foley, M. (1991), *American Political Ideas*, Manchester, Manchester University Press.

Henretta, J. A., W. E. Brownlee, D. Brody, and S. Ware (1993), *America's History*, New York, Worth Publishers.

King, D. S. and L. R. Jacobs (2010), 'Varieties of Obamaism: structure, agency, and the Obama presidency', *Perspectives on Politics*, 8, September, 793–802.

Lane, E. and M. Barnette (2011), *A Report Card on New York's Civic Literacy*, Brennan Center for Justice, http://brennan.3cdn.net/e9502c45a124420af3_r1m6beqp3.pdf.

Neustadt, R. E. (1991), *Presidential Power and the Modern Presidents: The Politics of Leadership from Roosevelt to Reagan*, New York, The Free Press.

Scialabba, G. (2002), 'Democracy-proof', *The American Prospect*, 1 July, www.prospect.org/print/V13/12/scialabba-g.html.

Skowronek, S. (1982), *Building a New American State: The Expansion of National Administrative Capacities, 1877–1920*, Cambridge: Cambridge University Press.

Sullivan, K. M. (1995), 'Constitutional amendmentitis', *The American Prospect*, 6:23, 21 September, www.prospect.org/print/V6/23/sullivan-k.html.

Wills, G. (1999), *A Necessary Evil: A History of American Distrust of Government*, New York, Simon and Schuster.

5

Congress and the passage of legislation

The US Congress is, according to the Constitution, the first branch of government. It has a *bicameral* structure and its powers include the passage of legislation, declarations of war, the ratification of treaties, the formulation of the annual budget, consent to major political appointments, and the oversight of executive departments and agencies. Members must, at the same time, respond to the concerns of countless individuals and organisations. Although the president can, at times, play a pivotal role in shaping Congressional decisions, it is always far from certain that his preferences will prevail.

This chapter will consider a number of questions. What are the powers of Congress? How effective is the oversight process? What are the differences between the House of Representatives and the Senate? How are laws made? What determines congressional voting behaviour? How important is party leadership? Should we think, as some argue, in terms of 'two Congresses' that play contrasting political roles and can be judged in different ways? Does Congress require reform?

Congress and the Constitution

The character of Congress, and its powers, were established and shaped by Article I of the Constitution, subsequent Supreme Court rulings, periods of crisis, the changing character of the economy and society, and the tensions between the different branches of government.

First, Congress is the national legislature and, as such, it is responsible for the making of federal law. The legislative role of Congress stems from the powers assigned to it by the Constitution. There are *enumerated* powers, such as the control of trade 'among the several States' (this has been understood as the power to regulate trade and business that crosses state lines and is known as 'the interstate commerce clause'), the regulation of foreign trade, and the raising of an army. However, as Chapter 4 established, the elastic character of some clauses in the Constitution, such as the 'necessary and proper' clause in Article I, Section 8, allowed the Supreme Court to establish that Congress also had *implied* powers (see p. 161). Furthermore, the scope of certain powers specified in the Constitution, such as those granted in the interstate commerce clause, has been extended. This has been partly because the economy has changed in character. During the late eighteenth century, most forms of trade and commerce were relatively small-scale in character. They served a local market. A modern economy rests instead upon national and global markets. Many contemporary firms, beyond small businesses, produce, distribute and sell their products across the nation or internationally. At the same time, another development 'stretched' the interstate commerce clause. For about sixty years, between the 1930s and the 1990s, the Supreme Court understood the clause in loose and expansive terms, enabling Congress to regulate almost every aspect of economic and social life.

Second, Congress not only makes law but also has the ability to pass resolutions. Concurrent resolutions are used to make or amend rules or express Congressional sentiments. A joint resolution, passed by both houses, and signed by the president, such as the 1964 Gulf of Tonkin resolution that provided the pretext for large-scale US intervention in Vietnam, has the force of law. Whereas the president has no formal role in the process, Congress can propose constitutional amendments, although, to be adopted, they require a two-thirds majority in both chambers and the assent of at least three-quarters of the states.

Third, Congress has the *power of the purse*. Article I, Section 8 of the Constitution specifically empowered Congress to raise taxes and impose duties. The Constitution specifies that bills 'for raising revenue' should originate in the House of Representatives, although they must, like all other legislation, also be passed in an identical form by the Senate. The annual budget is now, as Robert Singh has noted, of pivotal political and economic importance: 'The budget is the supreme political document, determining national priorities, shaping congressional and election debates, and allocating benefits to national, state, and local interests' (Singh, 2003: 249). The president submits a proposed budget to Congress at the beginning of each year. It covers the coming Fiscal Year that begins on 1 October. His proposals are drawn up by the Office of Management and Budget (OMB) within the White House on the basis of expenditure plans and projections submitted during the preceding year by the departments, agencies, and bureaux within the executive branch. Once under consideration within Congress, the budget is shaped by competing pressures and interests.[1] The Senate and House Appropriations Committees and their associated subcommittees play a particularly significant role. The budget is broken down into thirteen spending, or *appropriations*, bills. Each of these bills corresponds to one subcommittee's on the Appropriations Committees. Such is the power of these subcommittees, in so far as they decide how much government funding is allocated to, for example, defence, agriculture, or urban development, that the men and women chairing the House subcommittees have been dubbed the 'Cardinals'. As Paul Hilliar records: 'Mostly unknown outside of Washington Beltway, these "Cardinals" control the flow of hundreds of billions of dollars, which makes them some of the most powerful men in America' (Hilliar, 2002).

Fourth, as the 1946 Legislative Reorganization Act confirmed, Congress has *oversight* or scrutiny powers. It reviews and monitors the executive branch. This includes the White House as well as the myriad of departments, agencies, and bureaux that constitute the federal bureaucracy. Oversight or 'watchdog' work is undertaken through Congress's committee structure. Many of the standing committees that have legislative responsibilities also 'shadow' a particular executive department. Others oversee a less defined area of policy. The Senate, for example, has an armed services committee, a foreign relations committee, and an agriculture committee. The House too has an agriculture committee, but also a small business and science committee. While the standing committees exist on a permanent basis, select committees may also be created by either chamber or jointly on an *ad hoc* basis, so as to look at matters that fall outside the jurisdiction of the standing committees or in order to conduct a specific investigation. Oversight takes a number of forms. It includes formal and informal communication with administrators, committee hearings, the evaluation of a particular programme by congressional support agencies such as the Government Accountability Office (GAO) or the *Congressional Research Service*, or a requirement that an agency issue a report outlining and explaining aspects of its work.

Fifth, Congress has the constitutional power to remove 'the President, Vice President, and all civil officers of the United States' from office in cases of 'treason, bribery, or other high crimes and misdemeanors'. However, *impeachment* proceedings that may, if there is a conviction, lead to the official's removal from office have only ever become a consideration in the most exceptional circumstances. The process begins with a vote of the House to conduct an inquiry. The results of the inquiry, undertaken by the House Judiciary Committee, are presented to the full House. If the official is *impeached* by the House (and this requires only a majority vote), a trial is then conducted before the Senate. The Senators constitute a jury. A two-thirds majority (67 votes) is required if a public official is to be removed from office. The House of Representatives has since the founding of the US impeached only 19 officials (most of whom have been federal judges), and just eight of these were convicted and therefore removed from office.[2]

Two presidents have been impeached. The first was Andrew Johnson in 1868. In the aftermath of the Civil War, radical Republicans felt that he was over-sympathetic to the South, although Johnson's dismissal of his Secretary of War, in contravention of the Tenure of Office Act, offered the pretext. However, Johnson was acquitted. His accusers failed by a single vote to gain the required two-thirds majority in the Senate. In December 1998, the House voted to impeach President Bill Clinton following claims that the President had, through his alleged sexual misconduct and later actions, committed acts of perjury and obstructed justice. The Senate eventually acquitted Clinton by 55 to 45 and 50 to 50 on the two charges. In 1974, impeachment proceedings were initiated against President Richard Nixon, although he resigned before the matter was considered on the floor of the House. Nixon had been accused of obstructing justice by hiding White House involvement in an illegal break-in at Democratic Party offices.

Sixth, the Senate has 'advice and consent' powers. It can confirm or reject the appointment of senior federal officers such as cabinet secretaries, federal judges, and ambassadors. The Senate's 'advice and consent' powers also extend to the ratification of treaties signed by the president with foreign powers. Under the Constitution, these require a two-thirds majority. Although the president generally gains the assent of the Senate to his appointments and proposed treaties, there have been important exceptions. These are recorded in Chapter 6.

Seventh, the Constitution endows Congress with the power to declare war (Article I, Section 8). However, while US forces have been sent into action much more often, Congress has declared war only eleven times. As a *Congressional Quarterly* study records: 'Presidents have ordered the armed forces to protect settlers from Indians, repel bands of foreign outlaws, punish nations and groups for belligerent or criminal behavior, rescue US citizens abroad, support friendly governments and train their armies, fight pirates and terrorists, warn potential enemies against taking aggressive action, deliver humanitarian aid, and secure disputed lands' (*Congressional Quarterly*, 1997: 204). Congress sought to constrain the president with the War Powers Resolution of 1973. Amongst its provisions, this stipulated that Congressional assent must be given for medium- and long-term military actions overseas.

Comparing chambers

The US legislature is *bicameral*. In other words, it has two chambers. There are a number of similarities between them. Both chambers have oversight responsibilities. Both senators and members of the House devote extensive resources to addressing the problems and concerns of constituents. Although bills are considered separately and often at different times in the House and Senate, both chambers must agree upon identical forms of working if they are to become law. Furthermore, the working life of both chambers is organised around a committee structure. Standing committees exist on a permanent basis, and consider both legislation and the actions of the executive branch. Some Senate committees also hold hearings and make recommendations when the president puts forward nominees for either the administration or the federal courts.

Both chambers of Congress can draw upon the support of an extensive number of staff. Members of the House are given an annual allowance (the members' representational allowance) so as to pay 'staffers', maintain offices in both Congress itself and across their district, and pay for franked mailings to constituents. In the 2010 Fiscal Year, the totals averaged $1,522,114.10 for each member of the House (Brudnick, 2011: 3). They may employ up to 18 members of staff. The allowances for senators include a weighting for a state's population and funding for legislative assistance (each senator is given funding for three legislative assistants). The average allocation in the 2010 Fiscal Year was $3,343,867 (Brudnick, 2011: 7).

Nonetheless, although there are similarities, there are also important differences between the chambers. The House of Representatives and the Senate have their own distinct identities. They differ in their terms of office, constituencies, size, minimal qualifications, rules, partisanship, and collective identity. There are often differences of opinion, and there can be competition for power, between them.

The House of Representatives

The House is directly elected by the people in single-member constituencies drawn up on the basis of population. Those who serve have to be 25 years old or more, and have been a US citizen for at least seven years. Although the number is not specified in the Constitution, and is determined instead by law, the House has, since 1911, had 435 members. Each represents, following the 2010 Census, an average population of 709,760 (National Conference of State Legislatures, 2011).

The House is a large and heterogeneous chamber. Its members face re-election every two years, and they therefore have to be both district-oriented and campaign-oriented. Although members break ranks with their party on particular issues to a greater extent than in, for example, the British House of Commons, the House has traditionally been seen as the more partisan of the two chambers. Furthermore, it has become even more partisan in recent years (see p. 65).

House rules are detailed, formal, and comprehensive. Members tend to specialise in a limited number of policy areas and serve on only one or two standing committees. There will almost always be an association between a member's area of specialisation and the district that she or he represents. A congress member from a rural district would, for example, seek a place on the agriculture committee. The size of the institution has tended to give more power to party leaders and it is thus more centralised than the Senate. It is a *majoritarian* institution in so far as decision-making is based upon decision-making by a simple majority rather than through efforts to establish a consensus or secure a 'supermajority'. Furthermore, the rules of debate in the

House have a fairly restrictive character. Amendments to bills, for example, can be ruled out of order if not relevant, or germane, to the bill. Rulings on an amendment's 'germaneness' are guided by precedent.

The leader of the majority party in the House takes the post of speaker. Although the speaker will often preside, particularly on important occasions, the speakership is not, in contrast with its British counterpart, a ceremonial role. Instead, Speakers of the House, such as Nancy Pelosi and John Boehner, are active and influential partisans.

The Senate

The Senate has been, since 1913, directly elected by the people of the different states. Each state elects two Senators, regardless of its size. California has two senators, representing an estimated population of 37,253,956 in 2010. Wyoming's two senators speak for only 563,626 people (National Conference of State Legislatures, 2011). Therefore, there are, in total, 100 senators. The senator elected first in a particular state is referred to as the 'senior' senator whilst the other is described 'junior' senator. If a senator dies or resigns during his or her term of office, the governor of the state may, in most states, appoint a successor until a special election is held.

The Constitution stipulates that senators must be 30 years old or more, and have been citizens for nine years or more. One-third is elected every two years for terms of six years. Because elections are staggered in this way, partisan shifts may take a more gradual and less abrupt form than in the House.

Although the vice-president is, according to Article I of the Constitution, 'president' of the Senate, he takes the chair only if a tied vote seems likely. In these circumstances, the vice-president holds a casting vote. In March 2008, the Senate Historical Office calculated that 244 such votes had been cast since the founding of the US (Senate Historical Office, 2008).

The Constitution also allows the appointment of a president *pro tempore*, customarily the majority-party senator with the longest continuous service. In June 2010, the position was taken by the Hawaii senator Daniel Inouye. Although the post is regarded as an important honour, and the president *pro tempore* is third in the line of succession to the presidency (after the vice-president and the speaker of the House), he presides in the Senate only on an occasional basis. In practice, the president *pro tempore* appoints junior first-term senators to preside on a rotating basis throughout the day.

The comparatively small size of the Senate allows for a relatively intimate atmosphere in which, traditionally at least, connections and associations develop between members, many of which stretch across party lines. The Senate has customarily portrayed itself as more deliberative than the House. Senators tend to be more concerned with national and international interests and affairs than Congressmen. Their numbers do not allow for specialisation, and Senate members tend to have a more *generalist* approach. They serve on two or three standing committees. The Senate also has fewer formal rules. Senators are, for example, allowed more latitude than members of the House when bills are being considered on the floor of the chamber, and non-germane amendments can be permitted.

The customs of the chamber as well as its relative size ensure that each senator has much more influence than an individual House member. Party leaders have less leverage. In place of the House's majoritarianism, there was for a long period a tradition of consent, co-operation, and *individualism*. More is discussed on the Senate floor, and the chamber is less committee-based than the House. In the absence of unanimous consent agreements (see below), its deliberations are often slower and much less certain in character. A determined senator can attempt to block legislation by threatening to speak until a bill is dropped in a process known as a *filibuster*. In 1957 Senator Strom Thurmond, then a committed segregationist, spoke for 24 hours and 18 minutes so as to block a civil rights bill. Under Senate rules, debate can only be curtailed, and a threatened filibuster averted, if there is a three-fifths majority of the full Senate. The *cloture* procedure (enabling debate to be brought to an end and a vote taken) was introduced in 1917 for legislation and in 1949 for nominations (*New York Times*, 5 June 2003). In recent years the threat of a filibuster has become institutionalised, and all significant legislation now requires the backing of sixty senators.[3]

The Senate filibuster has at times been the subject of sustained controversy. It enables a minority of senators, perhaps representing the least populous states, to block the passage of legislation that may have the support of a popular majority. For this reason, some on the left regard the filibuster and the Senate itself as relics of an earlier anti-democratic era. They point out that, although the Democrats had a majority in the Senate in 2010, the passage of healthcare reform legislation was decided by a knife-edge vote and major concessions had to be made so as to secure the requisite 60 votes. There was talk of using *reconciliation*. This is the Senate procedure that is customarily reserved for budget matters for which a simple majority will suffice. Its usage is limited and governed by the 'Byrd rule'.[4]

Frustration with Senate procedure is not, however, restricted to the left. The Democrats' earlier use of the cloture rule to block President George W. Bush's judicial nominations provoked ire amongst Republicans. In retaliation, they made threats in 2005 to invoke the 'nuclear option' whereby a simple majority (which the Republicans then had in the Senate) would vote to suspend the requirement for a three-fifths vote for the president's nominations (see p. 155). Eric Schickler has captured the cumulative effect of Senate rules and traditions:

> Regardless of party, individual senators continue to insist on asserting their prerogatives under the Senate's rules and procedures. In addition to the right of unlimited debate, numerous senators use 'holds' (threats of a filibuster) to

delay – sometimes indefinitely – legislation and nominations they oppose. When legislation does reach the floor, individual senators typically resist limitation on amendments. (Schickler, 2002: 104)

Although the House and the Senate have been described as co-equal institutions, and the Constitution shares out responsibilities by assigning the House primacy in considering government finances and the Senate the principal responsibility for foreign affairs, the Senate has greater status. This stems, in part, from the smaller size of the Senate. A senator generally represents a larger number of people. She or he serves longer terms of office, faces fewer re-election contests, and has much more of a national profile. Although not historically an assurance of success, the Senate can thereby offer a more credible starting-point for those considering a presidential bid. It is significant that a member of the House will give up his or her seat so as to capture a Senate seat. A Senator would not, however, abandon his or her seat in pursuit of a place in the House.

How laws are made

The legislative process is long, complex, and difficult. The overwhelming majority of bills never have any prospect of becoming law but are put forward simply as a statement of belief or as a form of issue-promotion. The number of bills grew markedly from the mid-1990s onwards, and 10,537 bills were introduced in the 109th Congress (2005–6) (Harper, 2008). In the House, a member simply has to place the bill that she or he wishes to put forward in 'the hopper', a wooden box in the Chamber. Nearly all are, however, killed off in committee and are never considered by the chamber as a whole. The bills that survive emerge only in a heavily amended form. A bill has to pass through what many regard as an obstacle course to become law.

First, all bills are initiated or sponsored by members of Congress, who are described as the 'sponsors' of the measure. However, in the modern era defined by a more pro-active presidency, the 'executive communication' provides a basis for the legislative proposals that have a prospect of securing passage. This term 'executive communication' refers to a message or letter from a cabinet secretary, the head of an agency, or the president himself. Many of these follow on from the President's State of the Union address, the annual speech delivered to Congress which outlines the administration's goals and priorities. The chair or the ranking minority member of the appropriate committee, the most senior member of the minority party on that committee, customarily introduces the bill.

Second, bills may begin in either the House of Representatives or the Senate unless they are intended to raise revenue. (The Constitution specifies that revenue bills must originate in the House.) Bills are popularly known by the names of their principal sponsors. Indeed, the bill imposing more rigorous regulation of financial institutions which was passed in 2010 in the wake of the banking crisis was called the Dodd–Frank Wall Street Reform and Consumer Protection Act (Senator Chris Dodd and Congressman Barney Frank had originally proposed the measure).

Third, a bill will then be allocated, or *referred*, to a *standing committee* or committees for consideration. In the House, the Speaker decides which committee is appropriate.[5] In the Senate, the majority party leader has the power of referral. Both are however constrained by rules and earlier decisions establishing spheres of jurisdiction:

> Each committee's jurisdiction is defined by certain subject matter under the rules of each House and all measures are referred accordingly. For example, the Committee on the Judiciary in the House has jurisdiction over measures relating to judicial proceedings and 18 other categories, including constitutional amendments, immigration policy, bankruptcy, patents, copyrights, and trademarks. (The Library of Congress – THOMAS, 2007)

There are three stages to committee deliberations.

First, the committee chair decides whether the bill is to be referred to a subcommittee or *pigeonholed*. If it is pigeonholed by the chair, it cannot progress further. Nearly all bills die at this stage. For this reason, the committees are sometimes categorised by political commentators as 'gatekeepers'.

Second, the subcommittee will hold hearings to consider the bill with witnesses and presentations from relevant government departments, experts, and interest groups. These allow participation in the legislative process and, as Ross English notes: 'The primary function of hearings is to allow the committee members to gain enough knowledge to determine whether a change in the law is necessary, and if it is, what the details of the new law should be' (English, 2003: 67). There is, however, inequality of access. Only *some* interest groups can secure a place at committee hearings. As Kevin Leyden has established, groups that have their own lobbyists in Washington DC (and are therefore locked into political networks with the Congressional staffers who, in practice, make the decisions about who is invited) and those that have a political action committee (perhaps because they have contributed or might contribute to election campaign funding) are more likely to testify (Leyden, 1995: 438).[6]

Third, there will then be the consideration of the bill on a line-by-line basis. The writing of the detailed provisions is known as *mark-up*. Following a final vote, it will be reported to the full committee. There will be further mark-up and the bill is then *reported out*. If a House committee is reluctant to allow the bill to be reported out, the House can, in exceptional circumstances and if it can muster a majority, issue a discharge petition. This was used in 2002 to hasten the progress of the campaign finance reform bill (English, 2003: 79–80).

Once a bill has been reported out, time must be found to consider it in the chamber. Decisions to provide a place in the calendar and opportunities for debate and amendment are made by the House Rules Committee and, to a lesser extent, the Senate Majority Leader. The Rules Committee has been described as the House's 'traffic manager' (Griffith, 1976: 40). It determines the framework within which a bill is handled, the particulars of debate, time limits, and the conditions under which amendments can be submitted. There are three types of rule. An *open rule* allows amendments, while a *closed rule* prohibits them. A *modified rule* allows amendments when some sections of the bill, but not others, are being considered. The process takes a different form in the Senate, where unanimous consent agreements (which will be negotiated between the party leaderships) can be used to suspend rules and customs, set time limits, and specify the amendments to be considered. Individual senators can, however, use 'holds' to delay measures.

The bill is then considered and debated by the chamber as a whole. This is known as *floor action*. A bill must obtain a majority in both chambers. Voting is conducted by voice vote or, if sufficient numbers wish for it (the rules governing this differ between the House and the Senate), there may be a recorded *roll-call* vote using an electronic system.

However similar the bills introduced in the House and the Senate, there will almost certainly be significant differences between the versions passed in the two chambers. If they are to become law, bills must pass in an absolutely identical form. A *conference committee*, consisting of members from both houses, customarily drawn from the appropriate standing committees, will meet to seek a compromise between the different versions. This gives these members a pivotal role in shaping the final form of the legislation. However, it may not be an equal process. Most historical evidence suggests that, more often than not, the Senate conferees win where there is a gap between the two versions (Gross, 1980: 769).

If a compromise is agreed by a majority of both delegations, the bill must return to both chambers in its revised form for final approval. This is usually forthcoming, although there is a danger that members of either house may feel that too much has been conceded in conference negotiations. Amendments cannot be submitted at this stage.

Once it has been passed by the two chambers of Congress, the bill is submitted to the president. He may sign it or simply allow it to become law by allowing it to lie upon the table for ten days while Congress is in session. However, under the terms of the Constitution, the president can *veto* a bill. A veto can be overridden only if members of Congress can muster a two-thirds majority in both houses. George W. Bush cast eleven vetoes and was overridden four times. All the vetoes were cast between 2006 and the end of his presidency and all but one were cast after the Democrats secured majorities in both chambers. The veto power should not be underestimated, and the implicit threat of a veto may be sufficient in itself to force members of Congress to modify their original goals. The roles of the veto and the *pocket veto* are discussed further in Chapter 7.

What variables influence Congressional votes?

European observers are accustomed to voting discipline in national legislatures. Backbench revolts are regarded as a comparative rarity. However, even
in an era characterised by resurgent partisanship, US parties are less cohesive
than those in many other countries. Partisanship aside, what other variables
shape the ways in which members of Congress vote?

Although ideology and belief are closely tied to partisanship, they sometimes constitute an independent this is variable. Although this is increasingly
exceptional, there are times when members of Congress break ranks with their
party. In 2011, US military intervention against the Ghaddnfi regime in Libya
created significant intra-party fractures and inter-party coalitions. At the end
of June, 225 House Republicans joined anti-war Democrats to defeat a bill
that would have authorised 'limited' military action (Thrush and Hoskinson,
2011). The Republicans are pulled between 'neoconservatives', who stress
the need for the US to assert itself overseas so as to 'export' democratic values,
and those who fear that the country could become embroiled in conflicts in
which the US has no vital strategic interest. There also tensions within the
Democrats. Some want the US to play a part in multilateral coalitions with the
major European countries while others see military interventionism in regions
such as the Middle East as a form of imperialism.

Congressional 'staffers' may, in practice, also influence voting decisions.
John Kingdon has noted that 'a high probability exists that a congressman's
vote will reflect his or her staff position' (Woll, 1985: 189). The influence they
exert stems in part from the volume of work and the number of issues facing an
individual congressman or senator. She or he will inevitably depend to a large
extent guided by the recommendations of aides.

The role of lobbyists and organised interests (particularly corporations)
should also be considered. By 2005, the total number of registered lobbyists in
Washington DC (representing not only companies but many other interests)
had risen to 25,000. If corporate lobbyists are considered, the numbers with
offices in Washington DC grew from one in 1920 to 175 in 1968 to over 600
by 2005. Between 1998 and 2004, total expenditure on lobbying activity
(as reported under the provisions of the Lobbying Disclosure Act) rose at an
average rate of 8.2 per cent per annum (Repetto, 2006: 1–2).The companies
most involved in lobbying Congress (as well as the executive and judicial
branches of government) are the larger firms that have sufficient financial and
human resources. They are also those that are most affected by government
regulation (particularly those within the jurisdiction of regulatory commissions such as, for example, the Federal Communications Commission), those
for whom the federal government is a customer, those that have secured
government subsidies, or are particularly vulnerable to legislative changes.

The 'persuasion industry' utilises a range of techniques. Some will take
advantage of the sense of affinity that each of the parties has towards par-

ticular groupings. The trade unions held sway during the long years that the Democrats controlled Congress. Conversely, the Republican victories from 1994 onwards brought many business and conservative organisations further into the political mainstream. Interest groups can mobilise grassroots supporters. The Family Research Council, an important organisation within the Christian right, often asks those who back its campaigns to email or visit their Congress member. Through political action committees, interest groups and companies also make campaign contributions. Although the tobacco industry concentrates much of its resources on lobbying at state level (where policy towards smoking is largely determined), it still spent $4.1 million in campaign contributions in the 2008 election cycle (62 per cent of this was given to Republicans) (Mayer, 2009).

Within the president's party, and perhaps particularly when he has high approval ratings, the administration's support for a bill may also influence an individual senator or congress member.[7] Having said that, US history abounds with examples of a divide between the party in Congress and the White House. Despite Democratic majorities in both the House and the Senate during 1993 and 1994, President Clinton's healthcare reform plan had to be abandoned. President George W. Bush could not persuade Republican majorities to embrace Social Security reform. In 2009, there were tensions between President Obama and Congressional Democrats about military spending priorities and levels (Bendavid and Conkey, 2009).

The character of a state or district is significant. Although there is greater ideological homogeneity within both the parties, some Democrats, particularly in 'red' (or Republican-leaning) districts and states, have distanced themselves from the Democrats' legislation and its leadership. In the run-up to the November 2010 mid-term elections, two Democrats seeking re-election to the House of Representatives took out advertisements stating that they would not back the re-election of Nancy Pelosi as speaker (*Fox News*, 2010). When the vote was taken to choose a new speaker at the beginning of 2011, 20 Democrats failed to back her. When in 2009 the House of Representatives voted on the 'cap and trade' bill to limit carbon emissions, a key Democratic proposal, 44 Democrats voted against the measure. They were largely drawn from districts that were largely Republican or trending Republican in states such as Pennsylvania, West Virginia, Mississippi, and Arkansas (Trende, 2009).

Nonetheless, although these variables have at times been significant, partisan loyalties and partisanship are paramount. Although members' efforts will often be directed towards re-election, they also seek advancement in Congress. This depends, at least in part, on party loyalties and the character of a member's relationship with the party leadership. Some degree of loyalty is expected. Having said this, the part played by career-based incentives and disincentives is relatively limited. As noted in Chapter 2, the parties have in recent years acquired greater ideological homogeneity. For their part, the Republicans have established a more clearly defined conservative identity. At the same time, as they lost many of the conservatives from their ranks, the Democrats have for the most part placed themselves within a narrower range of beliefs and convictions. In other words, within both parties, there is less scope for policy disagreements. Given the importance of partisanship in the contemporary Congress, the parties should be considered in greater depth.

Parties and party leaders in Congress

When the 112th Congress convened at the beginning of January 2011, there were just two independents (Senators Bernie Sanders of Vermont and Joe Lieberman of Connecticut) and they both caucused with the Democrats. All the others belonged to either the Republican or the Democratic parties. The parties are organised within Congress through the Senate Republican and Democratic Conferences, the House Republican Conference, and the House Democratic Caucus. The House Democratic Caucus defines its role in these terms:

> The Caucus nominates and elects the House Democratic Leadership, approves committee assignments, makes Caucus rules, enforces party discipline, and serves as a forum to develop and communicate party policy and legislative priorities. It accomplishes these tasks through weekly Caucus Meetings, on-going Issue Task Forces, the yearly Caucus Issues Conference, periodic special events, and continual Member-to-Member communication. (House Democrats, 2011)

Three individuals play a key role in leading the majority party in the House. As was noted above, the speaker is responsible for the planning and implementation of the House's legislative agenda. His or her ability to chair proceedings allows him or her to rule upon contested points of order. However, administrative control extends far beyond this. The speaker influences decisions about the committee or committees to which a bill is assigned, and can place deadlines on committee action. He or she also has considerable powers of patronage, shapes the membership of select committees, and has since 1975 nominated majority party members to the all-important Rules Committee. Some speakers have used the position to stamp their personality and politics upon Congress as a whole. Arguably, Joe Cannon (1903–11), Sam Rayburn (1940–47, 1949–53, and 1955–63), Newt Gingrich (1995–99) and Nancy Pelosi (2007–2011) played particularly noteworthy roles (English, 2003: 90). The House majority leader structures and co-ordinates debate on the floor of the chamber and at the same time directs the party's strategy, intervenes in disputes among party members, and negotiates agreements with the minority party. The majority whip acts as a conduit of information between the executive and party members in the House, provides advice about the voting intentions of particular Congress members and, together with a team of assistant whips, encourages colleagues to vote with the party. The whip also provides information to members about forthcoming votes and the floor schedule. There are still memories of Tom DeLay, the Texas Republican who served as House majority leader from 2003 to 2005 and majority whip for eight years before then: he played a particularly significant role in marshalling the votes so as to ensure the passage of landmark legislation. Such was his reputation for imposing discipline on the party's ranks that he was popularly known as 'The Hammer'.

The greater individualism of the Senate has traditionally placed limits on the degree of leverage exercised by the party leaderships. Nonetheless, the Senate majority leader has an important role to play in co-ordinating party activity, managing day-to-day business on the floor of the chamber, establishing priorities, and negotiating time agreements and unanimous consent agreements with the minority leader that will set a timetable for the consideration of legislation.

Institutional variables

Chapter 3 argued that despite talk of 'party decline' there is much greater voting discipline in Congress than in earlier years. The proportion of 'party unity votes' has risen to around and sometimes in excess of 90 per cent. (These are roll-call votes where there is little voting across party lines and a majority of Democratic members are lined up against a majority of Republicans.) As noted above, partisanship is the pivotal variable in determining Congressional votes. Nonetheless, this is largely a consequence of ideological homogeneity. There are now fewer ideological differences within both of the parties. Although some Republicans who are centrist on a relatively small number of issues are derided as RINOs (Republican In Name Only), all Congressional Republicans would define themselves as conservative. The party no longer has a liberal wing. Although the Democrats embrace some differences between centrists and those who take more radical positions they are still more ideologically homogeneous than in earlier years when large numbers of highly conservative white southerners were in the party's ranks.

Despite the growth of Congressional partisanship, Congressional party leaders still have significantly less leverage than their counterparts in parliamentary systems. Party leadership plays a significant role in organising the procedures and the agenda of the chambers, but the leaders cannot command individual members to act. They can only seek to use their influence. Party group meetings, or caucuses, are infrequent and often of relatively little importance. Despite the number of party unity votes, there are, as has been seen, still issues (such as the 2011 intervention in Libya) that cut across the party divide.

Why do the Congressional parties lack the organisational strengths and resilience of the parliamentary parties in countries such as the United Kingdom? While the whips have some forms of patronage, including nominations for vacant committee assignments, participation in conference committees considering important bills, campaign contributions from leadership PACs (Political Action Committees established by prominent party figures so as to fund their own campaigns or those of others), or selection for foreign trips, they are, in contrast with their counterparts in the House of Commons, limited in the sanctions that they can impose upon dissidents. In contrast with Britain, where dissident MPs have, *in extremis*, been 'deselected' as party candidates, the party apparatus cannot prevent candidates who break ranks from gaining the party nomination. Instead, their fate depends upon their own ability to win and maintain the loyalty of primary voters. There are, however, other reasons why the parties play a relatively limited role.

First, the head of government in the US (the president) does not owe his or her position to votes in the legislature. In *parliamentary* systems the head of government (the prime minister) is elected by, accountable to, and dependent upon the legislature. In the UK House of Commons, the defeat of a major bill would lead to a vote of no confidence in the government, and, if this were carried, a general election would almost certainly be called. In the US system, the head of government – the president – is elected independently and retains office regardless of his performance or support in Congress. Legislators belonging to the same party can challenge the White House without the fear that the president may be forced to resign and the other party may gain office.

Second, Congress itself offers a career structure. In a parliamentary system, the career structure for those with ambition lies within the executive (the government). Upward mobility generally depends, however, upon an established record of loyalty towards the government and its leading members. In Congress, those who are ambitious do not generally look towards the executive branch. Instead, they seek a more powerful position, such as a committee chairmanship or membership of a more important committee, within Congress itself.

Third, Congress rests on a committee system that checks and limits the influence of the party leaderships. In the words of M. J. C. Vile: 'it is difficult to exaggerate the importance of these committees, for they are the sieve through which all legislation is poured, and what comes through and how it comes through, is largely in their hands' (quoted in Bennett, 1991: 17). Committee chairs are usually appointed on the basis of *seniority* rather than fidelity towards the party leadership. By tradition, the longest continuously serving majority party member of the committee takes the post. Similarly, membership of the most important and prestigious committees has customarily been reserved for those with the greatest seniority.

Fourth, there are other cross-cutting cleavages within Congress apart from the committee structures that curtail party authority. First, from the early 1970s onwards, Congress became more fragmented as a plethora of subcommittees assumed greater powers. Second, there are caucuses and task forces which are organised independently of the parties and cut across party lines. These include groupings based around the needs and interests of a particular industry, such as the Steel Caucus. It has, for example, campaigned on a bipartisan basis against steel imports from China. There are also state delegations. A Texan member of the House of Representatives has described the work of his delegation: 'we have a wide ideological spectrum . . . but we're able to close ranks and work together for any program that benefits any part of the state' (quoted in Woll, 1985: 183). Weight of numbers can give some delegations significant political leverage.

There is, therefore, a process of 'jostling' within Congress as different interests (the party leaderships, committee and subcommittee chairs and ranking members, the cross-party caucuses and task forces, organisations such as the Congressional Black Caucus, and established individuals) seek to assert themselves. Although the institutional character of Congress sets a framework, each of these interests has political resources that it can bring to the process. This was evident in 1975 when three House committee chairs were replaced, despite their seniority, by less senior Democratic colleagues. In the 1980s, Democratic speakers such as 'Tip' O'Neill and Jim Wright began to play more of a role in deciding which committees considered important bills and the conditions under which legislation was debated on the floor of the House (Owens, 1996: 16). After winning the 1994 mid-term elections, the House Republican leadership was committed to ensuring that conservative policy proposals would be adopted. It also bypassed the seniority principle by appointing chairs to the Appropriations, Commerce, and Judiciary Committees. At the same time, new (or 'freshmen') members who appeared to be the most committed to conservative principles were appointed to influential committees such as Appropriations, Ways and Means, and Rules. Those chairing committees were limited to a six-year period of tenure.

At the end of 2006, the incoming speaker Nancy Pelosi also made exceptions to the seniority principle by refusing to back Congresswoman Jane Harman (who had served on the committee for eight years) or Congressman Alcee Hastings (who had served for seven years) as chairman of the House Select Committee on Intelligence. There were political differences between Pelosi and Harman (Harman had backed the Iraq war) and Hastings faced ethics questions (*MSNBC*, 2006). However, despite these moves, the seniority principle was dented rather than destroyed. It remains the customary method of selection when committee chairs are decided upon.

Assessing Congress

Opinion polls suggest that people are critical of Congress as an institution, but, ironically, respect their own Congress member. In 2011, 17 per cent of

Americans expressed disapproval of Congress, while 54 per cent expressed approval of their own Congress member. Furthermore, sitting – or incumbent – members of Congress are almost always re-elected. The distinction between Congress as an institution and Congress as an aggregate of individual representatives has led some observers to talk of 'the two Congresses' (Davidson and Oleszek, 1998).

National legislatures fulfil different roles. They shape policy through the consideration of legislation, scrutinise the work of the executive branch (and in parliamentary systems hold the government to account), and engage in the 'redress of grievances'. These may be raised by either individuals or organised interests. More fundamentally, legislatures provide 'linkage' and representation. At least in the accounts typical of 'old institutionalism' (see Chapter 1), they offer a bridge between citizens and the government. To an extent at least, and the ways in which this is undertaken depends upon the model of representation upon which a particular political system rests, members of a legislature will convey the opinions of those they represent: 'legislatures act as a conduit of information allowing local-level demands to be heard by the central government and the policies and actions of the central government to be explained to citizens' (Kreppel, 2011: 125).

Given this, how should Congress be judged? First, how effective is Congress as a lawmaking institution? Few would draw positive conclusions. In contrast with parliamentary systems (or at least those where a party or coalition has a stable majority in the primary legislative chamber), Congress is much more effective at killing off legislation than passing it. Significant reforms have been passed. Welfare provision was fundamentally restructured and curtailed in 1996. Educational assessment was extended through the 2001 No Child Left Behind Act. The 2001 USA Patriot Act, which amongst its other provisions extended powers of surveillance, was enacted in the wake of the 11 September 2001 attacks. During the period between 2008 and 2010, Congress passed measures providing a $700 billion 'bailout' of the banking sector, a $787 billion fiscal stimulus, a far-reaching reform of financial institutions, and comprehensive healthcare reform. Yet, all of these were in many ways exceptional. There have been long periods of relative inactivity. There were few legislative achievements during both the Clinton and Bush presidencies. Clinton was unable to secure healthcare reform and Bush failed in his bid to secure the partial privatisation of Social Security. The period between January and June 2011 is perhaps representative. As *Politico* reported:

> Just 18 bills have become law through the first half of 2011, and 15 of those named a building after someone, temporarily extended expiring laws or appointed an official to the board of the Smithsonian Institution. Congress can't decide what to do on critical issues like Libya, spending or the nation's debt limit, and no compromise is in sight on a host of other issues. (Allen and Bresnahan, 2011)

The inability of Congress to pass legislation has at times, as legislators failed to reach agreement on the annual budget, led to a shutdown of government services and brought government to within hours of such a shutdown.

Why does a national legislature have such difficulty passing legislation? Part of the answer lies in the US Constitution. By definition, separated institutions create formidable barriers. Legislation requires the assent of the House of Representatives, the Senate (which unlike the upper chamber in many European countries has co-equal powers), and the president. Alongside the Constitution, the rules and customs that have evolved within Congress have also impeded the passage of legislation. The cloture rule whereby 60 votes are required to move to a vote is most obvious article. The cleavages and tensions between parties, committees, and subcommittees and at the same time national, sectoral, and constituency interests compound the problem.

There are, however, further difficulties. Henry Clay, who served in both chambers of Congress and as Secretary of State between 1825 and 1829, once said: 'all legislation is founded on the principle of mutual concession' (quoted in Brookings Institution, 2011: 44). Arguably, however, there are significant incentives *not* to compromise or make mutual concessions within the contemporary political process. They create the feelings of intense partisanship that characterise Congress and treat every disagreement 'like it's Armageddon' (Brookings Institution, 2011: 22).

Dan Glickman, a Democrat who served in the House of Representatives and as agriculture secretary in the Clinton administration, has pointed to some of these incentives. First, members of Congress are focused on raising campaign funds and are, Glickman has argued, indebted to donors. Those donors seek access once a member is elected but they are also seeking votes. In many cases, those who give donations will be seeking to protect benefits that they receive from the federal government. These benefits may be extended through the tax concessions that are offered to those in particular categories, or the entitlements that are, for example, provided for senior citizens, or the trade arrangements and subsidies that may be given to firms. This, in itself, 'leads to a risk-averse and sometimes paralytic political process' (Brookings Institution, 2011: 16). Second, the new media (cable news networks and the internet) offer a multiplicity of outlets, each tailored for a specific ideological grouping. Individuals engage in selective exposure. Conservatives will, for example, turn to *Fox News*. This reinforces existing beliefs and reduces the scope for compromise amongst a Congressman's grassroots supporters. Third, legislators spend less time on Capitol Hill and more within their district or state. Glickman has recalled the ways in which a shared life in Washington DC in earlier decades built up relationships between members from different parties:

When I was elected to Congress we worked five days a week. We lived in Washington, brought my kids to Washington, and I got to know and became good friends with most members of Congress, both sides of the aisle. They were my friends. Friendship and familiarity builds trust. (Brookings institution, 2011: 18)

Correspondingly, the weakening of social connectivity has reduced trust and co-operation. Fourth, there is a lack of leadership. Such is the political leverage of 'special interests', Congressional leaders will not challenge them. Like some other commentators, Glickman sees the protracted debates about federal government budget deficit reduction as indicative of this. Although all agree that the budget deficit and the national debt are at levels that jeopardise long-term economic growth, the party leaders are fearful of adopting measures that core constituencies might regard as a threat to their interests.

it's a failure of leadership . . . We didn't do it because our constituencies would not like various pieces of it. Our business constituencies would not like raising taxes in one way or the other. Our seniors wouldn't like Medicare or Social Security reforms, or whatever else it is. (Brookings Institution, 2011: 20)

Furthermore, when legislation is passed, it often includes 'earmarks'. Earmarks (sometimes described as 'pork' or 'pork-barrel politics') are amendments that reserve funding, resources, and employment for specific projects usually within a member's district or state. These will often be included as short items within the federal budget's annual appropriations bills. They usually evade close scrutiny. 'Pork-barrel politics', it is said, distort legislation and corrupt government programmes. In the aftermath of the *Challenger* space shuttle disaster in 2003, Senator John McCain suggested that $167 million of 'pork' had been added to legislation funding the National Aeronautics and Space Administration (NASA) and that this might have had an impact on NASA's safety programmes. He cited spending in particular districts and states: $15.5 million for the Institute for Scientific Research in West Virginia, $7.6 million for hydrogen research by the Florida State University System, and $1.35 million for the expansion of the earth science hall at the Maryland Science Center in Baltimore (*Washington Post*, 15 May 2003). Congress approved earmark spending projects amounting to more than $208 billion between 2000 and 2009.

Amidst widespread opprobrium about the practice and anger about government expenditure levels, both chambers of Congress moved during 2010 and 2011 towards a moratorium on earmarks and in his 2011 State of the Union Address President Obama said he would veto legislation that included earmarks (Boles, 2011). Nonetheless, the moratorium was of limited duration and there were, according to Citizens Against Government Waste (an advocacy organisation), sustained efforts to circumvent it (Kennedy, 2011). The oversight or scrutiny work undertaken by Congress should also be considered. Commentators are divided about the extent to which this is pursued and its effectiveness. Some point to Congress's role in subjecting US military operations in Vietnam to scrutiny and uncovering the Watergate scandal. From 1965 to 1970, the Senate Foreign Relations Committee, under the chairmanship of Senator J. William Fulbright, subjected the White House's military operations in South-east Asia to serious and increasingly bitter criticism. Just a few years later, in a chain of events that culminated in President Richard Nixon's resignation in August 1974, the Senate Select Committee on Presidential Campaign Activities, which was chaired by Senator Sam Ervin, played a pivotal role, along with newspapers such as the *Washington Post*, in unravelling the Watergate scandal and the subsequent White House cover-up. Joel D. Aberbach has argued that oversight work became even more important from the mid-1970s onwards (1990: 19, 72). This was because the political 'payoffs' for oversight work increased as public unease about the federal government grew.

There are examples that can be cited to illustrate this. In 1983, the head of the Environmental Protection Agency was censured and thereby compelled to resign after refusing to supply Congress with documents. In 1987–88, select committees drawn from both the House and the Senate charted the Iran–Contra scandal. (The scandal arose after revelations that the Reagan administration had pursued a secret policy of selling arms to the Iranian government so as to secure the release of western hostages and the provision of aid to right-wing guerrillas in Nicaragua.) Colonel Oliver North, who had worked for the National Security Council, was among those compelled to provide testimony. Twenty years later, the 110th Congress (2007–2009) was, at least in its early months, dubbed the 'Oversight Congress'. *Politico* reported on the forms that the oversight process was taking and the range of investigations that were launched:

> Some are high-profile, such as the leaking of Valerie Plame's CIA identity or the U.S. attorney firings, subjects that make for compelling cable news dramas But many more are mundane: inefficiency at the federal crop insurance program or conflicts of interest in FDA contracting. Some are pragmatic, such as an examination of food safety following outbreaks of illness caused by contaminated peanut butter and spinach. Others are tragic: the death of Army Ranger Pat Tillman and the misleading information the military provided to his family. (Hearn and Vandehei, 2007)

The ability of Congress to oversee and influence the actions of the bureaucracy was strengthened by the *legislative veto*. From 1932 onwards, legislation often included a provision that particular decisions and actions undertaken by the executive branch should be referred back to Congress. The first legislative veto permitted President Herbert Hoover to reorganise the executive agencies, but established a 90-day delay before any changes would take effect. During this period, the legislation allowed Congress to veto the organisational changes he had made. The overall effect of the legislative veto was to give

Congressional committees authority over day-to-day decisions by sections of the executive branch. In the 1950s, for example, a Congressional committee, the Joint Committee on Atomic Energy, decided where the Atomic Energy Commission should locate power stations and what forms of technology would be adopted. In June 1983, however, the US Supreme Court declared that the legislative veto was unconstitutional. In *Immigration and Naturalization Service v. Chadha* the Court found that, by giving Congress a power that was not subject to presidential concurrence, this form of veto breached the separation of powers. However, the overall impact of *Chadha* appears to have been limited. The status of laws passed between 1932 and 1983 that included a legislative veto remains uncertain. They have not been repealed and, furthermore, as Louis Fisher argues, more than 140 laws passed since 1983 have included a legislative veto (*Congressional Quarterly*, 1997: 18).

However, notwithstanding these developments, serious questions can be asked about the effectiveness of the oversight process. Peter Woll suggests that scrutiny of the executive branch offers relatively little to the individual members of Congress, the district or state that they represent, and their chances of re-election (1985: 146). In the same vein John Hart concludes that oversight is 'negligible'. Congress, he asserts, 'has neither the will nor the interest nor the incentive to reverse a half century of significant institutional development in American government' (1995: 237). Although he argues that Congress regards its 'watchdog' role in serious terms, Ross English notes that 'too many committees approach oversight with a "fire-fighter" approach, responding when a problem with the executive branch comes to light, rather than maintaining a more systematic style of surveillance' (English, 2003: 121).

Most fundamentally of all, Congressional oversight has been weakened by growing partisanship. Members of Congress are often reluctant to confront the White House if it is controlled by their own party. Ray LaHood, then a Republican member of the House who later went on to serve as transportation secretary in the Obama administration, summed up attitudes during the Bush years: 'Our party controls the levers of government. We're not about to go out and look beneath a bunch of rocks to try to cause heartburn' (quoted in Waxman, 2004). At the same time, there is evidence that members of Congress seek to tie down and impede the work of an administration if it is held by the opposing party. The California Congressman Henry Waxman, who became Chairman of the House Oversight and Government Reform Committee when the Democrats won back control of Congress in the November 2006 mid-term elections, wrote a bitter indictment of the ways in which, he claimed, the Republicans were approaching the oversight process:

> During the Clinton administration, Congress spent millions of tax dollars probing alleged White House wrongdoing. There was no accusation too minor to explore, no demand on the administration too intrusive to make . . . When President

Clinton was in office, Congress exercised its oversight powers with no sense of proportionality. But oversight of the Bush administration has been even worse: With few exceptions, Congress has abdicated oversight responsibility altogether. (Waxman, 2004)

What should be said about Congress and the representation of constituents in the districts and states? If its role in representing the opinions and views of the electorate is considered, there is a significant disconnect. As has been noted, there is intense polarisation between the parties in the contemporary Congress. Each of the parties (but particularly the Republicans) has become markedly more ideologically homogeneous. However, pictures of the electorate look very different. There has been a process of 'sorting' so that those who lean towards conservatism will back the Republicans (whereas half a century ago many particularly in the South would vote Democrat) and those who lean leftwards will be Democrats. Arguably, there has also been 'residential sorting' as individuals and families move into neighbourhoods with similar sorts of individuals and families. This creates more homogeneous districts, which makes them less electorally competitive. A Congress member representing such a district does not have to make political concessions to middle-ground voters or those who back the other party. Nonetheless, despite talk of a divide between a 'red' and a 'blue' America, when mass attitudes towards core political issues are considered, the polarisation that characterises Congress and the parties is largely absent. Indeed, large numbers occupy a moderate position. There are some differences between 'red' and 'blue' states but these are for the most part relatively small. For example, voters in both Republican-leaning and Democrat-leaning states support the death penalty in certain circumstances.

Abortion has become a significant faultline in US politics. Not only are the parties polarised but the issue has become, as Chapter 7 notes, a 'litmus test' for the appointment of federal court judges. However, surveys of public opinion reveal that a large proportion of the population favours the legal provision of abortion in some specified circumstances. Only a minority (albeit a large minority) support its availability on the basis of personal choice and only about one in seven argue that abortion should never be permitted (see Table 5.1).

Similarly, if survey respondents are asked about the federal government they also gravitate towards the middle. Although there were significant shifts between the middle categories in the aftermath of the 11 September 2001 attacks, only a handful are to be found at the extremes. Table 5.2 shows responses to a question about trust in the federal government.

The reasons for the disconnect between Congressional politics and public attitudes are to be found in other chapters. They are emphasised by Morris Fiorina. He points to the 'capture' of the nominating process by activists through the system of primaries and caucuses. He also points to the mass media which, he notes, construct and promote news stories around conflict (Fiorina with Abrams and Pope, 2005: 138–147). Wayne Baker, author of

Table 5.1 *Attitudes towards legal abortion, 1980–2008 (%)*

	1980	1990	2000	2004	2008
Never permitted	11	12	12	14	15
Permitted only in case of rape, incest, danger	32	33	31	32	27
Permitted only in case of clear need	18	14	15	18	18
Permitted always as personal choice	35	40	39	36	40
Don't know, other	4	2	2	1	1

Source: adapted from American National Election Studies (2011), *The ANES Guide to Public Opinion and Electoral Behavior*, http://www.electionstudies.org/nesguide/toptable/tab4c_2b.htm.

Table 5.2 *Attitudes towards trust in the federal government, 1980–2008 (%)*

	1980	1990	2000	2002	2004	2008
None of the time	4	2	1	0	1	2
Some of the time	69	69	55	44	52	68
Most of the time	23	25	40	51	43	25
Just about always	2	3	4	5	4	5
Don't know, depends	2	1	1	0	0	0

Source: adapted from American National Election Studies (2011), *The ANES Guide to Public Opinion and Electoral Behavior*, http://www.electionstudies.org/nesguide/toptable/tab5a_1.htm.

America's Crisis of Values, offers a parallel but more challenging explanation that has affinities with the work of Abraham Maslow (who put forward a hierarchy of human needs) and Ronald Inglehart (who considered the displacement of materialist by post-materialist values). Baker suggests that individuals are committed at the same time to both traditional and 'self-expression' values:

> Americans increasingly embrace self-expression values, which manifest themselves in rising environmental concerns, demands for equality, and the search for meaning and purpose in life beyond the mere consumption of goods and services. (Baker, 2004: 13)

Each of the parties pulls at one set of values. The Republicans are structured around traditional values. Conversely, since the mid-twentieth century, the Democrats have increasingly tied themselves to self-expression values.

However, although Congress is open to sustained criticism because of the way it handles legislation, oversight, and the representation of popular attitudes, it has substantial strengths in undertaking the 'redress of grievances'. Extensive resources are assigned to meeting the needs of individual constituents and accommodating the demands of organised interests. These include the provision of 'pork' that may distort (and in some eyes corrupt) the legislative process but is inevitably received well within a member's home district or state and contributes to the re-election prospects of incumbents. They address individual problems concerning government programmes particularly Social Security, Medicare and veterans' pensions but also act as an intermediary if the issue is within the jurisdiction of another tier of government. They maintain offices across the district or state and almost always have a high level of public visibility.

Conclusion

Legislators in other nations sometimes, it is said, look with envy upon the US Congress. In particular, they cite the number of staff working for members of the House and the Senate, the powers held by Congressional committees, and the frequent refusal of Congress to do the president's bidding. Nonetheless, there have been, most notably during the last-minute stand-off over the federal government's debt ceiling, increasing references to the 'dysfunctional' character of Congress and the wider political system. Arguably, these are legitimate claims. Indeed, it should be asked whether the legislative process continues to 'fit' the demands and needs of the US economy particularly in times of strain and crisis.

Notes

1 Note however that the budget-making process is subject to severe institutional constraints. See p. 99–100.
2 The figure includes one member of the Senate. There is debate about whether members of Congress can be constitutionally subject to impeachment proceedings.
3 If a cloture motion is passed, debate is then limited to 30 additional hours unless increased by a further three-fifths vote. If Senate seats are vacant (because of resignation as death) the voting numbers are reduced accordingly.
4 It was drawn up by the veteran senator for West Virginia, Robert Byrd.
5 From 1975 onwards, the speaker of the House has been able to refer a bill to multiple committees.
6 See p. 71.
7 Federal government departments and agencies maintain offices of Congressional relations so as to facilitate liaison.

References and further reading

Aberbach, J. D. (1990), *Keeping a Watchful Eye: The Politics of Congressional Oversight*, Washington DC, The Brookings Institution.

122 US politics today

Allen, J. and J. Bresnahan (2011), 'Dysfunctional Congress "worse" than ever?', *Politico*, 30 June, www.politico.com/news/stories/0611/58076.html#ixzz1Qpp4nmYn.

Baker, W. (2004), 'Is America really facing a crisis of values?', *Dividend*, Fall, 12–13, webuser.bus.umich.edu/wayneb/pdfs/culture/FacingCrisis.pdf.

Bendavid, N. and C. Conkey (2009), 'Obama, Democrats in Congress clash on spending', *The Wall Street Journal*, 27 June, http://online.wsj.com/article/SB124606398458663857.html.

Bennett, A. J. (1991), *American Government and Politics*, Godalming, the author.

Boles, C. (2011), 'Senate Democrats announce earmark moratorium', *The Wall Street Journal*, 1 February, http://online.wsj.com/article/SB100014240527487041245 04576118633989795702.html.

Brookings Institution (2011), *Congressional Leadership in an Era of Partisan Polarization*, Washington DC, The Brookings Institution, 8 April, www.brookings.edu/~/media/Files/events/2011/0408_congressional_polarization/20110408_congressional_leadership_transcript.pdf.

Brudnick, I. A. (2011), *Congressional Salaries and Allowances*, Congressional Research Service, 4 January, www.senate.gov/CRSReports/crs-publish.cfm?pid='0E%2C*PL%5B%3D%23P%20%20%0A.

Congressional Quarterly (1997), *Powers of the Presidency*, Washington DC, Congressional Quarterly.

Davidson, R. and W. Oleszek (1998), *Congress and Its Members*, Washington DC, Congressional Quarterly.

English, R. (2003), *The United States Congress*, Manchester, Manchester University Press.

Fiorina, M. P. with S. J. Abrams and J. C. Pope (2005), *Culture War? The Myth of a Polarized America*, New York: Pearson Longman.

Fox News (2010), 'Endangered House Democrats campaign against Pelosi', *Fox News*, 16 October, www.foxnews.com/politics/2010/10/16/endangered-house-democrats-campaign-pelosi/#ixzz1QgbOojbf.

Griffith, E. S. (1976), *The American System of Government*, London, Methuen.

Gross, D. A. (1980), 'House-Senate Conference Committees: a comparative state perspective', *American Journal of Political Science*, 24:4, November, 769.

Harper, J. (2008), '10,000 bills introduced in Congress, while government management goes neglected', *Washington Watch*, 3 August, www.washingtonwatch.com/blog/2008/08/03/10000-bills-introduced-in-congress-while-government-management-goes-neglected/.

Hart, J. (1995), *The Presidential Branch: From Washington to Clinton*, Chatham, Chatham House.

Hearn, J. and J. Vandehei (2007), 'The oversight Congress: trouble for Bush', *Politico*, 22 May, www.politico.com/news/stories/0507/4137.html.

Hilliar, P. (2002), *Caging the Cardinals, Citizens for a Sound Economy*, 3 December, www.cse.org/informed/issues_template.php/1192.htm.

House Democrats (2011), *The Democratic Caucus*, www.dems.gov/democratic-caucus.

Kennedy, S. (2011), 'Earmark moratorium backlash, citizens against government waste, 30 March, www.cagw.org/newsroom/waste-watcher/2011/march/earmark-moratorium-backlash.html.

Kreppel, A. (2011), 'Legislatures', in D. Caramani (ed.), *Comparative Politics – 2nd Edition*, Oxford, Oxford University Press.

Leyden, K. (1995), 'Interest group resources and testimony at Congressional hearings', *Legislative Studies Quarterly*, 20:3, August, 431–439.

Library of Congress – THOMAS (2007), *How Our Laws Are Made*, http://thomas.loc.gov/home/lawsmade.bysec/introtocomm.html.

Mayer, L. R. (2009), *Tobacco Lobby Lights Up Debate on Industry Regulation*, OpenSecrets (Center for Responsive Politics), 31 March, www.opensecrets.org/news/2009/03/tobacco-lobby-lights-up-debate.html.

MSNBC (2006), 'Pelosi won't pick Hastings to run intel panel', *MSNBC*, 28 November, www.msnbc.msn.com/id/15938168/ns/politics/t/pelosi-wont-pick-hastings-run-intel-panel/.

National Conference of State Legislatures (2011), *2010 Constituents Per State Legislative District Table*, www.ncsl.org/default.aspx?tabid=22292.

Owens, J. E. (1996), 'A return to party rule in the US Congress?', *Politics Review*, 6:1, September, 15–19.

Repetto, R. (2006), *Best Practice in Internal Oversight of Lobbying Practice*, Yale Center for Environmental Law and Policy, Working Paper No. 200601, http://envirocenter.research.yale.edu/uploads/workingpapers/WP200601-Repetto.pdf.

Schickler, E. (2002), 'Congress', in G. Peele, C. J. Bailey, B. Cain, and B. G. Peters, *Developments in American Politics*, Basingstoke, Palgrave, pp. 97–114.

Senate Historical Office (2008), *Occasions when Vice-presidents Have Voted to Break Tie Votes in the Senate*, www.senate.gov/artandhistory/history/resources/pdf/VPTies.pdf.

Singh, R. (2003), *American Government and Politics: A Concise Introduction*, London, Sage Publications.

Thrush, G. and C. Hoskinson (2011), 'Libya vote a rebuke the White House can live with', *Politico*, 24 June, www.politico.com/news/stories/0611/57744.html.

Trende, S. (2009), 'Cap and trade vote shows promise, peril for both parties', *Real Clear Politics*, 7 July, www.realclearpolitics.com/articles/2009/07/07/cap_and_trade_vote_shows_promise_peril_for_both_parties_97316.html.

Waxman, H. (2004), 'Free pass from Congress', *The Washington Post*, 6 July, A19, www.washingtonpost.com/wp-dyn/articles/A29810-2004Jul5.html.

Woll, P. (1985), *Congress*, Boston, Little, Brown and Company.

6

The president and the executive branch

The president is, by far, the most visible public representative of the American government. Congress seemed, particularly in the making of foreign policy, to have been consigned to the political sidelines. Furthermore, as 'chief executive', contemporary presidents head a large-scale government bureaucracy structured around departments, agencies, commissions and bureause. However, his authority does not go unchallenged and, in practice, he is subject to a considerable number of constraints. Indeed, there is a process of political 'haggling' between the president and other branches of government, particularly Congress. There are, furthermore, many other institutional constraints. This chapter surveys the president's powers and the limitations that the other branches, the character of the state apparatus, and the 'Institutional architecture' impose upon the office.

The Constitution and the presidency

The US Constitution assigns relatively few specific powers to the president. He is the head of state as well as head of government and, as such, undertakes ceremonial duties. He is commander-in-chief of the armed forces. He appoints senior government officials, Supreme Court justices, and those who serve as US ambassadors abroad. He can grant pardons. He has, in the words of the Constitution, the 'Power, by and with the Advice and Consent of the Senate, to make Treaties, provided two-thirds of the Senators present concur'. He may also 'give to the Congress Information on the State of the Union, and recommend to their Consideration such Measures as he shall judge necessary and expedient'. He can, furthermore, veto proposed laws passed by Congress.

However, many of these powers are matched, or 'checked', by powers assigned to one or both of the houses of Congress. Only Congress can declare war. Many of a president's appointments have to be confirmed by the Senate. As noted above, treaties are subject to ratification by a two-thirds majority in the Senate.[1] The making of law and financial control, known as the 'power of the purse', remain the prerogative of Congress. Furthermore, the president's ability to veto bills passed by Congress can be overridden by a two-thirds majority in both houses. Lastly, a president (along with other federal officials) can be impeached by the House of Representatives and then tried by the Senate for 'treason, bribery, or other high crimes and misdemeanors'. If convicted, the president is removed from office.

The president and foreign policy

Although the Constitution was delicately constructed around a *separation of powers* and a system of *checks and balances*, the authority of the president progressively grew during the course of the nineteenth and for much of the twentieth centuries. By the late 1960s and early 1970s, when Richard Nixon occupied the White House, the president had undoubted primacy or *hegemony* in the handling of defence policy and national security matters. He was also, as critics observed, able to use the apparatus of government to pursue personal political goals. This was the era of the 'imperial presidency', as Arthur Schlesinger Jr, a distinguished historian, described it in a celebrated phrase. Congress, although sometimes vocal in its comments, seemed to play a subordinate role.

The growth of presidential power was symbolised by US involvement in the Vietnam War. Despite the intensity of the conflict – which led to the loss of 58,000 American lives and embroiled neighbouring countries – there was never a declaration of war. Presidents Lyndon Johnson and Richard Nixon's only authority was the Gulf of Tonkin resolution passed by Congress in 1964, which backed retaliatory action in response to an alleged attack on American vessels by North Vietnamese forces.

Why did presidential power grow? Some words and phrases in the US Constitution have an 'elastic' character. Article II, for example, requires the president to 'take care that the laws be faithfully executed'. The meaning of these words has been progressively stretched, thereby allowing the president greater latitude and freedom of action.

Particular presidential styles or decisions by individual presidents set precedents that would be followed by their successors. Their actions enlarged the scope of the office and changed expectations about its nature. In 1803, President Thomas Jefferson (1801–9) authorised the purchase of French Louisiana. Although this more than doubled the size of US territory, he made the decision without consulting Congress. In the Civil War, President Abraham Lincoln (1861–65), ordered the blockade of southern ports and increased the numbers enlisted in the army without Congressional assent. Under Franklin D. Roosevelt (1933–45), the size and scale of the executive branch grew dramatically during the period of the New Deal, the economic recovery programme of the 1930s, and the Second World War. In particular, although there was some shrinkage during the 1990s, the Executive Office of the President (EOP) (the president's personal staff) expanded in terms of both size and authority. From the Roosevelt era onwards, the presidency consisted not of one individual, but was instead structured around a large number of aides, decision-makers, and administrators.

The president's constitutional role as commander-in-chief enabled him to dispatch US forces across the world without seeking a formal declaration of war from Congress. Although members of Congress retained the 'power of the purse', and could, where it disagreed with the president's objectives, threaten the withdrawal of funding, this could be seen, in periods of tension or conflict, as a betrayal of the country's armed forces. It has only been used on a limited number of occasions.[2] Congress has few other options. Although there have only been eleven declarations of war, in five separate wars, American forces were ordered into action abroad on hundreds of occasions from 1798 (when an undeclared naval war with France began) onwards (Grimmett, 2010: 1).

It can also be argued that Congress is structurally ill-placed to determine or even influence the character of US foreign and defence policy, particularly in the years after 1945 when the nature of war had been transformed by the stationing of American forces around the world and the development of missile technology. The national legislature is a slow, unwieldy, and bureaucratic institution. It is focuses on domestic policy issues (the terrain, it is said, on which elections are won or lost) and is structurally incapable of acting pro-actively. As Clinton Rossiter asserted in a celebrated phrase: 'secrecy, dispatch, unity, continuity, and access to information – the ingredients of successful diplomacy – are properties of his [the President's] office, and Congress . . . possesses none of them' (1963: 26).

At the same time, there is a degree of deference to the president on foreign policy and defence matters that despite growing partisanship usually stretches across party lines. The reason for this lies partly in the status and authority that US political culture assigns to the presidency. However, it is also rooted in the extent and scale of the consensus on foreign and defence policy goals that lasted between the late 1940s and the demise of the Soviet Union at the beginning of the 1990s. Although there were disagreements, throughout the Cold War years, about the specific character of particular operations, only a small handful of individuals on the radical edges of American politics challenged the belief that the US had an obligation to lead the 'free world' in the battle to contain communism. There was, similarly, in the immediate aftermath of the terrorist attacks on 11 September 2001 a renewed consensus on the need to take military action in Afghanistan. The consensus has at times been severely strained, most notably by the Bush administration's decision to invade Iraq in 2003 and the subsequent military occupation. Nonetheless, there is, in contrast to domestic policy issues, a greater hesitancy in challenging the White House's judgement. The president also has some latitude in deploying military forces. Under the terms of the Foreign Assistance Act of 1961, presidential determinations (which although similar should be distinguished from executive orders) allow the commitment of forces, funds, and assistance if, in the eyes of the president, urgency is required to safeguard US national interests. In such circumstances, Congress does not have to give specific authorisation. On 26 April 2011, President Obama made a determination that military action was required, in conjunction with other nations, to assist civilians under threat in Libya. It stated that the situation presented 'an unforeseen emergency' and that funds should be transferred from other government agencies so as to facilitate US military intervention and support partners (*The DISAM Journal*, 2011).

Although the Constitution stipulates that treaties require the 'advice and consent' of the Senate, successive presidents have circumvented this by drawing up executive agreements with the heads of foreign governments. Although such agreements do not have the legitimacy or authority of treaties and may not be maintained by subsequent presidents, and initially addressed only minor issues, some signed from the 1930s onwards have had far-reaching international implications. In 1940, President Franklin Roosevelt used an executive agreement to 'swap' fifty destroyers for air bases in the British Empire. This assisted the British war effort against Germany, and strengthened US strategic might in the Americas. Arguably, as Andrew Rudalevige suggests, the agreement was a violation of both a 1917 law prohibiting the transfer of warships to a belligerent nation and the 1940 Neutrality Act (Krutz and Peake, 2011: 39).

In 1973, an executive agreement signed between President Richard Nixon and South Vietnam promised that the US would 'respond with full force' to North Vietnamese violations of the Paris peace agreement that had ended American military intervention in Vietnam.[3] Although the case did not directly address executive agreements, the US Supreme Court's 1936 ruling in *United States v. Curtiss-Wright Export Corporation* bolstered their importance by asserting that, under the provisions of the Constitution, the president's powers in international affairs were 'plenary and exclusive' (Krutz and Peake, 2011: 41).

After Vietnam

There were some early efforts to rein in the use of executive agreements. In the first half of the 1950s, the Bricker Amendment (which was inspired by conservative fears that US sovereignty was being eroded) sought to end executive agreements. It faced fierce opposition from President Eisenhower and, amidst Cold War anxieties about a Soviet attack, was defeated.

The Vietnam War was, at least partially, a turning point. Like other postwar military ventures, it had been an undeclared war waged on the basis of

presidential authority alone. In so far as there had been Congressional engagement it had been limited in scope. The 1964 Gulf of Tonkin resolution authorised retaliation for an alleged attack on US naval vessels by North Vietnamese
forces. However, the harsh realities of withdrawal and defeat in South-east
Asia and diminution of presidential authority during the 'long, hot summers'
of the late 1960s led to a shift in the popular mood. There were increasing
efforts to rein in presidential authority.

In 1972, Congress passed the Case–Zablocki Act requiring that the Senate
and House Foreign Relations Committees be notified of all executive agreements within 60 days.[4] Then, in November 1973, the War Powers Act (a
joint resolution of Congress) became law after Congress overrode a veto by
President Richard Nixon. Through the Act, Congress sought to ensure that
members of both the Senate and the House of Representatives would play
a significant part in shaping future military conflicts. The stated purpose of
the War Powers Act was to ensure 'that the collective judgment of both the
Congress and the President will apply to the introduction of United States
Armed Forces into hostilities, or into situations where imminent involvement
in hostilities is clearly indicated by the circumstances, and to the continued
use of such forces in hostilities or in such situations' (quoted in Grimmett,
2004). So as to achieve this, the Act established that the president should only
send armed forces 'into situations of hostilities or imminent hostilities' when
there was a declaration of war, specific statutory authorisation, or 'a national
emergency created by attack upon the United States, its territories or possessions, or its armed forces'. Furthermore, the president should consult with
Congress before introducing troops 'in every possible instance' and provide an
appropriate report to Congress within 48 hours. Most significantly of all, the
Act specified that, in the absence of a declaration of war or specific statutory
authorisation, the use of military forces must be ended within 60 days (plus
a further 30 days withdrawal period) unless Congress authorises another
course of action.[5]

The War Powers Act has always been controversial. Both Republican
and Democratic presidents have held back from statements or actions that
might be seen as an acknowledgement of its constitutionality. They believed
that sections of the Act encroached upon their constitutional authority as
commander-in-chief (Lithwick, 2008). Nonetheless, although there were
questions about the War Powers Act's constitutionality, there were fewer
doubts at least when it was passed about its impact. For President Richard
Nixon, it removed 'authorities which the president had properly exercised
under the Constitution for almost 200 years'. He, and subsequent presidents,
denied its constitutionality. Henry Kissinger, President Nixon's national security adviser, also saw the Resolution, and the other measures adopted by
Congress, as a fundamental shift in the character of the relations between the
legislative and executive branches: 'The decade-long struggle in this country
over executive dominance in foreign affairs is over. The recognition that the

Congress is a co-equal branch is the dominant fact of national politics today'
(quoted in Foley and Owens, 1996: 372).

There is some evidence to support claims such as these. For the most part,
the provisions of the Act have been followed, albeit loosely. Successive presidents have submitted reports under its terms although the White House always
stated that such reports were 'consistent with' the Act rather than 'pursuant
to' it. Furthermore, until the period following the 11 September 2001 attacks,
when military action has been undertaken, it has for the most part been short-
term, structured around specific goals, and tied to an exit route. In October
1983, following a power struggle between different factions within the ruling
New Jewel movement on the Caribbean island of Grenada, the Reagan administration ordered US marines to occupy the island. The New Jewel movement
was removed from power. Congress, however, played a negligible role in all of
this. Rapid military success, and widespread public support for the invasion,
enabled the Reagan administration to keep Congress members relegated to
the sidelines. In April 1986, following a terrorist attack against American
servicemen and a clash between US and Libyan forces in the Mediterranean,
the Reagan administration ordered American air attacks on Tripoli and other
targets in Libya. Congressional leaders were invited to the White House only
as the US bombers were approaching Libya. President Reagan argued that
the action had been self-defence, and fell within his responsibilities as commander-in-chief. The Reagan administration also fought a covert and, critics
asserted, illegal war during this period. Although the Boland amendment had
been passed by Congress in 1984, cutting off funding for military and paramili-
tary aid to the Contras, a right-wing army seeking the overthrow of the radical
leftist Sandinista government in Nicaragua, they were backed and directed by
staff within the Reagan administration. They acquired funding for the venture
from secret arms sales to Iran and private donations.

In December 1989, President George H.W. Bush sent US troops into
Panama. The attack (Operation Just Cause) followed a period of tension
between the country's military ruler, General Manuel Noriega, who had been
accused of involvement in the international drug trade, and the United States.
Noriega was arrested by US forces at the beginning of January, and, after a trial
in Miami, imprisoned. President Bush ordered the withdrawal of the troops by
the end of February 1990. The invasion took place while Congress was out of
session.

In just a few instances, military action seemed to take a more open-ended
form. This led to tensions with Congress but direct clashes about the meaning
and relevance of the War Powers Act were averted. In 1983, President Reagan
sent US forces to the Lebanon. Congress responded by 'starting the clock'
established under the Act, although the President was given 18 months rather
than the 90 days specified by the Resolution. However, in the aftermath of a
brutally effective terrorist attack, when a suicide bombing led to the deaths
of 219 Americans, the President withdrew the troops. Congress took other

steps, aside from the War Powers Act, to rein in the president in his handling of foreign and defence policy. President George H.W. Bush sought Congressional backing before hostilities began in the 1991 Gulf War. On the eve of war, the House backed military action against the Iraqi forces by 250 to 83 votes. The Senate agreed by 52 to 40 votes. In 1999, President Bill Clinton continued the US bombing of Serbia for more than two weeks after the 60-day deadline specified in the Act as part of efforts to force Serbian withdrawal from Kosovo. The Clinton White House argued (seemingly in direct contravention of the Act's provisions) that the fact that Congress had authorised funding for military action constituted authorisation for the use of force.

The most significant exception, in the years before the 11 September 2001 attacks on New York and the Pentagon, was the 1991 Gulf War against Iraq. Operation Desert Storm was a very large-scale military operation. Although there was a defined exit route, it would, had Iraq forces not crumbled, have been an open-ended commitment to hostilities. Nonetheless, President George H.W. Bush took steps to secure Congressional backing. Just before the outbreak of war, he wrote to the Congressional leadership asking for the passage of a resolution endorsing the use of all necessary means to implement the United Nations Security Council Resolution that had condemned Iraq's invasion of Kuwait. Significantly, the President's request asked for Congressional 'support' and not for 'authority' to engage in military action (Grimmett, 2004). When signing the 2002 Congressional resolution that gave backing to the Iraq War, President George W. Bush stated that, while he had sought the backing that he secured from Congress, his actions did not constitute a recognition that the War Powers Act had constitutional authority:

> my request for it did not, and my signing this resolution does not, constitute any change in the long-standing positions of the executive branch on either the President's constitutional authority to use force to deter, prevent, or respond to aggression or other threats to U.S. interests or on the constitutionality of the War Powers Resolution. (quoted in Grimmett, 2004)

The terrorist attacks by Al-Qaeda operatives on the World Trade Center and the Pentagon on 11 September 2001 transformed the character of US policy and the presidency of George W. Bush. Urged on by neoconservatives and 'hawks' such as Paul Wolfowitz and Donald Rumsfeld at the Department of Defense, Bush committed the US to a broadly defined war on terror. He emphasised that the US would 'make no distinction between the terrorists who committed these acts and those who harbor them'. President Bush followed in his father's footsteps. Although the War Powers Act was not invoked, he sought Congressional backing. Three days after the 11 September 2001 attacks, at the White House's urging, Congress approved a resolution that was rather narrower in scope than that initially considered by the administration but it authorised the president to 'use all necessary and appropriate force against nations, organizations, or persons he determines planned, authorized, committed, or aided the terrorist attacks that occurred on September 11, 2001, or harbored such organizations or persons, in order to prevent any future acts of international terrorism against the United States by such nations, organizations or persons'. The votes for the resolution were 98–0 in the Senate and 420–1 in the House of Representatives. The lone dissenter was Barbara Lee, a black Democratic Congresswoman who represents the ninth district in California. Just over a year later, the 'war on terror' consensus had begun to fray. Undeterred by its failure to win specific authorisation from the United Nations and the opposition of countries such as France and Germany, the US maintained its assertion that Saddam Hussein's regime held chemical and biological weapons and, with allies such as the United Kingdom, invaded Iraq in March 2003. Military victory came within weeks and the US looked towards the political reshaping of the Middle East. Other 'rogue states', it was said, would recognise the 'new realities' of American might. In October 2002, the House of Representatives agreed to the use of force against Iraq by 296–133. The Senate vote was 77–23.

Having said this, however, the claim that the War Powers Act reined in the White House is open to question. It has been argued that, although the Act is widely seen as contributing to the demise of the 'imperial presidency' by imposing constraints upon the White House, it had inherent structural weaknesses that, in practice, bolstered presidential powers. According to Louis Fisher and David Gray Adler, 'it was ill conceived and badly compromised from the start, replete with tortured ambiguity and self-contradiction. The net result was to legalize a scope for independent presidential power that would have astonished the Framers, who vested the power to initiate hostilities exclusively in Congress' (Fisher and Adler, 1998:1).[6] In particular, by providing the president with a 90-day 'window' within which military operations could be conducted, it legalised and legitimised actions that had hitherto strained relations between Congress and the White House. Arthur J. Schlesinger Jr (who coined the phrase 'imperial presidency') argued that before 'the passage of the resolution, unilateral presidential war was a matter of usurpation. Now, at least for the first ninety days, it was a matter of law' (quoted in Fisher and Adler, 1998:1). Put another way, the Act made 'unilateral presidential action . . . routine' (Fisher and Adler, 1998:16).[7]

The Bush era

Presidential power, at least in the defence and 'homeland security' arena, was ratcheted upwards during George W. Bush's presidency as US forces battled with the Iraqi insurgency and the global 'War on Terror' seemed to require emergency measures.

There was increasing controversy about the use of presidential signing statements. These are the written comments issued by the president when a bill is signed. Although sometimes unexceptional, they may also include directions about the ways in which the statute should be interpreted and applied. They could even suggest that parts of a bill are or might be unconstitutional and will not therefore be acted upon. When, for example, at the end of 2001, President Bush signed the 'Intelligence Authorization Act for Fiscal Year 2002', he included the following paragraph in the signing statement emphasising what the administration regarded as its right, notwithstanding Congressional oversight mechanisms, to withhold sensitive information:

> Section 502 of the National Security Act as amended by section 305 of the Act shall be construed for all purposes, specifically including for the purpose of the establishment of standards and procedures under section 502(c) of the National Security Act by the Director of Central Intelligence, in a manner consistent with the President's constitutional authority to withhold information the disclosure of which could impair foreign relations, the national security, the deliberative processes of the Executive, or the performance of the Executive's constitutional duties. (quoted in Kaye, 2010)

Signing statements have a long history. Indeed, they have been dated back to President James Monroe (1817–1825). Furthermore, Bill Clinton issued large numbers. However, some commentators charge that Bush used signing statements not only to evade Congressional oversight but as a form of line-item veto so as to nullify particular laws. In 2006, *The Boston Globe* claimed that Bush had claimed the authority to circumvent more than 750 statutes (which were provisions Included in about 125 bills). As a senator and presidential candidate (like many liberals and some libertarian conservatives), Barack Obama was deeply critical of the Bush record on signing statements:

> That's not part of his power, but this is part of the whole theory of George Bush that he can make laws as he goes along . . . I disagree with that. I taught the Constitution for 10 years. I believe in the Constitution, and I will obey the Constitution of the United States. We're not going to use signing statements as a way of doing an end-run around Congress. (quoted in Youngman, 2011)

Some of Bush's signing statements went a stage further than what critics depicted as a line-item veto. Drawing upon Article II of the Constitution, the statements seemed to assert the 'unitary' character of the executive branch. Some within the Bush administration argued that, far from 'separated institutions sharing powers' (as Richard Neustadt suggested in his classic formulation), Congress and the federal courts had few powers over the executive branch activities and that officials within the executive branch are answerable to the president alone.

Such thinking took its most pronounced form in the arguments put forward by John Yoo, who at that time served in the Department of Justice. He stressed the president's power to interpret the Constitution and determine, on this basis, which laws the administration was required to follow. He argued, for example, that the use of waterboarding or other forms of 'enhanced interrogation techniques' on 'enemy combatants' held in the 'war on terror' was a matter for the president alone and that he, and those who acted on his authority, were immune from prosecution under laws prohibiting the use of torture. Indeed, according to a *Newsweek* report, Yoo believed 'that the president's war-making authority was so broad that he had the constitutional power to order a village to be "massacred"' (Isikoff, 2010).

The Obama record

The character of President Obama's record is harder to discern. Despite his criticisms of the Bush administration's record, he began to use signing statements, albeit for different political ends. In April 2011, when signing legislation defunding the informal policy advisers he had employed in the White House (sometimes dubbed 'czars' and not subject to Senate confirmation), he himself issued a signing statement refusing to accept a section of the bill he was signing:

> The president also has the prerogative to obtain advice that will assist him in carrying out his constitutional responsibilities, and do so not only from executive branch officials and employees outside the White House, but also from advisers within it . . . Therefore, the executive branch will construe section 2262 not to abrogate these Presidential prerogatives. (quoted in O'Brien, 2011)

Although executive orders were issued at the beginning of the Obama presidency, reversing some Bush-era policies towards detainees, the American Civil Liberties Union (ACLU) began to fear that the executive branch continued to exercise excessive powers. Notwithstanding efforts to close the Guantánamo camp, the principle of indefinite detention was upheld. Confidentiality was maintained, preventing effective Congressional oversight. And the administration asserted its right, particularly through drone attacks, to engage in targeted killing. The Bush administration's policies had, the ACLU argued, become the 'new normal' (American Civil Liberties Union, 2010).

The Obama administration's actions in the 2011 conflict with Libya also raised questions about executive power and the principle of checks and balances. After two months of military action against Colonel Moammar Ghaddafi's long-entrenched regime, Obama's critics on both the left and the right began to talk of taking action under the provisions of the War Powers Act.[8] This was tied to demands that the operation should become subject to

Congressional approval. In response, the White House sent a 32-page report to Congress in mid-June. It shied away from claiming that the War Powers Act was unconstitutional, but instead deployed a range of arguments in its efforts to assert that the Act did not apply to the Libyan crisis and the president would not therefore seek a Congressional vote. In particular, it sought to argue that the Act did not apply when the US was simply supporting a broader military alliance or using air power rather than ground troops:

> U.S. military operations are distinct from the kind of 'hostilities' contemplated by the Resolution's 60 day termination provision. U.S. forces are playing a constrained and supporting role in a multinational coalition . . . U.S. operations do not involve sustained fighting or active exchanges of fire with hostile forces, nor do they involve the presence of U.S. ground troops, U.S. casualties or a serious threat thereof. (The White House, 2011:25)

This triggered a wave of criticism. In an editorial, *The New York Times* said that the Obama administration's reasoning 'borders on sophistry . . . No word games can get him off the hook' (*New York Times*, 2011). There was, the newspaper argued, no legal or constitutional distinction whatsoever between the use of air power and the deployment of ground troops. On the Democratic left, Congressman Dennis Kucinich (who sought the party's presidential nomination in 2008) bitterly dismissed claims that the US was simply one participant among many: 'The fact remains that we're bombing another country and we pay, by far, the largest percentage of NATO's military bills . . . This is a war that we're leading – and it's a war that violates our Constitution and the War Powers Act' (Shaw, 2011). At the same time, John Boehner, the speaker of the House of Representatives who led the Republicans to victory in the 2010 mid-term elections, emphasised the importance of the Act and also began to issue veiled threats:

> Despite the constitutional concerns anyone may have with the statute, the War Powers Resolution is the law of the land and cannot be simply ignored. The White House's suggestion that there are no 'hostilities' taking place in Libya defies rational thought. From the outset of this operation, members of the House have demonstrated respect for the authority granted to the Commander-in-Chief. Unfortunately, the President has not exhibited a similar appreciation for Congress' important job of providing oversight and accountability. Over the coming week, our members will review all options available to hold the administration to account. (Speaker of the House John Boehner, 2011)

The president and domestic policy

Although the distinction between foreign and domestic policy is sometimes blurred (such as when trade agreements are under consideration), domestic policymaking has significantly different political dynamics. Arguably, a president has markedly less leverage in the domestic arena. Although the president has a range of formal and informal powers, there are significant *de facto* constraints.

He has prerogatives derived from the Constitution, subsequent laws passed by Congress, and Supreme Court rulings. He has, as is widely noted, the constitutional right to veto legislation passed by Congress. If he wishes to follow such a course, Article I specifies that he must send a statement to Congress within ten days of a bill being passed setting out his reasons for refusing to sign it. The president can in some circumstances also employ the *pocket veto*.[9] In other words, if the president does not sign a bill within a ten-day period, and Congress has, by the end of that time, adjourned, the bill does not pass into law.[10] At first sight, it might seem that the veto power is a measure of presidential capacity and strength. However, the veto is a *negative* instrument. It offers a way of blocking legislation, but it cannot be used to create the type of legislation that a president wishes to see. Furthermore, the use of the veto may be an indication of political weakness. Those presidents who have issued large numbers of vetoes (President Gerald Ford issued 48 regular vetoes and 18 pocket vetoes in the two-and-a-half years that he served) may have been compelled to adopt a confrontational approach because they lacked other political resources.

The president can also issue executive orders. Until 1933, such orders were generally confined to administrative matters; but, while they are still used to shape and mould the federal bureaucracy, they have since acquired a greater significance. On taking office in the midst of economic depression, President Franklin Roosevelt ordered a four-day closure of the banks. In 1942, Executive Order 9066 interned Japanese-Americans living in California when it was feared that they might assist Japanese military actions against the US. In 1948, President Truman used an executive order to desegregate the armed forces. In 1957, President Eisenhower used an executive order to 'federalise' the Arkansas National Guard so as to allow black students to enrol at Little Rock Central High School. President George W. Bush issued 291 executive orders. Barack Obama had issued 102 as of early November 2011. These included Executive Order 13505 (issued on 9 March 2009) which reversed President Bush's ban on federal government funding for embryonic stem cell research. Nonetheless, there are relatively narrow parameters within which executive orders can be issued. Although he can require agencies or individuals to undertake acts not specifically mandated by Congress, they have to be based on the powers assigned to the president under the Constitution, the broad framework of legislation already passed by Congress, or his role in heading the executive branch.

The power of appointment allows a president to shape the character of his administration and create a 'brand' for his period of office. It extends to cabinet members, other senior officials in the federal bureaucracy, and federal judges as well as ambassadors. However, although the power of appointment stretches far beyond the posts subject to appointment by a prime minister in, for example, the UK, there are important limits both on the appointment power itself and on the extent to which it enables a president to shape the character of the federal government. First, the power of appointment is subject to Senate confirmation. This is not necessarily straightforward. In 1987, President Reagan nominated a well-known conservative jurist, Robert Bork, to the Supreme Court bench. The Senate Judiciary Committee, guided by prominent Democrats such as the late Edward Kennedy and Joseph Biden (who became vice-president in the Obama administration), asserted that Bork's views disqualified him from serving on the Court. He was rejected. Subsequently, in 1989, President Bush nominated a former Senator, John Tower, as Secretary of Defense. However, in March 1989, allegations about Tower's personal life and his relationships with companies seeking military contracts led senators to reject the nomination by a 53–47 vote (Parmet, 1997: 379). Second, although an incoming administration will be besieged by applications from campaign supporters, the pool from which credible senior nominees can be drawn may be relatively small. They face intense vetting processes (which forced the withdrawal of former Senator Tom Daschle who was to have served as President Obama's Health and Human Services Secretary, and almost derailed, Tim Geithner's nomination as Treasury Secretary). Many in the private sector may be reluctant to take a career break. Members of Congress are required to relinquish their Congress position. And there is a premium on those who have some experience of government. To the chagrin of those of his supporters who had hoped for a radical policy departure, many of President Obama's nominees, such as his first White House Chief-of-Staff Rahm Emanuel, had a record in the Clinton administration during the 1990s. Third, and perhaps most importantly, presidential 'capacity', when the federal government 'apparatus' is considered, is limited (see Chapter 1). Although some commentators talk of the US having a 'small state', very large numbers are employed by the federal government. It has about two million civilian employees (excluding the Postal Service) and is the largest employer. (About 85 per cent of those who work for the government are employed outside the Washington DC area.)

It is tempting to regard the executive branch 'apparatus' as a mechanism through which White House policy can be implemented and a source of presidential power. As the late Richard Neustadt noted: 'Even Washington reporters, White House aides, and congressmen are not immune to the illusion that administrative agencies comprise a single structure, "the" executive branch, where presidential word is law, or ought to be' (Neustadt, 1991: 33–4). In contrast with parliamentary systems of government, where those who head executive branch departments are drawn from the legislature, the president's appointees are constitutionally prohibited from serving in Congress if they hold positions within the executive branch. Although those appointed are subject to Senate confirmation, the president often has a freer hand than prime ministers in making appointments. However, despite these representations and images, the structure and character of the executive branch are both labyrinthine and byzantine. It is organised around a network of interlocking and overlapping departments, bureaux, commissions, agencies, government corporations, such as the National Railroad Passenger Corporation (AMTRAK), and government-sponsored enterprises, such as the Federal National Mortgage Association (widely known as Fannie Mae).

Executive or cabinet-rank departments are responsible for broad areas of policy such as State, Defense, Commerce, Transportation, and Homeland Security. There are 15 such departments. Bureaux have more focused and narrowly defined responsibilities. The most familiar is the Federal Bureau of Investigation (FBI), which gained national recognition during the gangster era of the 1920s. The structural complexity of the bureaucracy is particularly evident when the position of the bureaux is considered. They are generally located *within* executive departments. There are, for example, nine bureaux and offices within the Department of the Interior including the Bureau of Indian Affairs and the National Park Service. Independent Regulatory Commissions (IRCs), such as the Federal Communications Commission (FCC), have quasi-legislative and quasi-judicial functions. There are also large numbers of other federal agencies, including the Central Intelligence Agency (CIA), the National Endowment for the Arts, and the National Aeronautics and Space Administration (NASA), which is responsible for the US space programme.

Structural complexity gives the federal government its unwieldy and unresponsive character. However, there are other reasons. Lines of accountability sometimes overlap and often lack certainty. Bureaux create particular problems of hierarchy and policy co-ordination. The FBI is, for example, located within the Department of Justice. The FBI Director is therefore answerable to the Attorney-General (the cabinet secretary who heads the Justice Department) but, because the FBI plays a pivotal role in crime-fighting and counter-terrorism, it also has a direct relationship with the president. At the same time, the departments, bureaux, and agencies owe a degree of allegiance to Congress. Congress plays a pivotal role in determining funding allocations. Furthermore, it has oversight responsibilities. And, it is Congress that, as the legislature, establishes federal government programmes or creates agencies.

Each department, bureau, and agency constitutes a constituency that will inevitably seek to maintain and perhaps extend its resources, status, and authority. At the same time, as noted in Chapter 1, government has a porous character. There is the 'revolving door' for senior personnel. The five thousand or so individuals who head the different agencies will sometimes have been appointed as a form of political reward. Or they may have secured their posts through their loyalty to and enthusiasm for the president's political goals. There will be an inevitable vacuum as nominees await Senate confirmation hearings and as they familiarise themselves with the demands of their new role. The career professionalism that generally characterises the civil service in advanced countries is largely absent. Robert Reich was appointed as President Clinton's Secretary of Labor in 1993:

> The Department of Labor is vast, its powers seemingly endless . . . I can barely comprehend it all . . . Every time a new president is elected, America assembles a new government . . . who only sometimes know the policies they're about to administer, rarely have experience managing large government bureaucracies, and almost never know the particular piece of it they're going to run . . . And they remain in office, on average, under two years – barely enough time to find the nearest bathroom. It's a miracle we don't screw it up worse than we do. (Reich, 1998: 52)

At the same time, *de facto* issue networks with 'client' groupings have emerged. (It has long been argued that the Department of Education has too close a relationship with teachers and the unions that represent them.) The consequences of this are political and administrative fragmentation. As B. Guy Peters noted: 'Each functional area tends to be governed as if it existed in splendid isolation from the remainder of government' (1986: 22). There are significant numbers of 'quasi-bureaucrats' who work on government programmes and are employed in firms and agencies that are supported by federal funding. They are not, however, directly answerable to senior civil servants. There are inevitably feuding and 'turf wars' as different agencies jostle with each other over funding and jurisdictional issues.

Much is made of the part played by the Executive Office of the President (EOP) in co-ordinating and structuring the work of the administration. Established in 1939, the EOP was an organisational response to the Brownlow Committee which had concluded that 'The President needs help'. Overseen by the White House Chief of Staff, it incorporates the National Security Council (NSC), Office of Management and Budget (OMB), and the White House Office (WHO). More than two thousand individuals serve the EOP although some will be formally employed by departments or agencies. The figure includes subject specialists who hold permanent positions, but also many presidential appointees. Some of the president's closest advisers, Most posts do not require Senate confirmation.

In some accounts the EOP provides a partial counterweight to the structural complexities that define much of the executive branch. As David Mervin concludes: 'Presidents have the gravest difficulties as it is in gaining control of a notoriously fractious political system; without the expertise and assistance of the EOP they would be helpless and the United States would be truly ungovernable' (1993: 78). Nonetheless, its role and ability to direct the president's work should not be overstated.

First, although those who direct the administration activity around a particular area of policy have been dubbed 'czars', those who staff the EOP are simply advisers to the president. As such, they do not have executive powers, and cannot therefore issue directives to those who work in the federal bureaucracy. In contrast, cabinet members (most of whom head a federal government department such as State or Defense) are empowered by legal authority and have a legitimacy that the White House staff inevitably lack (Bennett, 1996: 179). Second, there are sometimes tensions and rivalries between the EOP and the departments, bureaux, and agencies which can be destabilising for the administration and the implementation of policy. There were serious tensions between Condoleezza Rice (who served as National Security Adviser during President George W. Bush's first term of office), her aides, and Donald Rumsfeld, the Secretary of Defense. According to a report: 'he did not regard her as an equal and barely hid it. The opinions of her staff did not interest him' (quoted in Shipman, 2008). Third, the EOP can, in practice, constitute a 'mini-bureaucracy', presenting problems of management, direction, and control (Foley and Owens, 1996: 214–215). While presidents have responded to this by increasing the size of the White House Office, the process of expansion has not necessarily constituted a solution: 'presidents could not control cabinet departments, so they increased the size of the EOP. Because the EOP was itself too big and too diverse to control, presidents then expanded the WHO' (1996: 255). Considerations such as these have led James Pfiffner to conclude that the term 'Executive Office of the President' is a misnomer. It has a sprawling structure and lacks the power to direct events: 'The EOP is not really a single office, but rather a collection; and it is not really executive, since it contains units that are primarily advisory rather than executing' (Pfiffner, 2000: 87).

The modern presidency has also acquired emergency powers. These were rationalised and codified by the 1976 National Emergencies Act, which was passed during the post-Watergate period. The Act stated that, if an emergency is declared, the president must specify the laws under which powers are being exercised. The emergency is automatically terminated after a year unless he notifies Congress to the contrary. The president's powers include the restriction of travel by individuals to particular countries, the suspension of *habeas corpus*, which prevents arbitrary arrest, and the ability to declare martial law. Such powers are, however, limited by the extent and scale of *state capacity*. The concept refers to the effectiveness and scope of administration within its territorial area. Questions have legitimately been asked about US state capacity. An emergency was declared in New Orleans when Hurricane Katrina struck in 2005. However, it became painfully evident that federal as well as state agencies failed both in terms of preparedness and in terms of their ability to mount relief efforts.

The president's responsibilities and powers also extend to the annual federal government budget. Before passage of the 1921 Budget and Accounting Act, the Treasury Secretary forwarded departmental budget requests to Congress. However, the Act established that the president should to make budget proposals and created the Bureau of the Budget (which later became the Office of Management and Budget (OMB) to facilitate this. The Congressional Budget and Impoundment Control Act of 1974 made further changes to the process by establishing a fixed budget calendar that runs from 1 October to 30 September of the following calendar year, a budget committee in each house, and the Congressional Budget Office (CBO) so as to provide members of Congress with their own economic projections, cost estimates, and financial forecasts.[11] Although passage is the prerogative of Congress, the budget-making process is, as noted above, initiated within the executive branch. This in itself provides a measure of executive leverage. As Plano and Greenberg noted, the Budget's 'size and specificity tend to reduce legislative discretion' (1989: 163). However, this perhaps underestimates the concessions that a president may be compelled to make and the consequences of partisan divisions. President George H.W. Bush learned this lesson in an episode that contributed to his loss of the presidency. His 1988 election victory owed much to his celebrated soundbite: 'Read my lips. No new taxes.' Faced, however, with spending commitments and an entrenched budget deficit, the 1990 Budget included both tax increases and expenditure cuts. Opposed by both conservative Republicans, who opposed the tax increases, and Democrats, who rejected cuts in social provision, the initial budget was defeated in the House of Representatives. The White House and Congress agreed to a revised version, increasing tax revenues by $140 billion over a five-year period, which was passed at the end of October 1990. Fellow conservatives suggest that Bush's 'betrayal' demoralised his backers and contributed to his defeat in the 1992 presidential election. In April 2011, the federal government came within hours of a shutdown because agreement had not been reached between President Obama and Congressional Republicans. The crisis was averted only when the White House and Congressional Democrats agreed to $39billion in expenditure cuts. There are other limits upon the president's budgetary powers. The 1974 Congressional Budget and Impoundment Control Act (which was noted above) included provisions preventing a president withholding funds that had been allocated by Congress for a particular purpose. (President Nixon had, for example, cut about $9 billion from funds appropriated for the Environmental Protection Agency.) The Act specified that funds cannot be 'impounded' by the administration unless both houses of Congress give their assent to the action within 45 days. More significantly, the budget-making process is increasingly heavily constrained by earlier economic policy decisions, circumstances, and the consequences of demographic shifts. Increasing numbers of senior citizens have added to the costs of federal government programmes such as Social Security and Medicare. Tax cuts and an extensive patchwork of tax credits have reduced revenue levels. From late 2007 onwards, the recession took its toll on the budget by reducing revenue and creating further demands upon expenditure. The national debt has increased markedly. In other words, there is progressively less space for fiscal manoeuvre or discretionary policymaking.

Presidents have also gained informal powers through the expectation that they will serve as the nation's 'Chief Legislator'. Since Franklin Roosevelt assumed the presidency in 1933 and established the New Deal, it has been accepted that presidents should initiate and propose measures that they hope to see enacted into law. Harry Truman began the practice of presenting an annual package of legislative proposals (Mayhew, 1991: 6). What the president makes of his role as 'Chief Legislator' is another matter. George W. Bush's administration was pro-active both in 'selling' tax cuts as an answer to the economic downturn at the beginning of his years in office and in promoting the 'War on Terror'. President Obama was widely criticised, particularly by fellow Democrats, for what appeared to be a 'hands-off' approach to the passage of keynote legislation, particularly healthcare reform.

Contestation

The power of the presidency is often discussed in unyielding and rather strident terms. Arguably, the phrase 'the imperial presidency' was an exaggeration at the time it was coined, as President Nixon's retreat and downfall shortly thereafter suggest. Its periodic resurrection has taken the phrase to the edges of hyperbole. However, those who talked of the 'imperilled' or 'impaired' presidency are equally guilty. Joseph A. Califano Jr, who served in both Lyndon Johnson's and Jimmy Carter's administrations, claimed that Congress had 'become the King Kong of Washington's political jungle, dominating an executive branch that can no longer claim the co-equal status that the Founding Fathers saw as crucial' (1996: 112). In another allusion to a work of fiction, the president has been likened to Gulliver, who was held down by tiny Lilliputian ropes in Jonathan Swift's classic satire.

Having said this, power' is not a straightforward or unproblematic concept in this or any context. First, as is widely noted, it can be understood only in relational terms. Power involves the ability of an individual or group to induce another individual or group to behave in a way that it would not do otherwise. It is not sufficient to show that an individual or group favoured a particular course of action and others undertook it. In other words, a correlation does not, in itself, demonstrate power. Second, a distinction can be drawn between manifest and latent forms of power. Some displays of power are open and inducements are explicit. In other instances, individuals anticipate the wishes and intentions of others and adjust their preferences and actions accordingly. Third, there are different dimensions of power. It does not just involve decision-making processes. There is also 'agenda-setting'. This refers to the ability to determine or at least influence what issues are at the forefront of the political process and thus a subject for reform and change. Some theorists talk of 'structural power'. This is the often-hidden or latent form of power that arises from the institution, rules, and norms that define the overall political system. Left-leaning theorists suggest, for example, that the corporations have structural power and governments almost instinctively accommodate their interests.

Other commentators point to the ways in which popular preferences can be shaped through processes of cultural hegemony.

As has been noted, although there is no sharp dividing line, a distinction should be drawn between presidential power in the foreign and domestic policy arenas. For the most part, the president has greater leverage in the making of foreign, particularly 'homeland security', policy. Indeed, the late Aaron Wildavsky suggested that there were 'two presidencies'. There is a presidency for managing foreign affairs and a separate presidency for domestic policy formation. Each of these offers distinct opportunities and constraints.

However, there is, in both arenas, a process of formal and informal political contestation or 'jostling' between the two branches of government. This does not take place within a neutral framework. Instead, it takes place on a particular political terrain that is shaped by institutional variables and the legacy of earlier political decisions or processes. That terrain is shaped and contoured by interaction with other political actors, the legacy of earlier policy decisions, broader institutional variables, and the underlying economic and political context.[12]

These variables should be considered in greater depth. First, US Supreme Court rulings and perceptions of what the Court might or might not strike down have had an impact. Trends are always difficult to identify but, in broad terms, the Court has bolstered presidential power within the foreign and defence policy arena while reining it in within domestic policy. In 1936, in the case of *United States v. Curtiss-Wright Export Corporation*, the Supreme Court upheld a 1934 Act allowing the president to embargo arms shipments to foreign combatants in a South American war. In comments that had much wider implications, Justice George Sutherland asserted that the president was 'the sole organ of the federal government in . . . international relations' (*Congressional Quarterly*, 1997: 126). Yet, at the same time. significant parts of the New Deal were struck down in rulings such as *Schechter Poultry Corporation v. United States* (1935) and *United States v. Butler* (1936). The Court regarded the government interventionism upon which the New Deal rested as a threat to individual liberties and the rights of the states and based upon an over-expansive reading of the interstate commerce clause in Article I of the Constitution. President Truman's administration took control of steel mills when they were threatened by strike action (there were fears that industrial action would interrupt supplies destined for the Korean War effort). The Court ruled (in *Youngstown Sheet and Tube Company v. Sawyer*, 1952) that the president's action had been unconstitutional. In other words, the president's military powers did not extend to domestic matters. In 1974, the Supreme Court played a role in the Watergate crisis. Its judgement in *United States v. Richard M. Nixon* circumscribed the concept of 'executive privilege' by ruling that the president must release transcripts of the tape recordings that had been made of his conversations with aides. In the 1990s, the president's sphere of privacy was narrowed down still further. In a succession of court battles, arising from an allegation of sexual harassment against President Bill Clinton and Kenneth Starr's investigations, it was established that civil proceedings could be brought against a sitting president and White House political and legal advisers could be questioned and compelled to answer under oath.

Second, the president faces a further set of constraints. In contrast with those who lead nations that have a *unitary* structure, where sovereignty and core decision-making processes are centralised, the US has a *federal* structure. In a number of policy spheres, therefore, decision-making rests upon a bartering process between the president, Congress, state governors, and state legislatures. However, the character of that bartering and the amount of political space open to an administration shifts over time and is dependent upon court rulings, the political resources that are held, the logic of economic growth (which has tended to reduce regional and state-based disparities), and the prevailing national mood which has at times sought the imposition of national standards and rights.

Third, the changing character of the mass media (as well as the rise of think tanks and web-based outlets) has had consequences for the relative position of the presidency. As Michael Foley and John Owens note: 'Instead of a near monopoly of foreign policy information and reflexive Cold War deference to presidential judgement, presidents are now besieged by a multiplicity of groups and organisations not only with information sources and evaluation techniques of their own but with the means and willingness to challenge a president's foreign policy decisions on tactical, strategic, and ethical grounds' (1996: 380). This process has taken place in tandem with a long-term breakdown of public trust in many institutions and office-holders, including the presidency.

Fourth, as noted in Chapters 2 and 5, there have been significant shifts in the character of partisanship. These have had consequences for the White House. Although President Obama initially hoped that the fiscal stimulus package put before Congress just after he took office would win across substantial numbers of Republicans, it secured no Republican votes in the House of Representatives and just three in the Senate (although they were sufficient to cross the 60 vote threshold that is required under Senate rules). For Obama, it was an introduction to the harsh realities of contemporary partisanship. Whereas, a half-century ago, a presidential could reasonably hope to construct broad cross-party coalitions in Congress around particular measures, that prospect is now largely utopian.[13] At the same time, however, this does not mean that presidents are assured of legislative success if their own party holds majorities within Congress. Within both of the major parties, there is an acute sensitivity to core constituencies that impedes the granting of concessions and the process of compromise that is always required when legislation is under consideration. There is, for example, a reluctance to endorse measures that senior citizens might perceive as a threat to their interests. In other words, all the difficulties associated with governance have grown exponentially.

Indeed, there have been increasing references in media commentaries to the 'ungovernability' of the US.

Fifth, economic conditions and underlying economic variables (such as the long-term rate of economic growth or productivity trends) set parameters within which administrations (and legislators) have to function. This is partly because the state of the economy plays a significant part in shaping public opinion and a president's job approval ratings which in turn shape his bargaining abilities. It is also because short-term and long-term economic growth rates have an impact upon federal government revenue and expenditure levels. The period of sustained economic growth during the mid- and late 1990s (there was talk of the 'Goldilocks economy') enabled the Clinton administration to balance the federal government budget and provided a fiscal surplus that, in turn, permitted President George W. Bush to propose tax cuts in 2001.

Sixth, the part played by public opinion should be factored in. Many commentators suggest that public opinion plays a pivotal role in either strengthening or weakening a president. Congress is, as James Q. Wilson has argued, reluctant to oppose a popular president: 'Other things being equal, the more popular the president, the higher the proportion of his bills that Congress will pass' (1992: 344). This conclusion should perhaps be qualified. Poll ratings for the president and his party in Congress often move together. If his party holds the majority there are still opportunities for legislative success. President Obama's approval ratings had fallen from 63 per cent in the first poll taken after his inauguration to 45 per cent in a poll taken in March 2010 the day after the House of Representatives passed the Patient Protection and Affordable Care Act (PollingReport, 2011). At the same time, public opinion is of only limited significance at an aggregate level. Marginal shifts either within particular demographic categories or in particular districts and states have greater potential electoral importance. In other words, some 'publics' matter more than others. The impact of public opinion on the political process also interacts with temporal factors. Traditionally, it was said that there was a 'honeymoon' at the beginning of a presidency during which the passage of legislation was more likely.[14] There will, self-evidently, be a greater reluctance to adopt measures that are likely to be poorly received at the later stages of the electoral cycle. Furthermore, other variables can affect a president's legislative abilities to a rather greater extent than public opinion. As has been widely noted, presidents invariably face serious challenges towards the end of their second term. They become 'lame ducks' as political resources drift away. President Clinton had, despite the impeachment process, job approvals ratings of 60 per cent or more. Indeed, he left the presidency with the highest end-of-office job approval rating of any president since the Second World War. Yet, faced by an intransigent Congress, he was also a 'lame duck' and thereby forced, for want of other opportunities, to turn his attention to foreign affairs and 'statesmanship'.

Seventh, presidents and other political actors face a highly fragmented political system.[15] This does not stem only from the checks and balances imposed by formal institutional structures. It is also rooted in the piecemeal character of political development and social reform. Whereas many of the European countries introduced a 'welfare state' in relatively small number of very large-scale legislative reforms such as the 1946 National Service Act in the UK, the US implemented less far-reaching measures that were limited in scope. They have at the same time become embedded. Medicare, for example, offered assisted healthcare provision to senior citizens. Increasingly, seniors not only valued this form of provision but feared that its extension to other groupings might reduce the quality of the coverage that they were being offered. The US political landscape is littered with groupings and constituencies that have secured advantages, even if some are relatively limited, and will often oppose reforms that seem to place them in jeopardy.

The craft of persuasion

Many accounts stress the possibilities open to presidents despite these obstacles and barriers.

They suggest that a president's personal abilities can be pivotal. Drawing upon President Eisenhower's frustrations at the unresponsiveness of the government apparatus, Richard Neustadt concluded that much depends upon the skills of the individual office-holder:

> 'powers' are no guarantee of power . . . The President of the United States has an extraordinary range of formal powers, of authority in statute law and in the Constitution. Here is testimony that despite his 'powers' he does not obtain results by giving orders – or not, at any rate, merely by giving orders. He also has extraordinary status, *ex officio*, according to the customs of our government and politics. Here is testimony that despite his status he does not get action without argument. Presidential power is the power to persuade. (Neustadt, 1991: 10–11)

What is persuasiveness? It incorporates, Neustadt suggests, charm and the ability to offer a reasoned argument based upon logic. However, it goes beyond this. It involves the strategic use and application of the president's status and authority. It also rests upon the employment of bargaining skills. Governing is a two-way relationship between the president and others who must anticipate his reaction if he is defied or obstructed. For his part, the president can 'trade' the resources of his office: 'With hardly an exception, those who share in governing this country are aware that at some time, in some degree, the doing of *their* jobs, the furthering of *their* ambitions, may depend upon the President of the United States. Their need for presidential action, or their fear of it, is bound to be recurrent if not actually continuous. Their need or fear is his advantage' (Neustadt, 1991: 31).

From the perspective of Neustadt and his co-thinkers, there is, as Tim Hames records, 'almost no ceiling or floor to what a president might achieve. The incumbent may emulate Franklin D. Roosevelt or Warren Harding, depending on his political ability' (Hames, 2000: 67). Lyndon Johnson is widely regarded as a highly effective 'persuader'. A former Senate majority leader, he used his personal ties and skills to build coalitions of support for his civil rights legislation and the 'war on poverty'. Although he used very different forms of persuasion, President Reagan also had a significant measure of success in the early years of his presidency. His administration mobilised allied interest groups behind particular measures and, at the same time, adopted a strategy based on the setting of inflated goals. As Martin Anderson, the President's chief adviser on domestic and economic policy issues, notes, Reagan 'almost always got more than he would have been willing to settle for, because in the beginning he instinctively asked for far more than he could reasonably expect to get' (1988: 241).

There is, however, a very different perspective. There is a case for arguing that the stress that these accounts place on the capacity and abilities of individual office-holders is misplaced. Presidents and other elected officials are either constrained or empowered by context and circumstance. From this perspective, presidential 'success' (whether measured through legislative success, public approval or the opinions of historians) owes relatively little to personality or skill. Despite, for example, President Reagan's commitment to an all-embracing conservative revolution, he could secure only a small proportion of his overall political goals. Indeed, if the size of government is measured by considering government spending as a share of Gross Domestic Product (GDP), government was larger at the end of his period of office than at the time of his inauguration (US Government Spending, 2010).

For some, an emphasis on the constraints imposed by context and circumstance leads to claims that presidents can achieve relatively little. There is certainly evidence to support such an argument. There are long periods (including for example President Clinton's second term) when there were few landmark legislative achievements. When major reforms were enacted, such as the reform of welfare provision or the measures adopted during the period of economic crisis that hit the US from late 2007 onwards, it was because exceptional circumstances opened a 'window' of opportunity.

Other theorists instead suggest that there are long-term cyclical processes that periodically allow or indeed facilitate reform while at the same time curtailing the likelihood of substantive change for long periods. Their accounts are underpinned, either explicitly or implicitly, by a sense that there is an interaction between structural variables and human agency. In *The Politics that Presidents Make*, Stephen Skowronek argues that every president has to relate to an existing order or 'regime'.[16] He may be opposed to, or affiliated with, the regime. Skowronek represents their efforts to do this in terms of a typology based upon four types of presidential politics. These are the politics of reconstruction, the politics of articulation, the politics of disjunction, and the politics of pre-emption. As the name suggests, reconstructive presidents (such as Franklin Roosevelt or, before him, Andrew Jackson and Abraham Lincoln) challenge the existing regime and lead the political system and the electorate towards fundamental restructuring and reform. (Having said this, however, there has been a process of long-term institutional 'thickening' and the scope of reconstruction has necessarily become more limited.) Articulating presidents maintain the changed regime that they inherited at a time when it enjoys a broad coalition of support. Dwight Eisenhower and Lyndon Johnson loosely fit the category. What policy innovation there is builds upon what has gone before. Disjunctive presidents seek to hold together and maintain a weakened and vulnerable regime that is coming under political fire. (President Herbert Hoover is an oft-cited example.) Pre-emptive presidents oppose the existing regime but lack the opportunities for reconstruction. They cannot create sufficiently strong or broad coalitions (Skowronek, 1993).

Conclusion

News coverage in both the US and across the globe devotes endless attention to the personal attributes of Individual presidents. In much of western Europe, President George W. Bush was regarded in very critical terms while Barack Obama was seen, particularly in the early stages of his presidency, in almost adulatory terms. The importance of theoretical perspectives and models such as those introduced in studies such as *The Politics that Presidents Make* is that they stress the limits and constraints facing office-holders. They draw upon the *institutionalist* approaches. However, the difficulty that some institutionalist accounts face (and this is considered more fully in Chapter 8) is in explaining the motor (or driving force) of change and the degree of discretion (or choice) open to particular actors. In other words, are presidents prisoners of circumstances or do their personalities and approaches to decision-making matter?

Notes

1 In 1919–20, President Woodrow Wilson submitted the Treaty of Versailles to the US Senate. Fearful of further entanglements in European affairs, the Senate put forward amendments, and, following the rejection of these, refused ratification. In the wake of this, the US followed an isolationist course for the following two decades. In 1980, President Jimmy Carter withdrew SALT-II (the Strategic Arms Limitation Treaty that he had concluded with the USSR) once it had become clear that, in the aftermath of the Soviet invasion of Afghanistan, the Treaty

would be rejected by the Senate. The House of Representatives may also secure a role if a treaty has funding provisions or implications (Krutz and Peake, 2011: 29–30).

2 Despite the political hazards, Congress has also used its 'power of the purse'. In December 1970, it prohibited funding for combat troops in Cambodia and, in June 1973, this was extended to the remainder of South-east Asia. In 1976, Cuban military forces were deployed in Angola so as to support the Soviet-aligned government against western-oriented guerrilla armies. Although the US is traditionally fearful of Cuban operations, Congress was haunted by the prospect of another Vietnam, and specifically denied funding for military activities in the country. Control over funding was also used to hasten the withdrawal of US forces from the Lebanon in 1984.

3 It should be noted, however, that, although executive agreements often appear as examples of unilateral presidential power, a significant proportion rest upon the earlier passage of legislation by Congress or follow on from treaty obligations and have limits placed upon them (Krutz and Peake, 2011: 43).

4 There has, however, been a process of contestation or 'jostling' over measures such as the Case–Zablocki Act. The measure certainly did nothing to stem the flow of executive agreements. Indeed, between 1985 and 1989, the Reagan White House signed 1271 international agreements, only 47 of which were treaties. Furthermore, as John Dumbrell records, 'even the reporting provisions of the Case Act have been evaded and undermined by persistent executive delay' (1997: 135).

5 An exception is made if Congress is 'physically unable to meet as a result of an armed attack on the United States'.

6 According to Fisher and Adler, 'The Constitution vests in Congress the sole and exclusive authority to initiate military hostilities, including full-blown, total war, as well as lesser acts of armed force' (Fisher and Adler, 1998: 6).

7 Some also point to the absence of enforcement mechanisms in the War Powers Act. Should Congressional majorities wish to bring a military operation to a close, Congress can only impeach and try the president or bring legal proceedings. Small groups of Congress members have, in the past, on occasions sought to bring proceedings but without success. There were, for example, two suits against President Reagan, one against President George H.W. Bush, and one against President Clinton (Lemar, 2003: 1059).

8 The United Nations Security Council had authorised member states 'to take all necessary measures to protect civilians and civilian populated areas under threat of attack in the Libyan Arab Jamhariya, including Benghazi, while excluding an occupation force'.

9 Since the early 1970s, it has been accepted that the pocket veto can be used only immediately before the end of a two-year Congressional term, rather than during the days preceding a recess.

10 If Congress *is* in session, and the president takes no action, the bill becomes law at the end of the ten-day period. This mechanism can thus be used by a president to convey a lack of enthusiasm for a measure.

11 The budget calendar is, however, honoured more in the breach than the observance. 'Continuing resolutions' are used to fund the federal government if, as is commonplace, the budget process has not been completed by the end of September.

12 For his part, Charles O. Jones argues that presidents 'face the challenge of governing under the contrary political conditions set by the American voters, the competitive institutional conditions created by a reformed Congress, and the policy conditions resulting from the huge post-Great Society self-generating agenda' (1995: 55–56).

13 However, as noted in Chapter 5, Republicans presidents have had more success in winning across Congressional Democrats.

14 Some have attributed the 'honeymoon' to the 'coattails effect' (by which some members of the president's party of Congress owe their seats to the presidential campaign) or to patterns of deference towards the White House. Partisanship may, however, have destroyed the 'honeymoon'. President Obama's 'honeymoon' was short, perhaps non-existent.

15 See Chapter 1.

16 By 'regime', Skowronek is referring the dominant public philosophy (such as the commitment to government interventionism during the New Deal era), the policies that are pursued, and a 'carrier party' which is tied to both policies and philosophy. Skowronek suggests that there have been five 'regimes' in US history.

References and further reading

American Civil Liberties Union (2010), *Establishing a New Normal: National Security, Civil Liberties, and Human Rights under the Obama Administration*, New York: American Civil Liberties Union.

Anderson, M. (1988), *Revolution*, San Diego, Harcourt Brace Jovanovich.

Bennett, A. J. (1996), *The American President's Cabinet: From Kennedy to Bush*, Basingstoke, Macmillan.

Califano, J. A. (1996), 'Imperial Congress', in B. Stinebrickner (ed.), *American Government 96/97*, Guilford, CT, Dushkin Publishing Group, pp. 91–93.

Congressional Quarterly (1997), *Powers of the Presidency*, Washington DC, Congressional Quarterly.

Cooper, H. and S. L. Myers (2011), 'Obama takes hard line with Libya after shift by Clinton', *The New York Times*, 18 March, www.nytimes.com/2011/03/19/world/africa/19policy.html.

Dumbrell, J. (1997), *The Making of US Foreign Policy*, Manchester: Manchester University Press.

Fisher, L. and D. G. Adler (1998), 'The War Powers Resolution: time to say goodbye', *Political Science Quarterly*, 113:1, 1–20.

Foley, M. and J. E. Owens (1996), *Congress and the Presidency: Institutional Politics in a Separated System*, Manchester, Manchester University Press.

Grimmett, R. F. (2004), *RL32267 – The War Powers Resolution: After Thirty Years*, Washington DC: Congressional Research Service, www.fas.org/man/crs/RL32267.html.

Grimmett, R. F. (2010), *Instances of Use of United States Armed Forces Abroad, 1798–2009*, Congrerssional Research Service, 27 January.

Hames, T. (2000), 'Presidential power and the Clinton presidency', in A. Grant, '*American Politics: 2000 and Beyond*, Aldershot, Ashgate, pp. 65–83.

Isikoff, M. (2010), 'Report: Bush lawyer said president could order civilians to be "mas-sacred"', *Newsweek*, 20 February www.newsweek.com/blogs/declassified/2010/02/19/report-bush-lawyer-said-president-could-order-civilians-to-be-massacred.html.

Jones, C. O. (1995), *Separate but Equal Branches: Congress and the Presidency*, Chatham, Chatham House Publishers.

Kaye, J. (2010), 'Thwarting Congressional oversight via presidential signing state-ments', The Public Record, 28 April, http://pubrecord.org/politics/7515/thwarting-congressional-oversight/.

Krutz, G. S. and J. S. Peake (2011), *Treaty Politics and the Rise of Executive Agreements: International Commitments in a System of Shared Powers*, Ann Arbor: The University of Michigan Press.

Lemar, A. D. (2003), 'War powers: what are they good for?: Congressional disapproval of the president's military actions and the merits of a Congressional suit against the president', *Indiana Law Journal*, 78, 1045–1068.

Lithwick, D. (2008), 'Wrestling over war powers', *Newsweek*, 12 July, www.newsweek.com/2008/07/11/wrestling-over-war-powers.html.

Mayhew, D. R. (1991), *Divided We Govern: Party Control, Lawmaking and Investigations, 1946–1990*, New Haven, CT, Yale University Press.

Mervin, D. (1993), *The President of the United States*, New York, Harvester Wheatsheaf.

Neustadt, R. (1991), *Presidential Power and the Modern Presidents*, New York, The Free Press.

New York Times (2011), 'Libya and the War Powers Act', *The New York Times*, 16 June, www.nytimes.com/2011/06/17/opinion/17fri1.html.

O'Brien, M. (2011), 'Obama signs bill to keep government open, but protects "czars"', *The Hill*, 15 April, www.thehill.com/blogs/blog-briefing-room/news/156439-obama-signs-bill-to-keep-government-open-disregards-limit-on-czars.

Parmet, H. S. (1997), *George Bush: The Life of a Lone Star Yankee*, New York, Scribner.

Peters, B. G. (1986), *American Public Policy: Promise and Performance*, Basingstoke, Macmillan.

Pfiffner, J. (2000), *The Modern Presidency*, Boston, Bedford / St Martin's.

Plano, J. and M. Greenberg (1989), *The American Political Dictionary*, Fort Worth, TX, Holt, Rinehart and Winston.

PollingReport (2011), *President Obama: Job Ratings*, www.pollingreport.com/obama_job.htm.

Reich, R. B. (1998), *Locked in the Cabinet*, New York, Vintage Books.

Rossiter, C. (1963), *The American Presidency*, London, Harvest Books.

Shaw, D. (2011), 'GOP pulls Libya war powers resolution from the floor because it might pass', *OpenCongress*, 1 June, www.opencongress.org/articles/view/2305-GOP-Pulls-Libya-War-Powers-Resolution-from-the-Floor-Because-It-Might-Pass.

Shipman, T. (2008), 'Donald Rumsfeld made Condoleezza Rice cry in the White House', *The Daily Telegraph*, 20 September, www.telegraph.co.uk/news/worldnews/northamerica/usa/3023268/Donald-Rumsfeld-made-Condoleezza-Rice-cry-in-the-White-House.html.

Skowronek, S. (1993), *The Politics Presidents Make: Leadership from John Adams to George Bush*, Cambridge, MA, Belknap Press.

Speaker of the House John Boehner (2011), *Press Release - Statement by Speaker*

Boehner on Libya and the War Powers Resolution, 17 June, www.speaker.gov/News/ DocumentSingle.aspx?DocumentID=247461.

The DISAM Journal (2011), Presidential Determination, April 26, 2011 Drawdown in Support of Libya (Federal Register / Vol. 76, No. 93 / Friday, May 13, 2011 /), www. disamjournal.org/news/presidential-determination-april-26-2011-drawdown-in-support-of-libya-124.

The White House (2011), *United States Activities in Libya*, www.washingtonpost.com/ wp-srv/politics/documents/united-states-activities-libya.html.

US Government Spending (2010), *Time Series Chart of US Government Spending*, http:// www.usgovernmentspending.com/downchart_gs.php?year=1970_2009&view= 1&expand=&units=p&fy=fy11&chart=F0-total&bar=1&stack=1&size=m&title=& state=US&color=c&local=s.

Wilson, J. Q. (1992), *American Government: Institutions and Policies*, Lexington, MA, D. C. Heath.

Wilson, S. (2011), 'Obama administration: Libya action does not require congressional approval', *The Washington Post*, 15 June, www.washingtonpost.com/ politics/obama-administration-libya-action-does-not-require-congressional-approval/2011/06/15/AGLttOWH_story.html.

Youngman, S. (2011), 'White House: Obama's signing statements "entirely consistent", *The Hill*, 16 April, http://thehill.com/homenews/administration/156465-white-house-defends-obama-use-of-signing-statements-as-entirely-consistent.

7

The US Supreme Court, jurisprudence, and rights

Constitutions require interpretation. This is partly because particular words and phrases inevitably have an ambiguous or subjective character. The Preamble to the US Constitution specified that one of its purposes was to 'promote the general Welfare'. How narrowly or broadly should the term be understood? What does the 'equal protection of the laws', guaranteed in the Fourteenth Amendment, mean in practice? What conditions must be met if an individual accused of a crime is to be afforded 'due process of law' as required by the Fifth and Fourteenth Amendments? Difficulties also arise because the commonly accepted meaning of particular words and phrases has changed over time. What, today, constitutes the 'cruel and unusual punishment' that is prohibited by the Eighth Amendment? Should this be understood as its authors probably intended or should more modern forms of meaning be employed? The extent and scope of Constitutional provisions also has to be determined. Does, for example, the random checking of bags on a bus in a search for illegal drugs, by feeling their contents from the outside, breach the Fourth Amendment's prohibition of 'unreasonable searches and seizures'? Furthermore, words and phrases have implications that go beyond the immediate text. How far should these implications be considered or should those who interpret the Constitution attempt to disregard these?

All these questions are of far-reaching political importance. They shape public policy towards the powers of government and the rights of the individual. However, they are determined by the federal courts rather than the elected branches of government.[1] Their role is drawn from their power of *judicial review*. Although the Constitution assigned the Supreme Court and the lower federal courts other functions, including that of ruling on disputes involving the United States government, resolving controversies between states, and hearing cases arising under federal law, the courts can, if an appropriate case is brought before them, assess the *constitutionality* of any law passed, or action undertaken by either the federal government or the state governments. Laws and actions can be declared null and void, or *struck down*, if the courts conclude

that they are unconstitutional. While judicial review is not specifically identified in Article III of the Constitution, Supreme Court Chief Justice John Marshall
(who held the office from 1801 to 1835) claimed the right when ruling in the
case of *Marbury v. Madison* (1803). He asserted: 'It is emphatically the province
and duty of the judicial department to say what the law is.' The Court's power
of judicial review has been accepted and unchallenged ever since.

Since 1869, the Supreme Court has had a membership of nine. Most of
the cases that it considers will have first been heard by a lower federal court,
although it sometimes considers appeals that have been brought directly from
the state courts if constitutional issues are involved. The lower federal courts,
which hear cases arising under both the Constitution and federal law, consist of
the circuit courts of appeal and, on a lower tier, US district courts. There are 13
regional circuits, each of which has a court of appeals. They all consider appeals
from the US district courts located within their particular circuit. Furthermore,
the Court of Appeals for the Federal Circuit has national jurisdiction to hear
appeals in highly technical cases such as those involving patent laws.

For their part, the states have their own judicial systems that interpret and
apply state laws. Their courts have jurisdiction over almost all matters that are
not subject to federal jurisdiction. These Include most criminal and civil cases.
This chapter considers the role of the US Supreme Court and the lower federal
courts. It surveys the appointments process, and assesses the Court's powers.
It asks whether the US has 'government by judiciary' or if the Court is, as some
have claimed, 'the least dangerous branch'? It also considers other debates.
What approaches should judges on the Supreme Court bench adopt in making
their rulings? Some call for judicial activism, and argue that the Court should
use its powers in a pro-active way so as extend individual and collective rights.
Others, however, favour judicial restraint.

Appointing the judges

Federal judges are appointed by the president with 'the advice and consent
of the Senate' (Article II, Section 2). Although there are no official criteria, a
number of variables often play a part in the appointments process.

First, an appointee is almost always associated with the same political party
as the president. As Robert McKeever notes: 'An examination of the history of
presidential nominations to the Supreme Court reveals one overwhelming fact
. . . In only a handful of almost 150 nominations to the Court has the President
gone outside of his party for a Supreme Court nominee. This tradition was
firmly established by George Washington' (McKeever, 1997: 122).

Second, the president will appoint those who he believes broadly share his
political and judicial philosophy. The judges nominated during the Reagan era
were either moderate or more committed conservatives. Their ranks included
Antonin Scalia, while William Rehnquist was elevated to become Chief Justice.

Both were markedly unsympathetic towards affirmative action programmes and the rights of criminal suspects. Their rulings have had a consistently conservative character. For his part, President Barack Obama has selected Sonia Sotomayor and Elena Kagan, both forceful judges who were, like Obama himself, moderate liberals.[2]

Third, judges are expected to be legally qualified, to have practised law, and to have had judicial experience. From the days of President Eisenhower, the American Bar Association (ABA), the professional body for lawyers, was assigned a quasi-official role. For about fifty years, the administration sent the names of nominees to the ABA for scrutiny before they were publicly announced. Through its Standing Committee on Federal Judiciary, the ABA assessed the qualifications of, and assigned ratings for, potential appointees. Each was rated well qualified, qualified, or not qualified. This was decided, in the words of the Committee, on the basis of 'the professional competence, integrity, and judicial temperament of candidates'.

However, in March 2001 the Bush administration ended this practice. The White House announced that, from then on, the ABA was to lose its special role. Instead, the administration would invite comments on its nominees from a broad range of individuals and organisations (*New York Times*, 2001). From then on, and although the ABA continued to issue ratings of nominees, the Federalist Society, which is committed to a *strict constructionist* understanding of the US Constitution, secured much more of a role. The administration's decision reflected longstanding conservative criticism of the ABA. Despite its claim to be non-partisan, the Association is, they assert, guilty of liberal bias. Conservative nominees, they claim, have not been awarded the ratings that their judicial accomplishments merited. For example, to the chagrin of many on the right, Clarence Thomas, who was nominated by President Bush in 1991, was deemed only to be 'qualified'.

Fourth, it is now accepted that there should be a degree of diversity on the Supreme Court bench. Thurgood Marshall, the first African-American, was appointed in 1967. Sandra Day O'Connor, appointed by Reagan in 1981, was the first female Justice on the Supreme Court. Between 1916 and 1969, there was a 'Jewish seat' on the Court (McKeever, 1997: 124). President Obama's first two appointments to the US Supreme Court bench were both women. One of these nominees, perhaps reflecting the changing demographic character of the US, was also a Latina.

Fifth, abortion has become a pivotal or 'litmus test' issue. In practice, although other issues are also considered, a nominee's attitude towards abortion is critical. Although Republican presidents will, when making appointments, have to consider the composition of the Senate, their nominees will, at the least, be broadly sympathetic towards 'pro-life' arguments. A Democratic president's nominee will have broadly 'pro-choice' attitudes. Democrats have also increasingly looked for evidence in a nominee's record of empathy with lower-income groupings and the 'powerless' (see below).

Confirmation

Presidential nominations have traditionally been accepted by the Senate, but confirmation cannot be assured. Since the founding of the US, 11 nominations to the Supreme Court have been rejected and others have had to be withdrawn or postponed. However, only five of these rejections were in the twentieth century (Ragsdale, 1996: 422–423). In 1968, President Lyndon Johnson's nominee for Chief Justice, Abe Fortas, faced a filibuster. In 1969 and 1970, the Senate opposed two of Nixon's nominees, Clement F. Haynesworth and G. Harrold Carswell, who were accused of ethical violations and segregationist sympathies respectively.

Nonetheless, in recent decades, the confirmation process for US Supreme Court nominees (and for those who hope to serve on the lower courts) has become much more ideologically charged. The focus has shifted from personal failings to political issues. The Bork nomination is widely seen as a turning point. In 1987, Reagan nominated Robert Bork, a former law professor, a justice on the DC Court of Appeals and a leading advocate of judicial restraint who had criticised what he saw as social engineering by the courts. He faced fierce opposition from many on the left. If confirmed, it was said in television commercials produced by liberal advocacy organisations, Bork would seek to overturn the 1954 Brown ruling and take the US back to the days of segregation. The Senate rejected the nomination by 58 to 42 votes.[3] From then onwards, there was periodic talk of Senate efforts to 'Bork' presidential nominees.

Subsequent nominees also faced sustained ideological challenges. Although President George H.W. Bush won a narrow victory (by 52 to 48 votes) in 1991 when he nominated Clarence Thomas, a conservative black judge, to replace Thurgood Marshall, there was strong opposition on ideological grounds that echoed the arguments against Bork. There were also claims of sexual harassment by a former assistant. Thomas described his televised interrogation by the Senate Judiciary Committee as a 'high-tech lynching'. In 2005, following the retirement of Sandra Day O'Connor and the death of Chief Justice William Rehnquist, President George W. Bush nominated the White House Counsel Harriet Miers to take O'Connor's place. There was a wave of criticism, particularly from within the conservative movement. Miers was said to be inexperienced and, most importantly of all, there were doubts about her commitment to strict constructionism and her position on core issues such as abortion. There were fears that she could not withstand the demands of the Senate confirmation process. Just over three weeks after the nomination was made, Miers withdrew from consideration. President Bush's other nominations encountered less difficulty. John Roberts took William Rehnquist's place as Chief Justice by a 78-22 vote in the Senate (the Senate Democrats were split down the middle), and Samuel Alito, a much more committed conservative who was nominated following Miers's withdrawal, was sworn in after winning the Senate vote by 58-42. Those who opposed these nominations were concerned with the nominees' ideological dispositions, their basic instincts, and their records in both politics and jurisprudence. The newly elected junior senator for Illinois conveyed this as he explained why he was opposing the confirmation of John Roberts:

> what matters on the Supreme Court is those 5 percent of cases that are truly diffi-cult . . . In those 5 percent of hard cases, the constitutional text will not be directly on point. The language of the statute will not be perfectly clear. Legal process alone will not lead you to a rule of decision. In those circumstances, your deci-sions about whether affirmative action is an appropriate response to the history of discrimination in this country or whether a general right of privacy encom-passes a more specific right of women to control their reproductive decisions or whether the commerce clause empowers Congress to speak on those issues of broad national concern that may be only tangentially related to what is easily defined as interstate commerce, whether a person who is disabled has the right to be accommodated so they can work alongside those who are nondisabled – in those difficult cases, the critical ingredient is supplied by what is in the judge's heart. (*Wall Street Journal*, 2009)

Over time, Republican opposition to Democratic nominees has also become much more pronounced. Clinton had little trouble in his nominations of the centrist liberals Ruth Bader Ginsburg and Stephen G. Breyer, who were appointed in 1993 and 1994 respectively. They secured Senate confirma-tion by votes that a decade or so later seem to strain credulity: 96-3 and 87-9. President Obama had a very different experience. His nominees – Sonia Sotomayor and Elena Kagan – won confirmation by 68-31 and 63-37 respec-tively. Both faced determined Republican opposition, reflecting the intense partisanship and polarisation that characterises contemporary Congressional politics.[4] There were claims that both Sotomayor and Kagan would make social policy from the bench. Their ideas were said to be out-of-step with main-stream American opinion. In opposing her confirmation, Republican Senator Orrin Hatch (Utah) said that Kagan had 'endorsed, and praised those who endorse, an activist judicial philosophy' (quoted in Greenhouse, 2011).

The lower courts

Although the Supreme Court is usually the focus of attention, lower federal court nominations should also be considered. The Circuit Courts of Appeal are of particular importance. Because the US Supreme Court hears so few cases, the Courts of Appeal make rulings and often set precedents that have to be respected. Table 7.1 shows the confirmation rate (the proportion of those nominated by the president that is confirmed by the Senate) between 1977, when Jimmy Carter took office, and the end of George W. Bush's presidency in January 2009. As it suggests, although there have been fluctuations in the

Table 7.1 *The lower federal courts - nominations and Senate confirmations,*
1977–2009

	Courts of Appeal nominations	Confirmations	US district court nominations	Confirmations
Jimmy Carter	61	56 (92%)	223	203 (91%)
Ronald Reagan	94	83 (88%)	309	290 (94%)
George H.W. Bush	53	42 (79%)	187	148 (79%)
Bill Clinton	90	66 (73%)	348	305 (87%)
George W. Bush	84	60 (71%)	284	261 (92%)

Source: adapted from: Russell Wheeler (2011) *Judicial Nominations and Confirmations in the 111th Senate and What to Look For in the 112th* (Washington DC: Governance Studies at Brookings), 2, www.brookings.edu/~/media/Files/rc/papers/2011/0104_judicial_nominations_wheeler/0104_judicial_nominations_wheeler.pdf.

Table 7.2 *Lower federal court confirmation rates, 1993–2010*

	1993–94	2001–2	2003–4	2005–6	2007–8	2009–10
Courts of Appeal	86	52	55	57	45	67
US district courts	91	85	91	55	75	67

Source: adapted from: Russell Wheeler (2011) *Judicial Nominations and Confirmations in the 111th Senate and What to Look For in the 112th* (Washington DC: Governance Studies at Brookings), 2, http://www.brookings.edu/~/media/Files/rc/papers/2011/0104_judicial_nominations_wheeler/0104_judicial_nominations_wheeler.pdf.

confirmation rate for the district courts, there has been a consistent downward trend in the confirmation rate for the Circuit Courts of Appeal.

Presidents are in office for relatively long periods and attempts to assess trends on the basis of presidential tenure can hide significant variations. Table 7.2 considers confirmation rates in particular Congressional sessions. As it suggests, whereas there were very high confirmation rates at the beginning of Bill Clinton's presidency (a period when partisanship was less entrenched and of unified government whereby both the White House and Congress were under the control of the same party), they were markedly lower during much (although not all) of the Bush and Obama presidencies.

At the same time, the confirmation process slowed down. Indeed, as Table 7.3 shows, the time taken to confirm nominees more than doubled between the Clinton and Obama presidencies.

These figures reflect the increasingly bitter partisan divisions and the politicisation of the Senate confirmation process that was noted above. During both the Clinton and Bush administrations, there were accusations that the Senate was using delaying tactics so as to obstruct nominations to the district and appeal courts. In the latter half of the 1990s, the Republicans, it was said, used their majority to delay President Clinton's nominees. A study found that

Table 7.3 *Lower federal courts – average number of days between nomination and confirmation, 1993–2011*

	Courts of appeal	District courts to confirmation
Bill Clinton	103	76
George W. Bush	236	139
Barack Obama (until January 2011)	260	175

Source: adapted from: Russell Wheeler (2011) *Judicial Nominations and Confirmations in the 111th Senate and What to Look For in the 112th* (Washington DC: Governance Studies at Brookings), p. 9, www.brookings.edu/~/media/Files/rc/papers/2011/0104_judicial_nominations_ wheeler/0104_judicial_nominations_wheeler.pdf.

in 1992 the Democrat-controlled Senate took an average of 92 days to hold hearings on the Republican President George Bush's nominations for district judges. However, by 1998, the Republican Senate took an average of 160 days to hold hearings on Clinton's nominees (Ohio State University, 1999). In turn, once George Bush became president, the Democrats used Senate rules, in particular the ability to place a hold on a nominee and the threat of a filibuster, to obstruct his judicial appointments. Ten nominees to the Circuit Courts of Appeals were filibustered. In retaliation, Senate Republicans increasingly talked of using what was dubbed the 'nuclear option'. This would have changed the Senate rules so that judicial nominees simply required a majority vote. In the event, and despite a highly charged and partisan atmosphere, a compromise was reached between seven moderate senators from each of the parties (who became known as the 'Gang of 14'). It was agreed that the filibuster threat would be withdrawn for three of the nominees and the filibuster would not be used to obstruct future nominations unless there were 'extraordinary circumstances'. The agreement was, however, only temporary and it expired at the beginning of 2007 when the Democrats retook control of both Congressional chambers. A number of Bush nominees were blocked.

Hearing cases

In a limited number of spheres the Supreme Court has *original jurisdiction*. It can consider cases that are brought before it without having been earlier considered by a lower court. These spheres are specified in the Constitution and include 'controversies between two or more states' or cases involving the US government. However, the majority of cases are *appellate* cases, in which the Court may, at its discretion, consider appeals against decisions made by lower federal courts, state supreme courts, and the US Court of Military Appeals.

In a year, the Court typically receives over eight thousand petitions asking it to review a case (originally heard by a lower court). In 2008–9, there were

7,738 petitions. The decision to hear a case in this way is referred to as grant-ing writ of *certiorari* ('cert'). The judges (or Justices) themselves decide on the granting of 'cert' at weekly meetings. Under the 'rule of four', if at least four of the nine justices wish to consider a particular case, it is heard. Despite sugges-tions that, in practice, the clerks who assist the Justices play a pivotal role in determining which cases are considered, Robert McKeever argues that they do not impose their views: 'most see their role as carrying out the wishes of their Justice. Thus, when they have learned their Justice's tendencies with regard to grants of review, their recommendations will follow suit . . . It seems unlikely, then, that clerks are in a position to substitute their own views for those of the Justices' (McKeever, 1997: 79).

Nonetheless, since the mid-1990s, fewer than a hundred cases have been considered and decided upon annually. Indeed, in 2005–6, it fell to 69 cases although it had risen to 87 by 2009. What variables determine the granting of 'cert'?

- Some issues have long-term significance for society or the political process. This may persuade the Court to hear cases that address the powers of the federal government and the states, race and gender issues, and the counting of votes in the 2000 presidential election.
- A Justice may seek to deny 'cert' despite the importance of a case, if she or he fears that if the case is heard a ruling will be made with which she or he disagrees. As Linda Greenhouse (2006) argues, this becomes more likely on questions such as abortion on which the Court is deeply divided. Outcomes can be unpredictable.
- There are sometimes tensions between the circuit courts of appeal when they have made different rulings about similar cases. The Supreme Court may see it as its responsibility to resolve this by hearing the cases.
- The Court is more likely to hear a case if the federal government, repre-sented by the Solicitor General, is seeking the review of it.
- There are legal rules governing which cases may be heard. A case may, for example, be 'moot' if the circumstances that gave rise to it no longer hold. Those bringing a case must have 'standing', in so far as they must have been personally disadvantaged by a denial of constitutional rights and therefore be seeking redress.

Although oral arguments are put forward, and lawyers for each of the parties to the case are granted 30 minutes to present their case, they may play only a marginal role. It is also difficult to determine the role of *amicus curiae* briefs that may have been submitted by interest and advocacy groups that are lobbying for particular outcomes.[5] The more important deliberations take place in private both before and after the oral hearings. Case conferences are held. These are presided over by the Chief Justice but his powers are limited and he (so far all have been men) is not always in the majority.

Court decisions require only a simple majority, and 5–4 rulings, such as that made in *Bush v. Gore* (2000), are common. When the ruling is announced, written opinions are also published. These outline and explain the legal reasoning underpinning a vote. Opinions can take three forms: the *majority opinion*, which explains the basis for the Court's decision; a *concurring opinion*, which agrees with the decision but bases it on different legal grounds; and a *dissenting opinion*. This allows a minority to express its reasoning for opposing the decision. All the opinions are subject to considerable examination and debate. Between 20 and 30 per cent of cases are unanimous.

How much power?

Some commentators believe that the federal courts are too powerful. Raul Berger made this claim in *Government by Judiciary*, originally published in 1977. He asserts that the Supreme Court has been engaged, particularly through its rulings on the Fourteenth Amendment, in a 'continuing revision of the Constitution, under the guise of "interpretation" that has subverted our democratic institutions' (1997). Others argue that the federal courts have more limited powers. They echo the words of Alexander Hamilton in *The Federalist 78* (1788):

> the judiciary, from the nature of its functions, will always be the least dangerous to the political rights of the Constitution; because it will be least in a capacity to annoy or injure them . . . The judiciary . . . has no influence over either the sword or the purse; no direction either of the strength or of the wealth of the society; and can take no active resolution whatever. (Hamilton, 2002)

Those who stress the powers of the Court point to the scope and scale of its judgements. They have reshaped American society and the political process. Much of its history has been associated with three broad and often intertwined constitutional questions. These are the relationship between the federal government and the individual states (federalism), the power of government over the economy, the extent to which protections should be given to disadvantaged groupings, particularly women and minorities, and the rights of the individual.

The federal government and the states

During the early years of the US, there was uncertainty about the role of the national government and the rights of the states. Were the states semi-sovereign nations which had entered into a voluntary compact with each other through the US Constitution or was the US a single nation to which all owed allegiance? Under Chief Justice John Marshall who headed the Court between 1801 and 1835, there were landmark cases that bolstered the position of the federal government. In 1810, in the case of *Fletcher v. Peck*, the Court established that it had the right to declare a state law unconstitutional. Nine years later, in *McCulloch v. Maryland* (1819), the Court established the principle that the federal government had primacy over the states by recognising the right of Congress to create a national bank with a degree of authority over the states' banks. However, the importance of the ruling goes beyond this. Lawyers for the state of Maryland had maintained, because it was not specified in the Constitution, that the federal government did not have the constitutional power to establish a national bank. In rejecting this and making their ruling, the Justices drew upon the final sentence of Article I, Section 8. After listing the specific or 'enumerated' powers of Congress, it stated that Congress could 'make all laws which shall be necessary and proper for carrying into execution the foregoing powers, and all other powers vested by this Constitution in the government of the United States'. In *McCulloch v. Maryland*, the Court established that the 'necessary and proper' clause of the Constitution provided a basis for assigning the federal government a broad range of implied powers that went beyond the wording of the Constitution.

However, as the nineteenth century progressed, the Court became increasingly suspicious of federal government authority, and protective of 'states' rights'. Its rulings rested on notions of *dual federalism*. During the closing years of the century, this led the Court to acquiesce as white southerners regained much of the authority that they had held in the years preceding the Civil War, and imposed a system of segregation across the South. In the case of *Plessy v. Ferguson* (1896), the Court accepted the 'separate but equal' doctrine that underpinned segregation over the half-century that followed.

By the middle of the twentieth century, judicial attitudes had again shifted. The activism of the Warren and Burger Courts (1953–86) represented a sustained attempt to impose uniform standards of justice and citizenship across the nation. *Brown v. Board of Education (Topeka, Kansas)* (1954) declared segregated schooling to be unconstitutional. Although the southern states initially resisted the ruling, and used 'states' rights' as a rallying call, *Brown* eventually came to be accepted. *Baker v. Carr* (1962) established that the electoral districts for state legislatures had to be drawn on the basis of population. There had to be, the Court argued, periodic reapportionment to reflect population shifts. *Roe v. Wade* (1973) asserted that abortion was a constitutional right. In *Furman v. Georgia* (1972), the Court ruled that existing death penalty laws were unconstitutional because sentences were imposed in an arbitrary and random way. All these judgements reined in the decision-making powers and jurisdiction of the state legislatures, thereby triggering sustained protests by those who called for 'states' rights'. At times, this put the Court at odds with the White House. Although the Reagan administration was committed to curbing federal government powers, the Court maintained the centralising trend. In *Garcia v. San Antonio Metropolitan Transit Authority* (1985), the Court allowed the federal government to regulate the wages paid by the city authorities to local bus workers.

By the 1990s, however, there had been a significant shift in attitude on the part of the Court. It increasingly leant towards states' rights and curtailed federal government powers. In May 1995, Linda Greenhouse of the *New York Times* concluded on the basis of the Court's federalism rulings: 'it is only a slight exaggeration to say that . . . the Court [is] a single vote shy of reinstalling the Articles of Confederation' (quoted in Dinan, 2010: 163). This was undoubtedly an exaggeration but John Dinan rightly stresses the extent to which there was a departure from the jurisprudence of earlier years: 'only two congressional statutes were overturned on federalism grounds in the half-century prior to Rehnquist assuming the role of Chief Justice, and both rulings were soon reversed' (Dinan, 2010: 159).[6] The Court struck down a statute requiring states to establish sites for the disposal of radioactive waste generated by businesses. In 1995, the Court stressed the constitutional limits on the role of the federal government. In *United States v. Lopez*, the Court declared the Gun-Free School Zones Act unconstitutional. Washington, the Court argued, did not have the power that it had claimed under the interstate commerce clause of the Constitution to restrict the possession of a gun within 1000 feet of a school (McKeever, 1997: 45). Appropriate legislation was, the judges asserted, a matter for the individual states. The commitment to 'states' rights' that underpinned the *Lopez* ruling also informed a series of subsequent judgements such as *Kimel v. Florida Board of Regents* and *United States v. Morrison* (2000). *Kimel* established in a 5-4 ruling that states are protected from lawsuits alleging age discrimination. The states, the Court asserted, have sovereign immunity. The judgement struck down the Age Discrimination in Employment Act. The Court was stating, in effect, that state employees hoping for the redress of a grievance should seek a remedy under state discrimination laws rather than federal law. In *United States v. Morrison* (a 5-4 ruling), the Court struck down a core provision of the 1994 Violence Against Women Act, which stated that '[A]ll persons within the United States shall have the right to be free from crimes of violence motivated by gender' and allowed women to sue their attackers in federal courts. The Constitution, the Court asserted, did not permit the federal government to make laws on matters such as sexual violence that were the prerogatives of the states. As Chief Justice William Rehnquist asserted:

> We accordingly reject that argument that Congress may regulate non-economic, violent criminal conduct based solely on that conduct's aggregate effect on interstate commerce. The Constitution requires a distinction between what is truly national and what is truly local (Cornell University Law School, 2011)

Government and the economy

As the US became an industrial society, there were increasingly vocal calls for government intervention in economic affairs. The federal and state governments, it was said, should alleviate poverty and urban problems. Monopolies, cartels, and trusts should be restricted. Working hours particularly for those held to be particularly vulnerable should be regulated. The slums and tenement blocks should be cleared.

What role did the US Constitution assign to government? During the late nineteenth and early twentieth centuries, Court decisions reflected the view that it was severely limited. In *Lochner v. New York* (1905), the Court ruled that the state of the New York did *not* have the power to regulate working hours for bakery workers. Its ruling rested on the principle of 'substantive due process' in the Fourteenth Amendment. It was understood to protect the right of an employer to hire workers without external interference.

This limited, *laissez-faire* interpretation of the federal government's role was challenged by the activist interventionism of the New Deal era. Franklin Roosevelt's administration sought through the New Deal, a programme of economic reform and public works, to ensure that the country recovered from the Great Depression that had followed in the wake of the Wall Street Crash. Initially, the Court challenged the constitutionality of key elements in Roosevelt's programme. They were struck down. In May 1935, in *Schechter Poultry Corporation v. United States*, the Court declared that the National Recovery Administration (NRA) which had been created under the National Industrial Recovery Act had acted unconstitutionally by taking action against a Brooklyn business that had been selling diseased chickens. Under the Constitution, the federal government had the power to regulate only interstate, not intrastate, commerce. By defining 'interstate commerce' in a relatively narrow way, the Court placed much of the New Deal in jeopardy. Similarly, Roosevelt's agricultural programme, the 1933 Agricultural Adjustment Act, which restricted agricultural output and imposed a tax on food-processing businesses, was deemed in *United States v. Butler* (1936) to be an unconstitutional extension of the federal government's powers to intervene in the economy.

Roosevelt responded in 1937 by seeking to enlarge the Court beyond the existing nine members to 15. He proposed adding one new Justice to the Court for each existing Justice aged over 70. Although presented as a means by which the Court's workload could be eased, Roosevelt's 'court packing' plan would have enabled him, through the additional appointments, to have gained a majority which would have been sympathetic to the New Deal. However, the proposal met firm resistance in Congress. It was seen as a crude attack on the separation of powers. However, in the wake of the Roosevelt plan, the Court modified its approach and began to consider New Deal legislation in more positive terms. In April 1937, it ruled that the 1935 National Labor Relations Act which had required employers to negotiate with trade union representatives was constitutional. Similarly, Washington state's minimum wage legislation was upheld. The Court's apparent change of heart was described as 'a switch in time that saved nine'.

In the decades that followed the New Deal era, notwithstanding the circumscribed understanding of the interstate commerce clause from the mid-1990s onwards, the Court was cautious in challenging presidential and Congressional actions in the economic field. When the 'Great Recession' hit the US in the 1930s, triggering large-scale federal government intervention in both the financial sector and the broader 'real economy', the Court did not move to take up cases that challenged the constitutionality of the measures that were adopted. The historian Melvin Urofsky has drawn a contrast between the Court in the 1930s and the contemporary bench: 'It's a different Court . . . The Court of the 1930s was extremely conservative, and there was no history of federal involvement in the economy . . . The Court is used to massive intervention in the marketplace now' (quoted in Mauro, 2008).[7]

Equality, race, gender, and sexuality

For much of the nineteenth century, the Court backed the denial of the most basic rights of citizenship to African-Americans. In 1857, in *Dred Scott v. Sanford*, the Court, headed by Chief Justice Roger Taney, declared that the Missouri compromise, an Act of Congress that had allowed former slaves to be free in the new border territories created by westward expansion, was unconstitutional. The Court insisted that the slave, Dred Scott, who had been taken to a free state and had claimed his liberty, be returned to his former owner. The ruling endorsed the legitimacy of slavery and curtailed the rights of the federal government. The outrage that it created among those committed to the abolition of slavery contributed to the election of Abraham Lincoln as president in 1860 and the outbreak of the Civil War some months later.

In 1896, the Court accepted the constitutionality of segregation. In the closing decades of the nineteenth century, southern whites had, despite the victory of the north in the Civil War, progressively reasserted their power. Segregation laws were introduced across the southern states that relegated blacks to separate and invariably inferior public facilities. Segregation extended to education, shops, restaurants, transport, and even the graveyards. The Supreme Court declared in *Plessy v. Ferguson* that the segregation laws were a matter for the states. It was 58 years before the Court took a different view. In September 1953, President Eisenhower appointed the former Governor of California, Earl Warren, as Chief Justice. Despite expectations that it would pursue a conservative course, the Warren Court brought about a judicial revolution. The Court's rulings were pervaded by a spirit of judicial activism. In 1954, in *Brown v. Board of Education (Topeka, Kansas)*, the Court reversed the *Plessy* judgement and declared that segregated schooling was unconstitutional. The relegation of black children to separate schools conveyed a message of inferiority and caused psychological damage. It was a denial of the 'equal protection' required by the fourteenth amendment. A year later, the Court demanded that the desegregation of southern schools should proceed 'with all deliberate speed'.

Earl Warren was succeeded as Chief Justice by Warren E. Burger. While in some respects more cautious than the Warren Court, the Burger Court (1969–86) extended the 'civil rights revolution'. Although the southern states were finally desegregated a decade after the Brown ruling, the US remained a racially divided and unequal society. In both the South and the North, blacks and whites lived in different areas and districts. Even in the absence of restrictive laws, neighbourhood schools were predominantly white or black. Furthermore, blacks were underrepresented in higher education, business, and the professions. In 1971, in *Swann v. Charlotte-Mecklenburg Board of Education*, the Court ruled that school students should be taken by bus to different schools across a city so as to ensure a broad racial balance in each school. The Court also considered affirmative action. Such programmes are derived from a conception of equality based not on opportunity but on outcome. Their supporters assert that disparities of income and achievement between the races, ethnic groupings, and genders are, in themselves, evidence of institutionalised discrimination. In their most rigorous form, affirmative action programmes include numerical admissions quotas so as to increase minority representation in a certain field of employment or on a particular educational course. In *Griggs v. Duke Power Company* (1971), the Court outlawed selection tests that were not obviously job-related and produced different pass rates between the races. In making the judgement, Chief Justice Warren Burger focused on 'the *consequences* of employment practices, not simply the motivation' (Thernstrom and Thernstrom, 1997: 430). In *Regents of the University of California v. Allan Bakke* (1978), the Court did not accept the full affirmative action argument. Nevertheless, it ruled, albeit by a narrow majority, that, although concerns for racial equality were not to be the only consideration, educational institutions could include race as a factor when recruiting students. Subsequently, in 1980, in *Fullilove v. Klutznick*, the Court accepted the constitutionality of *set-asides* that awarded a fixed proportion of federal government construction contracts to minority-owned firms.

The civil rights era created the conditions for the emergence of the women's movement. Feminism established itself on the political and judicial agenda. Against this background, the Burger Court ruled in *Roe v. Wade* (1973) that a woman had an unfettered right to an abortion in the first three months of a pregnancy. States were allowed to impose only limited restrictions in the second trimester so as to protect the mother's health. In the final trimester, when the foetus may be viable outside the mother's womb, states might introduce laws restricting abortion, except when a woman's life or health was at risk. A companion ruling, issued on the same day, *Doe v. Bolton*, broadened the meaning of 'health' to include physical, emotional, psychological, and familial factors as well as the woman's age. This extended access to abortion still further. Prior to *Roe*, abortion regulations varied greatly between states, and this ruling circumscribed their ability to make their own laws. The ruling was based, at least for some of the Justices, on an implied right of privacy. Individuals, it was said, had the right to determine certain matters – particularly issues relating to their children – themselves, and the authorities should respect their personal autonomy. Although the concept of privacy is not to be found in the Constitution, the right was drawn, in the words of Justice William O. Douglas, from the 'penumbras and emanations' of the Constitution (McKeever, 1997: 15). The ruling had important consequences. Confirmation hearings increasingly focused on a nominee's attitude towards abortion. Many evangelical Christians were drawn still further towards the political process, creating the preconditions for the emergence of the 'religious right' as a significant political force during the 1980s and 1990s. *Roe* also led an intensification of pressure group activity and the mass mobilisation of both pro-life and pro-choice movements.

Although the overall character of the Court is shaped by other variables apart from the politics of the Chief Justice, the Rehnquist Court (1986–2005) was much more conservative in its thinking. Indeed, some have spoken of a judicial 'counter-revolution' or the 'rolling back' of the judgements made by the Warren and Burger Courts. Rehnquist and other judicial conservatives favour a 'strict constructionist' approach to the process of constitutional interpretation. The Constitution, they assert, should be read narrowly and literally. Uncertainties should be resolved by understanding the intentions of those who wrote the Constitution. Attempts to discern implied rights or apply the spirit of the Constitution to the modern era inevitably lead to the making of public policy on the basis of the judges' personal preferences. They argue for a much more restrictive conception of discrimination than that employed during the Warren and Burger years, one based upon individual instances of unfair treatment rather than on generalised claims that entire groups such as African-Americans have suffered institutionalised disadvantage. Judicial conservatives also emphasise the importance of 'states' rights' and the constraints that the Constitution imposes upon the powers of the national government.

However, while the Rehnquist Court had a broadly conservative stamp, its rulings were not entirely consistent or predictable in character. Instead, the composition of the majority and the minority changed to some extent according to the issue under consideration. Why was this? While Rehnquist, Antonin Scalia, and Clarence Thomas formed an important faction on the bench, conservatives failed to gain a clear majority during the Reagan and Bush era. Indeed, some of the moderate conservatives appointed in this period turned out to be 'swing votes' who sometimes sided with the more liberal members of the Court. Then, in the 1990s, President Clinton had the opportunity to appoint Stephen Breyer and Ruth Bader Ginsburg to the bench. This dashed conservative hopes of full-blown 'counter-revolution'.

These shifts are reflected in the Court's rulings on abortion. There was a partial but limited pull-back from the assertion of abortion rights in *Roe v. Wade*. The basic framework established by the *Roe* ruling did, however, remain intact. In July 1989, in *Webster v. Reproductive Health Services*, the Court upheld the constitutionality of a Missouri law prohibiting the use of state facilities and personnel in the performance of an abortion. Three years later, in June 1992, *Planned Parenthood of Southeastern Pennsylvania v. Casey* permitted states to impose a waiting period before an abortion is carried out, and to require unmarried women aged under 18 to gain the consent of a parent or judge (Hinkson Craig and O'Brien, 1993: 329–41). In 2000 (*Stenberg v. Carhart*), the Court overturned Nebraska's ban on so-called 'partial-birth' abortion. The Nebraska law, the Court asserted, included 'overly broad' language that threatened the continued availability of legal abortions.

The Court's judgements on the constitutionality of affirmative action programmes also had an uneven character. Although the circumstances in which such programmes can be employed have been progressively circumscribed since the *Griggs*, *Bakke* and *Fullilove* rulings (see p. 165), the Court did not, however, rule that they were unconstitutional. In 1989, the Court ruled in *Richmond v. J. A. Croson* that state and local governments could adopt a system of minority set-asides for contracts only if they were addressing specific instances of discrimination. They were to be 'strictly reserved for remedial settings' (Thernstrom and Thernstrom, 1997: 437). Other Court rulings imposed further constraints on affirmative action programmes. *Wards Cove Packing Company v. Antonio* (1989) looked again at company employment policies. It narrowed the grounds on which discrimination could be claimed, but at the same time broadened the basis on which employers could justify the use of particular selection tests and hiring practices. In 1995, *Adarand v. Pena* applied the arguments that underpinned the *Croson* ruling to the award of federal government contracts, and permitted minority set-asides in only narrowly prescribed circumstances. The Court had similar concerns about racial redistricting. In some states, the boundaries between electoral districts had been drawn so as to ensure that there were black or Hispanic majorities. This was intended to increase the overall level of minority representation in Congress. In *Shaw v. Reno* (1993) and *Miller v. Johnson* (1995), the Court rejected redistricting plans in which race was the 'predominant factor'.

A decade and a half later, the Court seemed to land further blows on policy decisions associated with affirmative action. In 2007, *Parents Involved in Community Schools v. Seattle School District No. 1* (and *Meredith v. Jefferson County Board of Education*) prohibited the allocation of students to particular schools solely for the purposes of achieving a racial mix (Findlaw, 2011). There was another significant case two years later. A test had been set for firefighters seeking promotion in New Haven, Connecticut. The test results were then disregarded because the African-American applicants had not achieved particularly high scores and the City of New Haven feared that a legal case could be brought. The firefighters with high scores then themselves brought a case alleging reverse discrimination which was upheld by the US Supreme Court in *Ricci v. DeStefano* (2009).

Nonetheless, these rulings should be placed in perspective. Despite earlier predictions that affirmative action programmes would be 'rolled back', the Rehnquist Court maintained its commitment to diversity as a goal and an acceptance that race could be used as a factor, albeit in a narrowly tailored way and alongside other factors, in the making of recruitment policies. In June 2003, in *Gratz v. Bollinger* and *Grutter v. Bollinger*, the Court reaffirmed the spirit of the *Bakke* ruling. It struck down the University of Michigan's under-graduate admissions policy, which assigned additional points to minority applicants, but allowed the University's Law School to continue considering race and diversity in its recruitment procedures, because these took a relatively flexible and pragmatic form. The *Parents Involved in Community Schools* ruling reiterated that institutions could address the effects of earlier discrimination (Findlaw, 2011).

Gay and lesbian rights have also come to the fore since the 'sexual revolu-tion' of the 1960s and 1970s. In 1986, in the case of *Bowers v. Hardwick*, the Court denied that the right to privacy that some asserted was implied in the Constitution extended to homosexuality. Instead, the legality of homosexual acts was left to the state legislatures. However, in a June 2003 ruling (*Lawrence et al. v. Texas*) that has wide-ranging implications, the Court reversed this. It decided that the right to privacy was broader than had been earlier understood and did include homosexual acts. Indeed, the *Lawrence* ruling spoke of a right to 'liberty'. It derived this from both earlier precedent including the *Griswold* case but also notions of 'substantive due process'. This suggests that the due process clauses in the Constitution offer more than procedural due process whereby the accused are assured of basic rights. Instead, it is based on the claim that due process places limits and imposes bounds upon government authority. The Texas law, which had outlawed gay sex, was thereby struck down. As Justice Anthony Kennedy argued: 'The petitioners are entitled to respect for their private lives. The State cannot demean their existence or control their destiny by making their private sexual conduct a crime' (*Washington Post*, 2003). Subsequent attempts to extend the legal bounds of consensual adult sexual activity have failed. Nonetheless, as Antonin Scalia predicted at the time of the *Lawrence* ruling, it may have begun to pave the way for the constitutional recognition of same-sex marriage. Claims that California's ban on same-sex marriage was unconstitutional have been upheld at US district court level.

Rights and liberties

The Bill of Rights established the basic liberties of the individual. However, since the earliest years of the US, the federal courts have also played a pivotal role in determining the practical meaning of those rights. A succession of cases focused on the rights of criminal suspects. *Gideon v. Wainwright* (1963) laid down that all defendants had a right to an attorney. To ensure this, the states would pay the expenses for those on a low income. Three years later, *Miranda v. Arizona* (1966) established that criminal suspects must be read their rights upon arrest. This ruling was derived from the protection of the right against self-incrimination in the Fifth Amendment.

During the years that have followed the Warren Court era, there has been much less of a readiness to extend the rights of the accused. Instead, the ability of the authorities to secure a conviction has been much more of a consideration. In 1991, in *Fulminante v. Arizona*, the Court ruled that, even if a confession is obtained by coercion, that fact does not necessarily invalidate a conviction based upon it.

The rights of those who have been convicted have also been circumscribed. In two 1989 cases (*Penry v. Lynaugh* and *Stanford v. Kentucky*), the Court ruled that it was constitutional to extend capital punishment to the mentally retarded and to those who committed murder as juveniles (McKeever, 1995: 283). The ability of the Court to consider appeals based on an alleged denial of constitutional rights by the state courts was also reined in. The most conservative judges on the Court, Antonin Scalia and Clarence Thomas, have taken the view that the Constitution, and therefore the Supreme Court, could not forbid 'the execution of an innocent man who has received, though to no avail, all the process that our society has traditionally deemed adequate' (quoted in Roberts, 1995: 155).

Nonetheless, the Court has also imposed limits upon the powers of the federal authorities. In *United States v. Bond* (2000), the Court held that the Fourth Amendment's prohibition of 'unreasonable searches and seizures' had been breached when a bus passenger's carry-on luggage was squeezed from the outside by a federal border agent in Texas, leading to the discovery of a 'brick' of methamphetamine.

In the wake of the 11 September 2001 attacks and the 'War on Terror' some important questions about individual rights merged with homeland security issues. In particular, the holding of detainees (dubbed 'enemy combatants') at the US military base at Guantánamo Bay provoked far-reaching debate that had constitutional implications.[8] In 2006, *Hamdan v. Rumsfeld* established that the military commissions created by the Bush administration so as to put enemy combatants on trial lacked 'the power to proceed because its structures and procedures violate both the Uniform Code of Military Justice and the four Geneva Conventions signed in 1949'.

Then, in June 2008, the Court ruled in *Boumediene v. Bush* that despite the earlier claims made by the Bush administration those held at Guantánamo were protected by the US Constitution. They could therefore appeal to courts in the US to challenge their indefinite detention without charge. Justice Anthony Kennedy, writing for the majority (it was a 5-4 ruling), said that, although there was a terrorist threat, the Constitution remained paramount: 'The laws and Constitution are designed to survive, and remain in force, in extraordinary times' (Associated Press, 2008).

The Court's rulings on freedom of speech and the First Amendment also had an uneven character. Some have extended the boundaries of the First Amendment. In June 1997, in *Reno v. the American Civil Liberties Union (ACLU)*, the US Supreme Court struck down the Communications Decency Act (CDA). The Act, which sought to prohibit 'indecency' on the internet, was deemed to be an unconstitutional restriction on free speech. Five years later, in April 2002, the Court also invalidated the Child Pornography Prevention Act of 1996 (*Ashcroft v. The Free Speech Coalition*), which had outlawed computer-generated images of children. However, the Court has also asserted that there are limits on speech. In a 2003 ruling (*Virginia v. Black*) made by 6 to 3, the Justices ruled that the burning of a cross, a ritual act undertaken by the Ku Klux Klan, may be prohibited by states if the purpose of it is to intimidate others. Although he offered a concurrent opinion in the case, Justice Clarence Thomas spoke for the majority when he asserted that the message of a burning flag was one of terror and lawlessness. It should not therefore be regarded as a form of protected expression: 'Just as one cannot burn down someone's house to make a political point and then seek refuge in the First Amendment, those who hate cannot terrorize and intimidate to make their point' (*New York Times*, 2003). It is also difficult to discern a clear trend when considering the Roberts Court. In 2010, by an 8-1 majority, the Court in (*United States v. Stevens*) struck down a federal law that made depictions of animal cruelty illegal. The law, the Court asserted, breached the First Amendment. Nonetheless, the Court also reiterated the limits to freedom of speech particularly so far as young people are concerned. *Morse v. Frederick* (2007) permitted schools to restrict student presentations advocating drug use. The Court also declined to hear a case concerning words on a T-shirt worn by a student. At district court level, the right of students to wear wristbands highlighting breast cancer issues was, however, upheld (Wheaton, 2011).

The concept of 'rights' extends beyond freedom of speech and protections for those accused of criminal offences. For conservatives (who often feel that excessive rights are granted to those in the criminal justice system), it also includes gun ownership and the citizen's right to buy, hold, and sell property. Those on the right therefore greeted the Supreme Court's 2008 and 2010 rulings *District of Columbia v. Heller* and *McDonald v. Chicago* with acclaim. *Heller* stuck down restrictive laws in Washington DC and affirmed the right to keep handguns for personal protection. It emphasised that the Second Amendment extended the right to 'bear arms' to individuals (and not, for example, only to those serving in a state militia). The McDonald ruling established that this applied to the states as well as the District of Columbia.

Although they have often applauded the Rehnquist and Roberts Courts, there was anxiety and anger among conservatives about their handling of issues relating to property rights. In particular, there have been concerns about 'eminent domain' (which is referred to as compulsory purchase in the

United Kingdom). In *Kelo v. City of New London* (2005), the Court upheld (in a
5-4 ruling) the right of a municipal authority to take possession of a privately
owned property and transfer it to a private developer which it hoped would
through business expansion eventually increase the authority's income. For
those on the right, individual property rights are at the core of American
freedom and as important as freedom of speech or religion. Sandra Day
O'Connor, who wrote the principal dissent, pointed to the wide-ranging implications of the *Kelo* ruling: 'Nothing is to prevent the State from replacing any
Motel 6 with a Ritz-Carlton, any home with a shopping mall, or any farm with
a factory' (quoted in Boaz, 2006).

Sources of power

The US Supreme Court has, through its rulings, had a far-reaching impact on
the US political process and American society. Some have, in particular, added
to the Court's importance.

First, notwithstanding the power of Congress to restrict the Court's ability
to rule on some issues (see above), it has wide jurisdiction. Article VI of
the Constitution established the Constitution and the laws of the US as the
supreme law of the land:

> This Constitution, and the Laws of the United States which shall be made in
> Pursuance thereof; and all Treaties made, or which shall be made, under the
> Authority of the United States, shall be the supreme Law of the Land; and the
> Judges in every State shall be bound thereby, any Thing in the Constitution or
> Laws of any State to the Contrary notwithstanding.

Second, the powers of the Court were confirmed through the evolution
of judicial review. By 1995, the Court had declared more than 125 acts of
Congress unconstitutional (Wetterau, 1995: 201). Its interpretations have
reshaped and changed the accepted meaning of many others.

Third, judicial review extends beyond law to the actions of government. The
president, Congress, executive departments, and government agencies can be
overruled. The Supreme Court's 1974 ruling that President Richard Nixon's
executive privilege did not protect the tape recordings of his conversations in the
White House led to his resignation.

Fourth, *Fletcher v. Peck* (1810) established that the principle of judicial
review also extended to state law and the actions of state officials. Furthermore,
the protections, such as the prohibition of 'unreasonable searches and seizures' and 'cruel and unusual punishments', included in the Bill of Rights were
progressively extended by the Court. They had originally been understood to
constrain the federal government alone. However, during the course of the
twentieth century, in cases such as *Wolf v. Colorado* (1949) and *Louisiana ex rel.*

Francis v. Resweber (1947), the Supreme Court increasingly drew on notions of 'substantive due process', (see p. 168) and asserted that the Bill of Rights also limited and bound the actions of the states. The Bill of Rights was thereby 'nationalised' (McKeever, 1997: 31–32).

Fifth, the Court's judgements can be reversed only through the process of constitutional amendment. This requires a *supermajority* in Congress and among the states. As a consequence, only five amendments have been passed so as to overrule Supreme Court decisions (Wetterau, 1995: 201).

Sixth, the Court has immense authority and prestige. Although the southern states obstructed the implementation of the *Brown* ruling, the Court's right to decide on constitutional questions is almost always unchallenged at least directly by those who disagree with its decisions.[9]

Seventh, because Supreme Court judges serve for life, or until they chose to retire, they are, in contrast with those who are subject to periodic re-election, protected from the pressures of public opinion. They can therefore make rulings that are profoundly unpopular with some groupings, such as the *Brown* or *Roe* judgements, without fear of electoral consequences.

Eighth, the federal courts have a wide range of remedies that can provide redress. One federal judge ordered that improvements be made to prisons in Alabama, at a cost of $40 million per annum, arguing that the conditions in them constituted a 'cruel and unusual' form of punishment prohibited under the Eighth Amendment.

Ninth, the federal courts also play an important role because the US is a relatively *litigious* society. Individuals, organisations, and corporations resort to the courts to protect what they regard as their rights. Many issues are taken to court, providing countless opportunities for judicial decision-making. Even in the first half of the nineteenth century, Alexis de Tocqueville remarked: 'Hardly any question arises in the United States that is not resolved sooner or later into a judicial question' (quoted in Bickel 1986: 199).

Tenth, the courts offer an access point for interest groups. Groups that have failed to achieve their goals in the political arena or have little hope of doing so will seek to realise them in the courts. Interest groups have, furthermore, backed individuals who have acted as petitioners and brought cases. Both the civil rights movement and pro-choice groups have both used this strategy. When not directly involved, interest groups will also submit *amicus curiae* ('friend of the court') briefs to the courts in support of a particular approach or ruling. In some years, there have been over three thousand of these (Wetterau, 1995: 206).

Eleventh, as government has become more and more involved in every aspect of life, the range of issues considered by the federal courts has been extended.[11] The legislative process is structured around compromise and issues are sometimes left in an ambiguous or unresolved form. The courts therefore have to clarify the meaning of particular provisions.

Constraints on power

Although some observers argue that the federal courts play an immensely influential role, others emphasise the constraints on their powers. They are limited in their ability to enforce their rulings. As Alexander Hamilton was to assert in *The Federalist Papers* (1788) they are, in practice, dependent upon the compliance of those whom the ruling affects or the backing of the executive branch: 'The judiciary . . . has no influence over either the sword or the purse . . . and can take no active resolution whatever. It may truly be said to have neither FORCE nor WILL, but merely judgment; and must ultimately depend upon the aid of the executive arm even for the efficacy of its judgments' (Hamilton, 2002).

Arguably, the events that followed *Brown v. Board of Education* in 1954 confirm the legitimacy of Hamilton's claims. Although the ruling called for the desegregation of public schooling, the process of implementation required the use of troops. There had been hostility from white crowds outside schools and the state authorities in the south pursued a strategy of non-compliance. In 1957, President Eisenhower had to send troops to the Central High School in Little Rock, Arkansas, so as to ensure that nine black students could attend classes alongside whites. Segregation and the 'Jim Crow' laws that enforced it came to an end in the southern states only once Congress agreed to the 1964 Civil Rights Act and the 1965 Voting Rights Act. Furthermore, the Supreme Court has no power of initiative and cannot consider hypothetical legal questions. It is to all intents and purposes an appeals court and can therefore only react to cases that are submitted to it. It cannot identify a law or action that it considers unconstitutional and express an opinion. Instead, it must await an appellant with 'standing' who claims that his or her constitutional rights have been denied.

As has been noted, Congress has powers over the federal courts. It has the ability to alter the number of judges, both on the Supreme Court and in the lower courts. Although the number of Supreme Court Justices has been stable at nine since 1869, there have been substantial increases in the overall number of federal judges. Congress can also broaden or restrict the jurisdiction of lower courts and create new courts. At the same time, although it cannot circumvent the requirements of the Constitution, if Congress feels that the laws that it has passed have been misinterpreted by the courts, it can amend its own statutes so as to clarify its intentions and wishes.

Congress also has the power of impeachment, but this is very rarely used. Since the founding of the US, 15 federal judges have been impeached, and eight subsequently convicted (three others resigned). Furthermore, in almost all these cases, Congress was responding to accusations of personal misconduct. Its actions were not challenges to judicial rulings. In 2010, for example, Thomas Porteous, a federal judge in Louisiana, was impeached and removed from office amidst accusations of financial wrongdoing and corruption.

Although the process is fraught with political difficulty, Congress and the states can initiate a constitutional amendment if they oppose a ruling by the Supreme Court. In 1895, the Supreme Court declared a federal income tax unconstitutional. The Sixteenth Amendment was ratified in 1913, specifically authorising such a tax.

The Court cannot, in the long run, disregard public opinion although attitudes towards rulings are often fraught with ambiguity. Like other political institutions, its legitimacy depends upon its popular credibility. In 1972, in *Furman v. Georgia*, the Court declared all existing death penalty laws unconstitutional, largely because of the arbitrary, random, and chance way in which the death penalty was imposed. Chief Justice Warren Burger concluded from the *Furman* ruling that capital punishment had been abolished in the US (McKeever, 1997: 145–146). However, there is widespread backing for the death penalty across much of the US. This led many state legislatures to pass revised legislation whereby the imposition of the death penalty depended less on chance. In *Gregg v. Georgia* (1976), the Court retreated from its original position and accepted the constitutionality of the amended legislation. The overwhelming majority of states now include the death penalty in their statutes.

In some instances the judges exercise a degree of self-restraint. They are reluctant to enter 'the political thicket'. As appointees, there is a feeling that they should, in most circumstances, defer to the elected branches of government. According to rules laid down by Justice Louis D. Brandeis in 1936, the Court should interpret a statute so as to avoid ruling it unconstitutional 'even if a serious doubt of constitutionality is raised' (Witt, 1993: 216). Notions of self-restraint have been particularly evident in times of war and during periods of national crisis. During the First World War, Congress passed legislation prescribing fines and imprisonment for opponents of the War, principally radical socialists, who sought to interfere with the recruitment of troops or campaigned against the war effort. Despite claims that such measures contravened the First Amendment's assurance of free speech, the Supreme Court Justice Oliver Wendell Holmes wrote that 'in many places and in ordinary times' the socialists would be within their constitutional rights. But the Bill of Rights does not protect words creating a 'clear and present danger' of 'evils that Congress has a right to prevent'. Eighty years later, in the aftermath of the 11 September 2001 attacks, Congress passed the Patriot Act, which, critics asserted, curtailed individual liberties. However, the Supreme Court has not for the most part heard cases challenging the Act's provisions. When it did consider a part of the Act, which prohibited the provision of 'material support' to designated terrorist organisations, it ruled that even though this might include those who sought to persuade terrorists to adopt more peaceful approaches. For the Court minority, this constituted a breach of the First Amendment and its guarantee of free speech (Richey, 2010).

The Courts are constrained by precedent. Decisions are guided by previous rulings or those reached in the lower courts. This is known as the principle of *stare decisis*. As Justice David Souter recorded: 'The Court (and, I think, the country) loses when important precedent is overruled without good reason' (Silverstein, 2009). The importance attached to precedent is evident in the Supreme Court's reluctance to overturn *Roe v. Wade*, even though a majority of current judges on the Court would almost certainly not have decided the case in the same way as the Burger Court.

Originalism

On what basis should judges make their rulings? There are, in very broad terms, two schools of thought about the principles that should guide the way in which judges reach their rulings. There are those who are committed to originalism, which is tied to conservative thinking, and those who are for the most part associated with liberal thinking who assert that the meaning of the Constitution evolves over time. The phrase 'living Constitution' is sometimes used.

Many conservatives argue that a constitutional provision is to be understood by discerning the original intent of those who wrote the original Constitution and its later amendments and by considering the meaning of particular words and phrases at the time that they were used. Originalism is often (although not necessarily) allied with strict constructionism, which insists upon a close and literal reading of constitutional text. Originalists such as Supreme Court judges Antonin Scalia, Clarence Thomas (and, to a lesser extent, Samuel Alito and John Roberts) and those in the Federalist Society put forward five interconnected arguments.

First, there is profound suspicion towards those who seek out the 'penumbras and emanations' of the Constitution that Justice William O. Douglas discerned in establishing a constitutional right of privacy: 'the originalist point of view is clear . . . No provision of the Constitution guaranteed the right to abortion, homosexual sodomy or assisted suicide, and nothing prohibited the death penalty' (Virginia Law, 2010).

Second, alternative forms of judicial interpretation such as those based on 'evolving standards' or notions of a 'living constitution' assign too much of a role to the personal ideological preferences of judges. They thereby allow judges to rule on too broad a range of issues and to engage in social engineering. Conservatives sometimes refer to an 'imperial judiciary'.

Third, the process of historical inquiry, so as to discern earlier forms of intent and meaning, is from an originalist perspective, relatively straightforward. The Supreme Court's 2008 ruling *District of Columbia v. Heller*, which struck down many of the restrictions in the District of Columbia on the keeping of handguns, was based upon the right to 'bear arms' established in the Second Amendment. Although liberals argued that gun rights were intended only to be exercised within a militia or some other formally organised force, historical texts have showed, originalists have argued, that the right to keep arms for personal use was a principle rooted in seventeenth-century England and the early American settlements. Originalists would not claim that history necessarily identifies 'truth' but argue that the seeking out of original intent has greater validity as a basis for jurisprudence than other approaches. As Justice Antonin Scalia has said: 'My burden is not to show that originalism is perfect, but that it beats the other alternatives, and that, believe me, is not difficult . . . in ease of lawyerly application, never mind legitimacy and predictability, it far surpasses the competition . . . History is a rock-solid science compared to moral philosophy' (Virginia Law, 2010).

Fourth, court rulings based upon the personal preferences of judges (although disguised by talk of a 'living constitution') not only are an illegitimate usurpation of power but also impose poorly devised and ill-considered forms of policy. As Judge Robert Bork has argued, judges are not equipped to make public policy, particularly social policy. Judicial activism has led the courts towards the making of social policy.

Fifth, the imposition of personal ideological preferences by liberal judges reduces the credibility of the courts in the eyes of the public. The legitimacy of the courts depends on the acceptance of their rulings by the people.

The 'living Constitution'

The process of judicial interpretation can, however, be seen very differently. One of the most well-known judges associated with judicial activism was Thurgood Marshall (1967–91), the first African-American to serve on the Supreme Court bench. A leading contemporary academic advocate is Professor Laurence Tribe. The school is sometimes called non-interpretivist. Some have talked of a 'living Constitution' that can adapt over time without requiring amendment.

From this perspective, judicial meanings evolve over time just as the political process, the economy, and society have also changed. Although Article I of the Constitution gave Congress the power 'to regulate Commerce . . . among the several States' the meaning of this has been extended as the economy has become more advanced and complex. Lawrence Tribe has noted the ways in which the Supreme Court's understanding of the interstate commerce clause shifted over the years:

> Since the New Deal, the court has consistently held that Congress has broad constitutional power to regulate interstate commerce. This includes authority over not just goods moving across state lines, but also the economic choices of individuals within states that have significant effects on interstate markets. (Tribe, 2011)

Conclusion

Many politics textbooks (considering either a single country such as the US, a continent such as Latin America or Europe, or comparative political structures on a multi-nation basis) are structured around an implicit or sometimes explicit *functionalism*. They suggest or at least imply that there is a 'fit' between the different components of a political system and a broader 'fit' between the political system and society more generally. There are in other words complementarities. As earlier chapters of this book have argued, the search for a 'fit' or compatibility may be illusory. Arguably, political systems (and perhaps the US more than most) are characterised by internal disorder and '*dis*complementarities'. 'Fits' are few and far between. This is, in large part, because political processes are established, or laws passed, or decisions made at different times, by different political actors, for different purposes, and in different circumstances. The US Supreme Court exemplifies this. Most of those (sometimes all) serving on the Court were appointed by earlier presidents and confirmed by the Senate when it had a markedly different composition and character. The justices may well have been chosen because of long past political pressures and to fulfil political needs long forgotten. In such conditions, a 'fit' is improbable and the existence of complementarities with the other branches of government is, to say the least, unlikely.

Notes

1 It should be noted, however, that the federal courts deal with only a relatively small proportion of criminal and civil cases. There are about 1600 federal judges but some 30,000 state judges. Furthermore, only a handful of cases heard in the federal courts have constitutional implications.
2 Some have questioned this. There were suggestions that Sonia Sotomayor's judicial record, at least in hearing cases concerning police actions and law enforcement, was to the right of her predecessor, David Souter (Bravin and Koppel, 2009).
3 A further nominee for the post, Douglas H. Ginsburg, withdrew his nomination in 1987 after admitting to having smoked marijuana many years earlier.
4 The fact that they secured a handful of Republican votes (and the Democratic votes for President George W. Bush's nominees) suggests that judicial appointments are not quite as polarised as some other areas of contemporary decision-making.
5 The US government, the states, and individuals may also submit *amicus* briefs. When the rights of detainees held by the US at Guantánamo Bay were under consideration, both houses of the UK Parliament submitted a brief.
6 Having said this, there is a need, as John Dinan records, to place the Rehnquist Court's commitment to federalism in perspective. Although the Court reined in Congress's use of the interstate commerce clause, there were limits to its rulings. He cites Mark Tushnet's comment: 'Scholars of real revolution would be amused by the Rehnquist Court's federalism revolution. Not a single central feature of

the New Deal's regulatory regime was overturned in that revolution, nor were central elements of the Great Society's programs displaced' (quoted in Dinan, 2010: 163–164).

7 Nonetheless, the constitutionality of the Patient Protection and Affordable Health Care Act 2010 (often dubbed 'Obamacare') has been questioned. In particular, there have been challenges to the individual mandate (the principle that almost everyone should be required to have a health insurance policy). Although, it has been said, the federal government has the constitutional power to regulate interstate commerce it cannot oblige citizens to engage in a particular form of economic activity. (This is sometimes dubbed the 'broccoli argument'. If, it is said, government can compel an individual to purchase health insurance against his or her will it can also require individuals to consume broccoli.) In June 2011, the US Court of Appeals for the 6th Circuit in Cincinnati upheld the individual mandate and asserted that the interstate commerce clause could indeed be used in this way because health provision affects interstate commerce 'in a substantial way' (quoted in Sargent, 2011).

8 Guantánamo Bay is on the Cuban coast but US territory. It was, however, held to be outside US legal jurisdiction.

9 There are, however, less direct ways of challenging or at least reining in US Supreme Court rulings. Although the 1973 *Roe* ruling established abortion as a constitutional right, many state laws have been passed that seek to restrict access to abortion. Some, for example, require that women seeking an abortion are told that they can have an ultrasound of the foetus while other states require that a woman is given an ultrasound before an abortion. The sight of the ultrasound image will, they hope, deter women from going ahead with an abortion (Guttmacher Institute, 2011: 1). In June 2011, *The New York Times* reported that six states, including Nebraska and Indiana, had passed laws banning abortions after 20 weeks of a pregnancy. This was a frontal assault on the *Roe* ruling but pro-choice campaigners seemed reluctant to mount a court challenge because of fears that *Roe* might be overturned (Eckholm, 2011).

References and further reading

Associated Press (2008), 'Supreme Court backs Guantanamo detainees', *MSNBC. com*, 12 June, www.msnbc.msn.com/id/25117953/ns/world_news-terrorism/t/ supreme-court-backs-guantanamo-detainees/#.

Berger, R. (1997), *Government by Judiciary: The Transformation of the Fourteenth Amendment*, Indianapolis, IN, Liberty Fund.

Bickel, A. M. (1986), *The Least Dangerous Branch: The Supreme Court at the Bar of Politics*, New Haven, CT, Yale University Press.

Boaz, D. (2006), 'One year after *Kelo*, good news and bad news', Cato@Liberty, 24 June, http://www.cato-at-liberty.org/one-year-after-kelo-good-news-and-bad-news/.

Bravin, J. and N. Koppel (2009), 'Nominee's criminal rulings tilt to right of Souter', *The Wall Street Journal*, 5 June, http://online.wsj.com/article/ SB124415867263187033.html.

Cornell University Law School (2011), *Supreme Court – United States v. Morrison*, www. law.cornell.edu/supct/html/99-5.ZO.html.

Dinan, J. (2010), 'The Rehnquist Court's federalism decisions', *Publius*, 41:1,158–167.

Eckholm, E. (2011), 'Several states forbid abortion after 20 week', *The New York Times*, 26 June, www.nytimes.com/2011/06/27/us/27abortion.html?_r=1&hpw.

Findlaw (2011), *Parents Involved in Community Schools v. Seattle School District No. 1*, http://caselaw.lp.findlaw.com/scripts/getcase.l?court=US&vol=000&invol= 05-908.

Greenhouse, L. (2006), 'Dwindling docket mystifies supreme Court', *The New York Times*, 7 December.

Greenhouse, L. (2011), 'Activists by invitation', The New York Times, 15 June, http:// opinionator.blogs.nytimes.com/2011/06/15/activists-by-invitation/?hp.

Guttmacher Institute (2011), *State Policies in Brief – Requirements for Ultrasound*, www. guttmacher.org/statecenter/spibs/spib_RFU.pdf.

Hamilton, A. (2002), *Federalist No. 78 – The Judiciary Department*, www.foundingfa-thers.info/federalistpapers/fed78.htm.

Hinkson Craig, B. and D. M. O'Brien (1993), *Abortion and American Politics*, Chatham, Chatham House.

McKeever, R. (1995), *Raw Judicial Power? The Supreme Court and American Society*, Manchester, Manchester University Press.

McKeever, R. (1997), *The United States Supreme Court: A Political and Legal Analysis*, Manchester, Manchester University Press.

Mauro, T. (2008), 'Supreme Court stays above economic fray – for now', *Law. com*, 1 October, www.law.com/jsp/article.jsp?id=1202424921625&slreturn= 1&hbxlogin=1.

Ohio State University (1999), *Study Finds Unprecedented Delay in Appointing Federal Judges*, 25 April, www.acs.ohio-state.edu/units/research/archive/fedjudg htm8/25/99.

Ragsdale, L. (1996), *Vital Statistics on the Presidency: Washington to Clinton*, Washington DC, Congressional Quarterly Inc.

Richey, W. (2010), 'Supreme Court upholds controversial part of Patriot Act', *The Christian Science Monitor*, 21 June, www.csmonitor.com/USA/Justice/2010/0621/ Supreme-Court-upholds-controversial-part-of-Patriot-Act.

Robert, R. S. (1995), *Clarence Thomas and the Tough Love Crowd: Counterfeit Heroes and Unhappy Truths*, New York, New York University Press.

Sargent, G. (2011), 'A big blow to the conservative legal case against health reform', *The Washington Post – Opinions*, 29 June, www.washingtonpost.com/blogs/plum-line/ post/a-big-blow-to-the-conservative-legal-case-against-health-reform/2011/ 03/03/AGhgN1qH_blog.html?hpid=z3.

Silverstein, G. (2009), 'The last conservative', *The New Republic*, 1 May, http://www. tnr.com/article/politics/the-last-conservative.

Thernstrom, S. and A. Thernstrom (1997), *America in Black and White: One Nation Indivisible*, New York, Simon and Schuster.

Tribe, L. (2011), 'On health care, justice will prevail', *The New York Times*, 7 February, www.nytimes.com/2011/02/08/opinion/08tribe.html?_r=1&scp=2&sq=tribe& st=cse.

Virginia Law (2010), *Scalia Defends Originalism as Best Methodology for Judging Law*, 20 April, http://www.law.virginia.edu/html/news/2010_spr/scalia.htm.

Wall Street Journal (2009), 'Why Obama voted against roberts', *The Wall Street Journal*, 2 June, http://online.wsj.com/article/SB124390047073474499.html.

Wetterau, B. (1995), *Desk Reference on American Government*, Washington DC, Congressional Quarterly Inc.

Wheaton, S. (2011), 'Bands promote awareness, and giggles, but aren't lewd', *The New York Times*, 14 April, www.nytimes.com/2011/04/15/us/15bracelet.html.

Witt, E. (1993), *Congressional Quarterly's Guide to the US Supreme Court*, Washington DC, CQ Press.

8

Theories, perspectives, and concepts

Much has been written, and will continue to be written, about US political processes and institutions. Both attract immense amounts of coverage in the US itself and across the globe. The 2008 presidential election campaign was as closely followed in Europe and beyond as it was amongst those who cast a vote.

Having said this, there is, however, a significant divide between the types of scholarly study of US politics undertaken on the two continents. Although university-level researchers may consider the same topics (such as Congress, the Supreme Court, and the presidency), the research process takes markedly differently forms. There is also at the same time a gap between the study of US politics in Europe and research in many of the other fields and sub-fields within European political science. For the most part, European researchers who study US politics and their counterparts in US universities (and those working in other politics sub-fields in Europe) employ very different approaches and methodologies. Indeed, in many European universities, those who study US politics will not be located in politics or political science departments but will instead be based in American Studies (which is often dominated by those drawn from literature and cultural studies), history, 'area studies', or (outside of the UK and Ireland) an English language department. This chapter looks at the character of US politics as an academic subject in both the US itself and Europe, considers the extent and character of these methodological gaps and assesses their consequences. It also introduces the different theories and perspectives that govern the study of the subject.

'Old institutionalism'

In many parts of Europe, politics was (as a university subject) a late developer. The Political Studies Association (UK) was formed only in 1950. (The American Political Science Association had been founded in 1903.)

There were reasons for this. As Kenneth Newton and Josep Valles have argued, the emergence and development of politics as an academic subject required a broadly democratic society (Newton and Valles, 1991: 227). For much of the twentieth century, fascist, authoritarian and communist regimes across Europe prevented politics research progressing beyond either ideologically 'safe' micro-level studies or works that served a propaganda function for the governing regime. However, the difficulties went further. Even in democratic countries, politics was as a discipline subsumed within philosophy, law, or history. Even in 1966, almost 40 per cent of those teaching politics at university level in Britain had history as their first degree subject (Kavanagh, 2003: 597). Furthermore, it was not well regarded. In 1932, the study of politics at the University of Oxford was described in the following terms: 'The subject is taught by a very few specialists and a large number of philosophers and historians who approach it with varying degrees of enthusiasm or disgust' (quoted in Hayward, 1991: 301).

The picture was different in some other European countries but the study of politics was still held back. Often it was structured around public administration and the training of those who would, in different capacities, work for governments and the state. In so far as politics emerged as a discipline, there were different and diverse approaches. Some of those who studied politics were drawn to 'grand theory'. Others focused on the character of the state apparatus. There were normative essays advocating particular political outcomes. There were those (such as the Fabians in Britain) who based their work on what they saw as the need for extensive social, political, and economic planning by government. The most influential of the early theorists contributed broad conceptual studies that, for example, considered the formation of states and nations (Stein Rokkan), the 'social fabric' of British politics and comparative government (Jean Blondel), and the structures of political parties (Maurice Duverger).

Alongside this work, there were many studies of the different national political systems, structures, and processes. These considered both the countries of Europe and the US. Some took a textbook form while others were research monographs. For the most part, they tended towards what has subsequently been dubbed the 'old institutionalism'.[1] Studies were often based largely upon 'official' accounts of procedures and processes. Books and articles concentrated on formal institutions and outlined the ways in which they seemed to work. Against this background, institutional systems, structures, and rules were considered in depth. As Stephen Bell records:

> the emphasis in this kind of 'old' institutionalist political science was on charting the formal-legal and administrative arrangements of government and the public sector. From today's perspective, the old institutionalism displayed little interest in cumulative theory building . . . The main emphasis was on description, not on explanation or theory building. (Bell, 2002: 4)

The 'old' institutionalism was not, as Vivien Lowndes has argued, a reflective approach. Theory and methodology were almost seen as distractions that interrupted the narrative flow:

> The silence regarding theory and methods actually tells us something about the approach – that it was generally unreflective on issues of theory and method, took 'facts' (and values) for granted, and flourished as a kind of 'common sense' within political science. (Lowndes, 2010: 62)[2]

In Britain (where there was a particular aversion to generalised theoretical constructions and *Weltanschauungen*), many 'old' institutionalist accounts of the UK rested on the 'Westminster model'. This stressed the triumphs of the British political process in creating a parliamentary system resting upon parliamentary sovereignty, the rule of law, and a balance between accountable and effective forms of governance (Kavanagh, 2003: 602). Later accounts offered alternatives although they tended to be normative prescriptions rather than detached analysis. Some argued that liberty rested upon the dispersal of power rather than a balanced constitution while others asserted that the state could play an important role in remoulding society. There was however a reluctance to challenge the defining tenets of the Westminster model. Although there was sometimes a critical engagement with it, nearly all of those who asked questions or raised criticisms remained within the same paradigmatic framework. Those who in the 1960s talked of cabinet government being displaced by prime ministerial power or feared the entrenched power of the civil service saw political relationships and the parameters within which those relationships occurred in the same way as the Westminster model. They simply wished to rid the model of the forces that weakened or corrupted it. Only a handful of authors (perhaps most notably Harold Laski, who brought in social class and the role of established elites) considered the exercise of power outside of formal political categories.

The study of US politics in Britain and in other European countries (including those where equivalents to the Westminster model held comparatively little sway) was for the most part shaped by 'old institutionalist' approaches. The parameters of the 'institution' as a concept were drawn relatively narrowly. Although there was always an understanding of the part played by individual state governments, studies often failed to look beyond the structures of government on Capitol Hill and within the executive branch. Accounts of Congressional politics would, for example, list the stages that bill had to pass so as to become law. Studies of the Electoral College, which formally chooses the president, similarly concentrated on its workings and mechanisms. The use of evidence and the process of verification (and broader forms of theory) tended to be a haphazard process. When claims or arguments were constructed, there was little or no consideration of the extent to which particular forms of evidence had greater legitimacy or credibility than others.

This is not to say that the study of the US political process remained static. While, with the passage of time, such 'official' accounts remained an implicit or explicit starting point for the exploration of topics, they began to incorporate an understanding of more informal processes and a sense of contestation. Congressional studies, for example, increasingly acknowledged that surveys of legislative procedures had to incorporate the tensions between party networks and committee structures and the ways in which they formed layers of complexity and unpredictability 'on top' of 'official' processes. All of this was however 'contained' within an implied functionalism (see p. 177). It was assumed that the political system was, at root, ordered and there was a 'fit' between its different components.

Behaviouralism

In the US, the study of politics took a radically different evolutionary path. There was a transformative process often described as the 'behaviouralist revolution' (although it was perhaps too slow and uneven to justify allusions to revolution). Some place the 'revolution' in the first half or even the beginning of the twentieth century. Others suggest a later date. Whatever is decided upon, the locus of attention in the study of politics had by the 1950s and 1960s become focused on the behaviour of individuals, aggregates of individuals, and aggregates of individuals within particular categories. Elected officials and voters attracted particular attention.

The more important shift was, however, in terms of methodologies. Political analysis increasingly employed quasi-scientific methodologies resting on the operationalisation of concepts, the construction of formalised testable hypotheses, and structured forms of data collection.[3] Case studies in politics began to resemble the experiments undertaken in the natural sciences. Through this, the discipline had, it was said, become value-free. This allowed the study of politics to proclaim itself, without too many feelings of presumption or status inferiority, to be 'political science'. Writing critically at the end of the 1950s, Bernard Crick noted the scale of the shift that he argued had been evident in the US from the 1930s onwards. He was bitterly critical of what he saw as a false 'scientism', the focus on methodologies alone and the neglect of broader contextual study (Adcock and Bevir, 2005: 1).

> And the education of the American teacher of politics in the 'thirties became more and more a training in research techniques and less and less an education in history and philosophy. His gains in sociological techniques were all too often at the expense of cutting away the very foundations (inadequate though they were in themselves) of any genuine sociological knowledge . . . Men who had a profound ignorance even of the history of their own national politics, men who knew little but technique, were trained and began to teach. (Crick, 2002)

What did the behavioural revolution mean in practice? Within 'political science', there was a focus on bivariate and multivariate correlations and tests of statistical significance. Indeed, research questions rested upon these. For example, just how close a relationship was there between ethnicity and race and voting behaviour? What were the most significant variables when roll-call votes were taken in Congress? Were those members of Congress who backed interventionist forms of foreign and defence policy drawn from particular districts, states, or regions?

In the US today, behaviouralist approaches still remain dominant. Although political science is now divided between areas such as public administration and public policy and there has been a proliferation of sub-fields as the profession has expanded and to meet the challenges posed by social change and the rise of new social movements (most obviously the growth of feminism), a process that some have depicted as fragmentation, nearly all are structured around behaviouralist methodologies.[4] In most of the fields and sub-fields that collectively comprise political science, studies have little or no credibility unless they are structured around formalised hypotheses and quantitative data.

European shifts

There was, albeit belatedly, a shift as European political science began to ape developments in the US (see below). It took different forms and moved at different speeds. Broad theoretical issues continued to occupy much more of a place than in the US.

The rate of change often depended on the character of particular university systems and the extent to which there were 'native' political studies that had secured a hold within them. Indeed, there were differences even within the comparatively small Nordic region. Whereas Sweden, where political studies had long had a presence, held out, Denmark and Norway (where it had been weaker) absorbed the behaviouralist revolution much more quickly and extensively (Newton and Valles, 1991: 234).

As in the US, behaviouralism brought with it a turn to the methodologies associated with the natural sciences and the use of quantifiable data. Election outcomes were, for example, increasingly studied in terms of quantifiable variables (such as the unemployment level, rates of economic growth, or the results of preceding elections), rather than through broad accounts of events and trends. Such models could, it was said, be applied to any political system. Indeed, the widest possible would be a test of a model's 'robustness'.

There were other shifts in the study of the subject. Over time, the nation-state was increasingly displaced as the primary focus of analysis by comparative studies and thematically defined research. Indeed, there was a growing assumption within the profession that the nation-state could not serve as a legitimate unit or framework of analysis. From this perspective, the use of national frameworks suggested that national-specific variables played the determining role in shaping political structures and processes. Increasingly, scholars looked instead towards variables and sub-fields of study that had little or no respect for national boundaries.

Although Britain held out for a much longer period than most other European countries, there was a discernible shift in the character of most university politics departments. Although there were and continue to be 'hold outs', behaviouralist approaches were increasingly the norm. The increasing weight given to theory and methodology led to a turn away from the nation-state as a unit of analysis and a focus on comparative methodologies. Whereas they had (at least up until the 1970s) been populated by those who specialised in geographically defined sub-fields (such as 'French politics', German politics', 'US politics', or perhaps the politics of the European Union), those who held these posts were on retirement replaced by researchers in for example 'govern-ance and policy', 'global political economy', 'executive-legislature relations', 'party systems' or 'civil society'.[5] The use and application of quantitative techniques increasingly became a part of the discipline's standard operating procedure.

Despite this, there has been only a limited process of reappraisal amongst those studying US politics (and perhaps others involved in the study of particu-lar nation-states or territories). Pre-behaviouralist frameworks of analysis con-tinued to hold sway among the approximately hundred individuals estimated in 1991 to be studying the subject across Europe (McKay, 1991: 462).[6]

Having said that, there were shifts. Although remnants of the 'old institu-tionalist' paradigm were always there in the background, scholarly studies increasingly gave greater weight to both informal processes and human agency. Indeed, in some accounts, the discretion open to individuals and the different ways in which they chose to act upon their political preferences became pivotal. However, in the absence of methodological self-reflection, there was little discussion of the relationship between institutional structures and agency.

There is in other words a significant transatlantic methodological divide. It has been said, with only some flippancy, that while in Europe the study of US politics is a sub-field within history, particularly contemporary history, it is in the US a sub-field of mathematics.[7]

New institutionalism

Although behaviouralism is still hegemonic within US political science, there have been further shifts. Arguably, as a consequence, those who study US politics in Europe are increasingly not just one intellectual 'generation' behind American scholars but perhaps two or even three.

Within the US, behaviouralism has been subject to criticisms and challenges. As some have noted, while behaviouralist approaches stress the importance of methodological rigour they often shy away from broader theoretical perspectives. In other words, they tend to discuss propositions rather than theories. They seek to establish correlations and levels of significance but the question 'why' can remain unexplored or at least under-explored. Correlation and causation are sometimes blurred. The focus on the use of quantitative data has led to the 'mathematicisation' of the discipline, and as a consequence, some charge, an increasing proportion of research findings can be understood only by relatively small numbers. And it might be argued that the claim that politics can function as a value-free 'science' is in itself an ideological manoeuvre.

From a different perspective, rational choice theorists have suggested that political science can and should go beyond the adoption of quasi-scientific methodologies. They argue that the assumptions that underpin microeconomics, in particular the depiction of individuals as rational utility-maximisers who undertake a form of cost-benefit analysis before committing themselves to an action, and the assertion that organisations, groups, and movements are simply aggregates of individuals, can be applied to political processes.

The critique offered by 'new institutionalist' approaches goes rather further.[8] They do not seek to build upon behaviouralism but instead challenge its governing assumptions. Historical institutionalism stresses the ways in which political opportunity and the room for manoeuvre that particular political actors (such as the president) may have is shaped and constrained by long-term patterns of historical development. Many institutionalist accounts acknowledge the importance of formal institutions and institutional arrangements (such as Congress and the rules that govern its legislative procedures) but also emphasise the importance of less formal structures and processes. Peter Hall has defined institutions as 'the formal rules, compliance procedures, and standard operating practices that structure the relationship between individuals in various units of the polity and economy.' Asbjorn Norgaard has referred even more broadly to 'legal arrangements, routines, procedures, conventions, norms, and organizational forms that shape and inform human interaction' (quoted in Aspinwall and Schneider, n.d.: 4).

Within institutionalist accounts, the concept of *path dependence* is pivotal. Over time, rules, arrangements, systems, and procedures become 'sticky'. Particular political outcomes, in particular those at 'critical junctures', create 'feedback mechanisms' that lock in or reinforce the structures and patterns established by those outcomes. In simple terms, the political (and perhaps economic) costs of changing course become prohibitive. In many of its variants, new institutionalism, furthermore, stresses the idea of institutional incoherence. Different policy structures and institutional arrangements will have been established at different times, in different contexts, and for different purposes. In contrast, the 'old' institutionalism tended to suggest that, although political processes often produced sub-optimal outcomes or conflicts, these would, given appropriate reforms or far-sighted office-holders, be minimised. Coherence was, in other words, the default position.

When applied to the US political process, institutionalist perspectives generally emphasise the limits on the abilities of presidents to achieve the goals that they have set because of the enduring resistance of political, social and economic structures that will not bend easily to the presidential will (Pierson, 1994).[9] They often point, for example, to the separation of powers, the bicameral character of Congress, the rules governing lawmaking in the Senate, and federalism. Sven Steinmo and Jon Watts's study of President Bill Clinton's efforts to introduce healthcare reform in 1993 is instructive. They reject claims that the defeat of the Clinton plan was rooted in the strength and resilience of popular values such as 'individualism' or anti-government sentiments. Nor do they believe that flaws in the legislative strategy chosen by the president and his advisers were the critical feature of the plan's downfall. Instead, they argue that the structural obstacles created by the US Constitution meant that the health reform plan was all but doomed from the start despite the fact that there was widespread support at that point for healthcare reform. In particular, Steinmo and Watts point to the separated institutions created by the Constitution's authors:

> The game of politics in America is institutionally rigged against those who would use government – for good or evil. James Madison's system of checks and balances, the very size and diversity of the nation, the Progressive reforms which undermined strong and programmatic political parties and the many generations of congressional reforms have all worked to fragment political power in America. (Steinmo and Watts, 1995: 363)

In overall terms, they emphasise the ways in which institutional barriers compound the difficulties facing reformers. For example, the use of the cloture rule in the Senate has become routine in recent decades so that legislation almost always requires a supermajority of 60.[10]

However, many institutionalist scholars also emphasise, to a rather greater extent, the institutional forms that lie beyond Capitol Hill. These include the networks of formal and informal forms of organization and structures that create the setting and context within which policymaking is undertaken. At the same time, it has been argued that public policies can often have as much 'staying power' as formalised institutional structures (Pierson, 2006: 117–120).

At the same time, historical institutionalism considers the part played by the constituencies and interests created as a result of earlier policy changes. In his classic 1935 account of US tariff policy, E. E. Schattschneider reversed customary representations of causality and spelled out the ways in which 'new policies create a new politics' (Schattschneider, 1963: 288). Protectionist trade policies such as those adopted in the wake of the Wall Street Crash through the Smoot–Hawley Act of 1930 always, he asserted, have unintended consequences. They laid the basis for the growth of economic interests (under the 'shelter' of tariffs) that then sought to maintain those tariffs and other restrictions on trade. These industries 'form the fighting legions behind the policy'. They gain further traction and influence because, at the same time, 'the losers adapt themselves to the new conditions imposed upon them, find themselves without the means to continue the struggle, or become discouraged and go out of business'.

The thinking behind Schattschneider's study of tariff policy has informed recent studies. In her account of President George W. Bush's 2005 attempt to reform Social Security, Fiona Ross notes that, while it may have appeared as if Bush, who was at the time flanked by conservative Republican majorities in both chambers of Congress, had a real chance of enacting a partial privatisation, the embedded nature of the existing policy regime and the value attached to it by important political constituencies (most notably senior citizens) meant that reform was never feasible (Ross, 2007).

Although institutional variables can in some circumstances facilitate change, they often seem to curtail and limit reform. There are, as noted above, processes of path dependence. For many scholars, these explain, in part, why so many presidents, members of Congress, and other political actors fail to secure the goals that they set in their election campaigns and disappoint those who initially backed them. Why do institutional variables limit the opportunities open to actors? Why is there path dependence in US politics?

First, particular policies (or legislative changes) create constituencies that have distinct and separate interests. Such interests will use the many access points offered by the US system of government to defend and promote these. For example, the creation of Medicare in 1965 established assisted healthcare provision for senior citizens and some others. Subsequently, many senior citizens have been anxious to ensure that Medicare is protected from budget cuts and have also been fearful that healthcare reform would, by extending coverage to other groupings, reduce the quality of the provision that they received (Henry J. Kaiser Family Foundation, 2010: 3). Senior citizens are a sizeable political constituency and their anxieties restrict the options open to policymakers seeking political change.

In other words, the process of ending or even circumscribing a government expenditure programme, once it has established a client base, is fraught with political difficulty whatever the budgetary constraints. Thomas Donohue, President of the US Chamber of Commerce, reflected on this tendency of government spending programmes to become self-perpetuating during the debate about the passage of the American Recovery and Reinvestment Act (ARRA), the $787 billion fiscal stimulus enacted a month after President Obama took office. Despite the Chamber of Commerce's support for the measure Donohue asked: 'Who is in charge of saying, two years from now, "OK, we aren't doing that anymore"?' (quoted in Cummings, 2009). Therefore, even if the policymakers responsible for choosing a particular policy path consider a measure to be only a short-term step, that could later be revisited and revised, those initial decisions can have enduring consequences because constituencies will coalesce around the institutions created and these groupings may well come to see their interests as tied to the continuation of those policy paths (Pierson, 2000; 2004).

There are countless interests, constituencies, organisations, interlocking networks, and clusters (or institutions nested inside other institutions) embedded within particular institutional contexts (Hall and Thelen, 2009: 10). Indeed, the US institutional landscape is extraordinarily cluttered. This clutter makes decisive change difficult to achieve, even at times of apparent crisis.

Second, a particular institutional configuration lays the basis for the social construction of political rationality and establishes ideological and cultural parameters for 'the art of the possible'. In other words, institutional structures influence and to some extent constrain ideas.

Third, once particular institutional arrangements are in place, *institutional complementarities* take shape. In other words, as those associated with the 'Varieties of Capitalism' school, which draws a sharp distinction between liberal market economies such as the US (and the UK) and co-ordinated market economies such as Germany, stress, different sectors increasingly interlock with each other over time. Put another way, they form an 'interlocking ensemble' (Howell, 2003: 106). Reform or change in one sector can be held back or abandoned because of the consequences that it might have in other areas. At the least, the relative cost of a path-departing measure will increase.

From this perspective, there are formidable barriers to substantive change. Indeed, some institutionalist accounts tend to explain periods of far-reaching change and reform only by falling back on exogenous variables. (The term refers to those events and developments that take place outside of the political system but have consequences for it.) From this perspective, although has been a recent turn amongst institutionalist scholars towards a focus on relatively slow endogenous determinants of change (in other words those that arise from within the system), it often takes an external shock or rupture to bring about significant political reform.

American political development

The scholars associated with American Political Development (a methodological school) are amongst those applying the methods and approaches associated with institutionalism (particularly historical institutionalism) to the long-term development of US political structures.

APD has focused, for the most part, on the character of the American state apparatus.[11] At federal level, this involves the departments, agencies, bureau, and commissions as well as the structures within the White House, most notably the Executive Office of the President. The character of these structure the opportunities that policymakers have to develop new forms of policy and the extent to which particular outside interests have access to the policymaking process.

In contrast with behaviouralist approaches, there is a scepticism towards the models that are widely used in US political science and a conviction that studies of behaviour do not pay sufficient attention to the structural contexts within which that behaviour takes place. There is instead an emphasis on processes of policy feedback and moments of crisis and the structural consequences they bring about.

At the same time, APD tends to pull away from methodologies that suggest or imply that arrangements and relationships tend towards order or some form of equilibrium. All too often, despite efforts to create an 'iconography of order', the polity is characterised by a substantial degree of disorder, incongruity, and fragmentation. APD research 'exposes sources of disorder, introduces incongruity and fragmentation into depictions of the political norm, and pushes to the foreground an essentially dynamic view of the polity as a whole' (Orren and Skowronek, 2004: 14). Many studies use a comparative framework so that the differences and similarities between the different national paths pursued in the US and other countries can be considered and assessed.

What does all of this mean in practice? Studies of the New Deal in the 1930s pay less attention to President Franklin Roosevelt's ambitions or tactics and more to the ways in which state structures offered opportunities to new forms of economic thinking and permitted particular political coalitions to form. From this perspective, presidential power should be considered afresh. It is insufficient simply to consider the relationship between the president and Congress. Instead, broader sets of institutional arrangements play a role.

Issues and questions

Only a minority of scholars within the US considering the American political process (and very few indeed in Europe) have turned to the methodologies associated with historical institutionalism and APD. In the US, most scholars and researchers draw upon behaviouralist approaches. A cursory look at the agendas and programmes for the conferences convened by the American Political Science Association reveals that the most of the research papers being presented consider and assess the relationship between particular variables through the use of mulitivariate correlations or tests of statistical significance. They often draw valuable conclusions by establishing the relative strength of the relationships between different variables and by looking at what is, or is not, significant.

Nonetheless, despite the methodological rigour of such studies, the broader context and the underlying reasons for political processes are sometimes lost. The 'new institutionalism' has in its different forms sought to fill that gap. Nonetheless, historical institutionalism faces some difficulties of its own and issues remain unresolved.

First, the term 'institution' is the basis of institutionalism. And yet there is often a degree of uncertainty about the meaning of the word. It is sometimes used in a way that is reminiscent of the 'old institutionalism' to refer to formal structures alone. Therefore, at a federal level, Congress, the US Supreme Court, the presidency, the Department of State are all institutions. But some extend the concept of an 'institution' further. They include informal as well as formal structures. From this perspective, loose affiliations based upon perceptions of a shared interest and a common identity or even perhaps laws and norms have institutional characteristics. In this context, a seemingly flippant but very important question has been asked. Does an institution, to be acknowledged as such, need to 'have a phone number'?

Second, historical institutionalism has for the most part edged away from the mathematisation of political analysis. This does however raise methodological issues about the character of verification. In the absence of quantification, what forms of evidence can be regarded as sufficient to draw conclusions or make generalisations?

Third, institutionalist arguments and those associated with APD can sometimes seem to be relatively deterministic in character. They sometimes appear to deny the possibility that individual or group actions can bring about significant forms of change. Although APD scholars have charted ideas extensively, the beliefs that individuals hold or the ideologies to which they adhere often appear to be disregarded. However, in reality, most institutionalist accounts make more limited claims than it may sometimes seem. As John L. Campbell notes: 'The important point in much of this [historical institutional] work is not that institutions directly determine outcomes . . . but more modestly, that institutions constrain them' (Campbell, 2004: 24). Some recall Karl Marx's celebrated but melodramatic words in *The 18th Brumaire of Louis Bonaparte* about the relationship between structure and agency:

> Men make their own history, but they do not make it just as they please; they do not make it under circumstances chosen by themselves, but under circumstances directly encountered, given and transmitted from the past. The tradition of all the dead generations weighs like a nightmare on the brain of the living.[12]

This might be taken to suggest that structural forces open up periodic 'windows' or a form of short-term 'release' within which human agency acquires primacy. However, this perhaps neglects the ways in which the policymaking that is undertaken during periods of opportunity is shaped, structured, and contoured by the tradition of both dead and living generations and the institutional forms and forms of path dependency that they created or reproduced. Lawrence Jacobs and Desmond King point to the ways in which institutional frameworks and the self-conscious actions of individuals and groups interact with each other so as to create opportunities for change. They talk of 'structured agency'. Reform and presidential 'success' is brought about at 'the intersection of agency and structure . . . Presidents have opportunities to lead, but not under the circumstances they choose or control' (Jacobs and King, 2010: 794).

Fourth, alongside the place of human agency, the role of ideas and cultural processes is also hard to pin down. In some accounts, ideas are almost peripheral. They do not have an autonomous existence but are simply an expression of group or individual interests. Others, however, talk of 'discourse' rather than ideas. 'Discourse' includes but goes beyond ideas. It 'encompasses not only the substantive content of ideas but also the interactive processes by which ideas are conveyed' (Schmidt, 2008: 305). The character of framing processes can, in particular, contribute to explaining why change does or does not take place and in accounting for the form that it takes.

Conclusion

Many of these theoretical debates and concerns are relatively abstract. They can be difficult to follow. They may at first sight seem to have only limited relevance to the topics considered in the other chapters of the book such as presidential power, Congress, and the US Supreme Court. Indeed, these theories are far removed from the content of most course specifications. Nonetheless, some of these theoretical frameworks offer a basis for exploring topics such as the presidency in a broader context, deciding upon the variables or causal factors that require attention, and reflecting upon their relative weight. They are, in other words, a starting point for more rigorous forms of analysis.

Beyond this, institutionalism and APD (see p. 191) introduce a further consideration. The question of order and agreement has appeared and periodically reappeared throughout the book. As has been noted, political observers tend to assume that they are the norm. The study of politics has been said to be about processes of reconciliation and compromise. The bitter disagreements, polarisation, and talk of 'ungovernability' that characterise the contemporary US political process are depicted as a deviation from an order that otherwise brings forth co-operation and consensus.

In so far as there is defining argument in this book (and it might be that the inclusion of a defining argument goes beyond the proper functions of a textbook) it is that the norm rests upon disorder, tension, fragmentation, and 'discomplementarities'. Instead of looking at 'how systems work' we should perhaps consider how and why systems fail to work.

Notes

1 The terms 'old' and 'new' institutionalism have different meanings within economics.
2 There is, however, always a danger of setting up a 'straw man'. Some studies from the 'old' institutionalist era were much more sophisticated (through, for example, comparative analysis) than others (Lowndes, 2010: 62).
3 The 'operationalisation' of concepts refers to the ways in which a concept can be translated into forms that are measurable.
4 The study of political theory is a significant exception.
5 Nonetheless, it could be argued that the 'revolution' has been incomplete in parts of Europe. As noted above, the principal academic politics organization in the UK is the Political Studies Association. The continent-wide organisation is the European Consortium for Political Research. In the US it is the American Political Science Association.
6 The figure includes those who studied US politics as well as other topics and themes. McKay reported that 'only a handful' studied the US exclusively (McKay, 1991: 466, note 4). That 'handful' has been further reduced in size during subsequent years.
7 The comment was, I believe, made by Tim Hames at a conference organised by the American Politics Group of the Political Studies Association (UK).
8 The focus in this chapter is on historical institutionalism and the ways in which institutional arrangements have developed over time. It should be acknowledged that there are other institutionalist approaches within political studies. Both discursive institutionalism and rational choice institutionalism have influenced scholars and shaped their work (Schmidt, 2010).
9 Institutionalist accounts also, however, recognise and acknowledge the ways in which institutional arrangements can empower as well as constrain political actors.
10 Budget bills are, however, exempt from the danger of a filibuster. A simple majority suffices.
11 The word 'state' always poses difficulties when US political structures and processes are considered. It is easy to understand it as a reference to the 50 individual states. However, the term 'state' is generally employed more broadly in political studies. It refers to the governing institutions (administrative, legal, or military) within a particular territory.
12 'Structure' refers to the constraints upon individual decision-making while 'agency' emphasises the capacity of political actors to shape events and processes.

References and further reading

Adcock, R. and M. Bevir (2005), 'The history of political science', Political Studies Review, 3, 1–16.
Aspinwall, M. D. and G. Schneider (n.d.), Same Menu, Separate Tables: The Institutionalist Turn in Political Science and the Study of European Integration, www.uned.es/dcpa/old_doctorado_2004-2005/cursos/subprograma_ue_2005/lecturas_closa/52closa_Aspinwall%20y%20Schneider%201999.pdf.

Bell, S. (2002), 'Institutionalism: old and new', in J. Summers (ed.), *Government, Politics, Power and Policy in Australia*, 7th ed, Australia: Pearson Education, pp.363–380.

Campbell, J. L. (2004), *Institutional Change and Globalization*, Princeton: Princeton University Press.

Crick, B. (2002) *American Science of Politics*, Abingdon: Routledge.

Cummings, J. (2009), 'Stimulus: Boost or budget buster?', *Politico.com*, 15 January, www.politico.com/news/stories/0109/17473.html.

Hall, P. A. and K. Thelen (2009), 'Institutional change in varieties of capitalism', *Socio-Economic Review*, 7, 7–34.

Hayward, J. (1991), 'Political science in Britain', *European Journal of Political Research*, 20, 301–322.

Henry J. Kaiser Family Foundation (2010), *Kaiser Health Tracking Poll*, December, www.kff.org/kaiserpolls/upload/8127-F.pdf.

Howell, C. (2003) 'Varieties of capitalism – and then there was one', *Comparative Politics*, 36:1, October, 103–124.

Jacobs, L. R. and D. S. King (2010), 'Varieties of Obamaism: structure, agency, and the Obama presidency', *Perspectives on Politics*, 8:3, 793–802.

Kavanagh, D. (2003), 'British political science in the inter-war years: the emergence of the founding fathers', *British Journal of Politics and International Relations*, 5:4, November, 594–613.

Lowndes, V. (2010), 'The institutional approach', in D. Marsh and G. Stoker, *Theory and Methods in Political Science*, New York: Palgrave Macmillan, pp. 60–79.

McKay, D. (1991), 'Is European political science inferior to or different from American political science?', *European Journal of Political Research*, 20, 459–466.

Newton, K. and J.M. Valles (1991), 'Introduction: political science in western Europe, 1960–1990', *European Journal of Political Research*, 20, 227–238.

Orren, K. and Skowronek, S. (2004), *The Search for American Political Development*, New York: Cambridge University Press.

Pierson, P. (1994), *Dismantling the Welfare State. Reagan, Thatcher, and the Politics of Retrenchment*, Cambridge: Cambridge University Press.

Pierson, P. (2000), 'Increasing returns, path dependence, and the study of politics', *American Political Science Review*, 94:2, June, 251–267.

Pierson, P. (2004), *Politics in Time: Politics in Time: History, Institutions, and Social Analysis*, Princeton: Princeton University Press.

Pierson, P. (2006), 'Public policies as institutions', in G. Daniel, I. Shapiro and S. Skowronek (eds), *Rethinking Political Institutions: The Art of the State*, New York: New York City University Press, 114–134.

Ross, F. (2007), 'Policy histories and partisan leadership in presidential studies: the case of social security', in G. C. Edwards III and D. S. King (eds), *The Polarized Presidency of George W. Bush*, New York: Oxford University Press, pp. 419–446.

Schattschneider, E. E. (1963, orig. 1935), *Politics, Pressures and the Tariff: A Study of Free Private Enterprise in Pressure Politics, as Shown in the 1929–1930 Revision of the Tariff*, Hamden: Archon Books.

Schmidt, V. A. (2008), 'Discursive institutionalism: the explanatory power of ideas and discourse', *Annual Review of Political Science*, 11, 303–326.

Schmidt, V. A. (2010), 'Give peace a chance: reconciling the four (not three) new institutionalisms', in D. Béland and R. Henry Cox (eds), *Ideas and Politics in Social Science Research*, New York: Oxford University Press, pp. 1–37.

Steinmo, S. and J. Watts (1995), 'It's the institutions, stupid! Why comprehensive national health insurance always fails in America', *Journal of Health Politics, Policy and Law*, 20:2, 329–372.

Index